Strategic HRM

HRMT 295 - Strategic HRM

MacEwan University

NELSON

NELSON

ISBN-13: 978-0-17-678448-5
ISBN-10: 0-17-678448-9

Consists of Selections from:

Strategic Human Resources Planning, Sixth Edition
Monica Belcourt, Kenneth J. McBey
ISBN-10: 0-17-657030-6, © 2016

Managing Human Resources, Eighth Canadian Edition
Monica Belcourt, Parbudyal Singh, Scott A. Snell, Shad S. Morris, George Bohlander
ISBN-10: 0-17-657026-8, © 2017

Cover Credit:

STILLFX/Shutterstock

Contents

CHAPTER

STRATEGIC MANAGEMENT

CHAPTER LEARNING OUTCOMES

AFTER READING THIS CHAPTER, YOU SHOULD BE ABLE TO:

- Discuss why managers need to examine the human resources implications of their organizational strategies.
- Discuss why human resources managers need to understand strategy.
- Understand the various terms used to define strategy and its processes.
- Describe organizational strategies, including restructuring, growth, and maintenance.
- Define business strategy and discuss how it differs from corporate strategy.
- Discuss the steps used in strategic planning.
- List the benefits of strategic planning.

Hudson's Bay Company (HBC) is Canada's oldest organization, established in 1670 as a fur trading company. It has survived for over 300 years by adapting its strategy to changing environmental conditions, both threats and opportunities. The following condensed history will demonstrate that it has experienced nearly all of the strategic options described in this chapter.

In 1821, HBC merged with its main rival, the North West Company. The declining demand for fur influenced the decision to change the fur trading posts to retail stores, and HBC launched its department store business in 1913. The company also had a diversification strategy and at various times throughout its history sold liquor, salmon, coffee, tobacco, and real estate. The economic downturn of the 1980s caused HBC to rethink its priorities and, like many other firms, return to its core business. Nonretail businesses were sold off and retail businesses added. The pace of retail acquisition increased with takeovers of Zellers (1978), Simpsons (1978), Fields (1978), Robinson's (1979), Towers/Bonimart (1990), Woodward's (1994), and Kmart Canada (1998) following in the tradition of Cairns (1921), Morgan's (1960), and Freiman's (1971). Even HBC's subsidiaries had to adopt new business-level strategies. For example, when Walmart entered the Canadian retail market in 1994, competing head-on with Zellers, the latter had to reposition itself from a low-cost business strategy to a differentiation strategy by selling exclusive and slightly upscale products such as Martha Stewart Everyday. Other retailers, such as Eaton's and Consumer Distributors, did not make good strategic decisions, and went bankrupt.

In 2005, HBC adopted a corporate growth strategy and a business-level strategy of differentiation coupled with low cost by opening new store concepts such as Home Outfitters and DealsOutlet.ca. Online shopping was introduced in 2000. In 2006, American billionaire Jerry Zucker bought HBC. Thanks to HBC's talent management and succession planning systems in place, HBC was able to quickly generate a new executive team from within. When Zucker died, his estate sold HBC to NRDC (owners of the Lord & Taylor department store). The recent economic recession again forced HBC to focus on its department store and specialty store businesses to drive growth. In 2011, HBC decided to spin off 220 stores of its weakest chain, Zellers, to Target for $1.825 billion. Currently, HBC is focusing on the luxury market, with the acquisition of other retailers such as Lord and Taylor and Saks Fifth Avenue.[1]

The HBC example highlights the strategic decisions made by organizations in their attempts to survive and become profitable. Each strategic choice has implications for the management of human resources. We start in this chapter by establishing a common understanding of strategy, its importance, and its link to human resources management (HRM).

// A NEED FOR STRATEGIC HRM

Read any Canadian newspaper and you will see stories such as these:

- Burger King takes over Tim Horton's in a deal worth $12.5 billion.
- Scotiabank eliminates 1500 jobs and closes branches.
- Loblaws acquires Shoppers Drug Mart for $12.4 billion in cash and shares.
- Canadian fashion retailer Jacobs, with 1000 employees, liquidated its 92 stores and filed for bankruptcy.
- Four Quest Energy Inc., an oil sands service producer increased its sales 7300 percent from 2008 to 2013.

The common theme in these stories is the adoption of a strategy that has serious HRM implications. In most cases, unless the HRM strategy, for example, internationalization or downsizing, is appropriately formulated and skillfully implemented, the success of the organizational strategy is at risk.

We have written this book to provide answers to questions about the proper alignment of HR policies with organizational strategies. Managers who have implemented any kind of change within their organizations realize the importance of matching HRM practices with organizational goals. There is a growing acknowledgment that the strategic management of people within organizations affects important organizational outcomes such as survival, profitability, customer satisfaction levels, and employee performance. Our goal is to help readers understand strategy and the HRM programs and policies that enable organizations to achieve that strategy. We discuss strategy at some length, because HR professionals have been criticized for not understanding nor using the language of business when discussing the value of HR programs. HR managers have to use strategy terms to show how their HR practices support organizational strategies.

STRATEGY

Strategy is the formulation of organizational objectives, competitive scopes, and action plans for gaining advantage.[2] Strategy is the plan for how the organization intends to achieve its goals. The means it will use, the courses of action it will take, and how it will generally operate and compete constitute the organization's strategy.[3]

We have presented one definition of strategy, but there are many others. A sampling is found in HR Planning Notebook 1.1.

> **Strategy**
> The formulation of organizational objectives, scopes, and action plans for gaining advantage

---

HR PLANNING NOTEBOOK 1.1

DESCRIPTIONS OF STRATEGY

Concepts of strategy are numerous. Here is a guide to some common terms used throughout the text and in the organizations where you work:

Strategy: A declaration of intent

Strategic intent: A tangible corporate goal; a point of view about the competitive positions a company hopes to build over a decade

Strategic planning: The systematic determination of goals and the plans to achieve them

Strategy formulation: The entire process of conceptualizing the mission of an organization, identifying the strategy, and developing long-range performance goals

Strategy implementation: Those activities that employees and managers of an organization undertake to enact the strategic plan and achieve the performance goals

Objectives: The end, the goals

Plans: The product of strategy, the means to the end

Strategic plan: A written statement that outlines the future goals of an organization, including long-term performance goals

Policies: Broad guidelines to action, which establish the parameters or rules

---

The top management team determines strategy through a process of environmental analysis (which is discussed in Chapter 3) and discussions. The strategy and objectives developed by senior management are then approved by the board, and negotiated and revised as they filter throughout the organization. The organization then develops plans, which include HRM programs, to achieve those goals. This does not suggest,

however, that strategic planning is a unilateral or one-time process. Various organizational outcomes provide a feedback loop to the strategic planning process led by senior management, who will also continuously monitor the dynamic environment to make adjustments to the strategy.

Strategic planning requires thinking about the future. In a perfect world, some experts believe that the strategic planner would establish an objective for five to ten years and then formulate plans for achieving the goals. However, other experts do not perceive strategy in such a simplistic, linear fashion. They assert that the future is not that predictable. Planning for the long term (i.e., more than ten years) is difficult and would be more appropriately judged as a best guess. For example, the nuclear power industry in Japan could not have predicted the 2011 Tohoku earthquake and tsunami, nor could financial analysts have predicted the 2008 economic meltdown on Wall Street. Besides catastrophic events, there are more typical shocks to the competitive environment that trigger a change in strategy, such as changing market conditions, new technology, emerging markets, and new moves of competitors etc. Some other organizational events that precede strategic change are outlined in HR Planning Notebook 1.2.

Because of the unpredictability of trigger events, many planners look at a relatively shorter period of time, a more predictable term of three to five years. Because of the uncertainty, their plans are formulated to be somewhat flexible so that they can respond to changes in the environment. Thus, strategic planning must be viewed as a dynamic process, moving, shifting, and evolving as conditions warrant changes. The process of subtly redirecting strategy to accommodate these changes is called logical incrementalism.[4] Rather than calling for a straight path to the goal, this strategy calls for a series of actions to react to changes in competitor actions or new legislation. Another name for this reactive process is **emergent strategy**. This cumulative process can look like a dramatic revolutionary change to those on the outside, but to those on the inside, the strategy has been incrementally implemented.[5] Firms can wait passively for these changes to occur and then react, or they can anticipate these moves and adopt a proactive stance.

Writers on strategy sometimes distinguish between intended strategy and realized strategy. The **intended strategy** is the one that was formulated at the beginning of the period. The **realized strategy** is, of course, what actually happened.

Figure 1.1 illustrates these various concepts of strategy.

You may be asking: Why develop a strategy if the organization must continually change it to accommodate unforeseen changes? Think of strategy as a game plan or a flight plan. A pilot's flight plan looks relatively simple: fly from Ottawa to Edmonton. However, before departure, he or she is aware of the environment and the capacities (or competencies) of the plane. On the basis of these external and internal factors, the pilot develops a strategy for a safe flight. While on the voyage, however, environmental changes, such as strong winds or a blizzard, may require a change of plans. Even internal factors, such as a passenger suffering a heart attack, may necessitate such a change. But the plane and/or its passengers will somehow, at some time, arrive in Edmonton. This is what is meant by incremental adjustments to the strategy, adjustments that do not require changing the focus of the desired result. There is no strategy so finely crafted that adjustments aren't needed. The general rule is that, unless there is a crisis, it should not be necessary to make quantum leaps in strategies. Thus, these strategies should withstand the test of time and be durable for several years.

A good strategy recognizes the complexity of these realities. To be effective, strategic management anticipates future problems, provides an alignment with external contingencies and internal competencies, recognizes multiple stakeholders, and is concerned with measurable performance[6]–just like the flight plan.

Emergent strategy
The plan that changes incrementally due to environmental changes

Intended strategy
The formulated plan

Realized strategy
The implemented plan

TRIGGERING EVENTS TO STIMULATE A CHANGE IN STRATEGY

Here are some common examples of events that trigger a change in strategy within organizations:

- *New CEO:* May ask questions about the assumptions underlying the strategy and challenge the status quo

- *Threat of a change in ownership:* Similarly to a change in CEO, new owners (or a threat of new ownership) cause a reconsideration of the effectiveness of the strategy

- *External intervention:* Examples are a customer who accounts for a large portion of sales defecting to another company or lodging a serious complaint about a defect

- *Performance gap:* When sales or profit targets are not being met, most organizations will review the strategy

- *Strategic inflection point:* Rapid changes in technology (for example when Yellow Pages had to go digital), customer preferences, or industry regulations will trigger a change in strategy

Sources: Adapted from S.S. Gordon, W.H. Stewart, R. Sweo, and W.A. Luker, "Convergence versus Strategic Reorientation: The Antecedents of Fast-Paced Organizational Change," *Journal of Management*, Vol. 26. No. 5 (2000), pp. 911–945; and T.L. Wheelen and J.D. Hunger, *Concepts in Strategic Management and Business Policy*, 11th edition, 2008, Toronto: Prentice Hall, p. 19.

FIGURE 1.1

THE REALITY OF THE STRATEGIC PROCESS

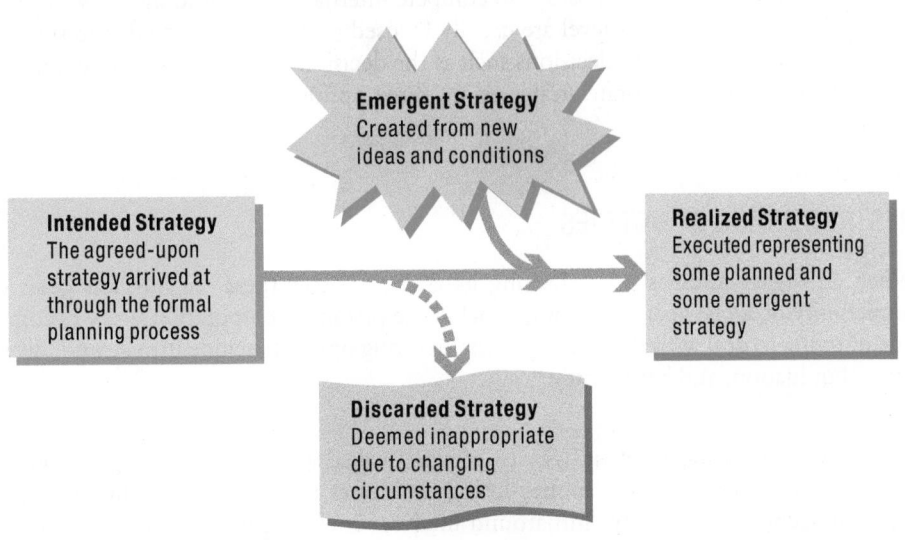

Source: Adapted from work by Henry Mintzberg. Used with permission.

The fundamental premise of this book is that different organizational strategies demand different HR policies and practices. Therefore, before we can discuss HRM strategies, you need to understand the different types of strategies that organizations formulate and implement.

// STRATEGIC TYPES

Many executives and senior managers put in an incredible number of hours forging the strategy for the firm, and they believe the strategy they developed, with much sweat and tears, is unique to their organizations. In one sense, pure, unique organizational strategies do exist, because organizations are extremely complex and no two are identical. In another sense, they do not, because it is possible to group strategies into categories or generic types. Just as we can group our friends into personality categories of introvert and extrovert, so we can group organizations by strategy. By virtue of their simplicity, these *typologies*, or classification schemes, aid our understanding. The more we add variables to approximate the reality of an organization, the more unwieldy the typology becomes.[7] Organizational theorists use classification schemes not only to help us understand how organizations work but also to enable us to test the concepts, leading us to better information about how to manage.

These identifiable, basic strategies can be classified into (1) corporate strategies and (2) business strategies.

CORPORATE STRATEGIES

Company-wide strategies, sometimes referred to as **corporate strategies**, are focused on overall strategy for the company and all of its businesses or interests. Examples of corporate strategies include decisions to compete internationally or to merge with other companies. Strategies at this level are usually focused on long-term growth and survival goals and will include major decisions such as the decision to acquire another company.

Grouped within corporate strategies are three options: restructuring, growth, and stability.

> **Corporate strategy**
> Organizational-level decisions that focus on long-term survival

RESTRUCTURING STRATEGIES

When an organization is not achieving its goals, whether these are business goals of profitability or social goals of helping rehabilitate prisoners, corporate strategy becomes one of trying to deal with the problem. Restructuring options include turnaround, divestiture, liquidation, and bankruptcy.

TURNAROUND A **turnaround strategy** (sometimes called a *retrenchment strategy*) is one in which managers try to restore money-losing businesses to healthy profitability or government agencies to viability. Turnaround methods include getting rid of unprofitable products, imposing layoffs, making the organization more efficient, or attempting to reposition it with new products. For example, many cable companies were once near bankruptcy and have now turned around. See also HR Planning Today 1.1 for a history of the turnaround efforts of McDonald's.

> **Turnaround strategy**
> An attempt to increase the viability of an organization

DIVESTITURE **Divestiture** refers to spinning off a business as a financially and managerially independent company or selling it outright.[8] For example, Nokia divested its smartphone business to Microsoft. Here in Canada, the private equity fund NRDC acquired Hudson's Bay for roughly $1.1 billion in 2008. In 2011, it divested one of HBC's weakest chains, Zellers, which was sold to Target for more than $1.8 billion, much higher than the price NRDC paid for HBC.[9]

LIQUIDATION The least attractive alternative is **liquidation**, in which plants are closed, employees released, and goods auctioned off. There is little return to shareholders under this option. Nevertheless, an early liquidation may allow some resources (including human resources) to be salvaged, whereas a bankruptcy does not. Jacobs, mentioned earlier in the chapter, and Radio Shack are recent examples of liquidation.

BANKRUPTCY **Bankruptcy** occurs when a company can no longer pay its creditors, and, usually, one of them calls a loan. The company ceases to exist, and its assets are divided among its creditors. The list of companies that have filed for bankruptcy is long and includes CanWest, Quebecor, Sam the Record Man, and Tilden Rent a car.

> **Divestiture**
> The sale of a division or part of an organization

> **Liquidation**
> The termination of a business and the sale of its assets
>
> **Bankruptcy**
> A formal procedure in which an appointed trustee in bankruptcy takes possession of a business's assets and disposes of them in an orderly fashion

HR PLANNING TODAY 1.1

TURNAROUND AT MCDONALD'S

The McDonald's burger chain has, for several decades, been a success story. Every year saw increases in outlets, people served, profits, and shareholder value. But in 2003, restaurant sales were down nearly 5 percent and profits were down by 11 percent. McDonald's had since made several attempts to revive its success.

One effort focused on making its food healthier through continuous innovation. It introduced premium salads in 2003, snack wraps in 2006, and real-fruit smoothies and frappés in 2010. Related to these introductions was its switch to trans-fat–free cooking oil for french fries and the use of organic milks. The company also introduced a food and nutrition website, and created a mobile app that allows customers to calculate the nutrients in their meal choices.

Another effort attempted to tap regional food interests. The company has McArabias (grilled chicken in Arabic bread) in the Middle East, Shogun Burgers (teriyaki pork) in Hong Kong, McShawarmas (kosher meat) in Israel, Bulgogi Burgers in South Korea, and McSpicy Paneer in India.

A third attempt was to diversify; McDonald's added high-margin McCafé coffees in 2009 and Chipotle BBQ in 2011 to broaden its customer base.

Finally, as consumers were facing the economic recession, McDonald's boosted its low-price dollar-menu items, which included a double cheeseburger or a hot fudge sundae. At a recent presentation at Ryerson University, the Canadian CEO admitted to making mistakes such as introducing too many products (menu creep). For example, a launch of custom made meals ("Create your taste") resulted in wait times of seven minutes, compared to two minutes for its fast-food bestsellers (fries, burgers, nuggets) McDonalds decided to focus on a core item: coffee. It now controls 11 percent of the brewed coffee market in Canada. However, sales and profits are declining and McDonald's executive team is responding by drastically reducing menu items, and perhaps will become another turnaround story.

Sources: Adapted from www.canadianbusiness.com/companies-and-industries/mccomeback, retrieved November 17, 2014; Olive, D. "Don't Count the Behemoth Out Yet," *The Toronto Star*, December 12, 2014; D. Goold, "McDonald's Woes a Matter of Taste," *The Globe and Mail*, November 28, 2002, p. B9; "McDonald's Said Ready for More Restructuring," *The Globe and Mail*, March 24, 2003, p. B1; www.economist.com/blogs/schumpeter/2011/06/fast-food-and-cultural-sensitivity; and -company fact sheets, www.mcdonalds.com, retrieved July 26, 2011.

Restructuring strategies, like growth strategies, have profound effects on human resources issues, such as managed turnover, selective layoffs, transfers, increased demands on remaining employees, and renegotiated labour contracts. These issues are described in Chapter 10.

GROWTH STRATEGIES

Many organizations in the private-sector target growth as their number-one strategy. By this they mean growth in revenues, sales, market share, customers, orders, and so on. To a large extent, the implications of a growth strategy for HR practices are profound. A firm in a growth stage is engaged in job creation, aggressive recruitment and selection, rapidly rising wages, and expanded orientation and training budgets, depending on how the organization chooses to grow. Amazon and Alibaba are good examples of companies with growth strategies.

Growth can be achieved in several ways: incrementally, internationally, or by mergers and acquisitions.

INCREMENTAL GROWTH Incremental growth can be attained by expanding the client base, increasing the products or services, changing the distribution networks, or using technology. Procter & Gamble uses all these methods:

- Expanding the client base (by introducing skin-care lotion and hair conditioner for babies)
- Increasing the products (by adding Pringles potato chips to a product mix of cleaning and health care products)
- Changing the distribution networks (by adding drugstores to grocery stores).
- Using technology to manage just-in-time customer purchasing

INTERNATIONAL GROWTH Seeking new customers or markets by expanding internationally is another growth option. Operating a business in a foreign country, particularly one that is not in North America or Europe, may be challenging for the Western HR manager. The HR implications for an international strategy are described in Chapter 11.

MERGERS AND ACQUISITIONS Quantum leaps in growth can be achieved through acquisitions, mergers, or joint ventures. An **acquisition** occurs when one company buys another, whereas a **merger** typically is seen as two organizations merging to achieve economies of scale. Acquisitions and mergers have an obvious impact on HR: they eliminate the duplication of functions, meld benefits and labour relations practices, and, most importantly, create a common culture. The complexity of merging two companies is outlined in Chapter 12.

Acquisition
The purchase of one company by another

Merger
Two organizations combine resources and become one

Burger King acquired Tim Hortons to become a fast-food giant.

STABILITY STRATEGIES

Some organizations may choose stability over growth. For many reasons, some executives, particularly small business owners in relatively stable markets, wish to maintain the status quo. They do not wish to see their companies grow. The executive team is content to keep market share, doing what it has always been doing. HRM practices remain constant, as they are presumed to be effective for current strategy. Others see this as a temporary strategy ("Pause and proceed with caution") until environmental conditions are more favourable for growth. Or perhaps the organization grew very rapidly, and needs time to manage all the changes. Both Microsoft and Apple had rapid growth, and are now growing more slowly. We have not included chapters on stability strategies, because the HRM issues would, by definition, be subsumed under another generic strategy.

Executives in other companies, recognizing that a current profitable situation will not last forever, choose to milk the investment. This harvest strategy can also be seen as a retrenchment strategy, because no investment or efforts will be made to make the business grow; therefore, the goal will be restructuring.

Businesses can pursue several strategies over time or concurrently. Read HR Planning Today 1.2 about the strategies implemented by Cara Operations.

HR PLANNING TODAY   1.2
MULTIPLE STRATEGIES

The mission statement of Cara Operations declares that its aim is to be Canada's leading integrated restaurant company. Cara owns or controls food outlets such as Harvey's, Swiss Chalet, and Milestones Grill and Bar. Cara is an example of a company employing multiple corporate strategies—through acquisition, divestiture, and new concept development—to achieve increased sales and profitability.

- *Acquisitions:* Cara began an aggressive acquisitions strategy in 1999 when it bought 61 percent of Kelsey's, a Canadian company that owned 74 restaurants including Kelsey's, Montana's, and Outback. In 2002, Cara bought the Second Cup coffee chain and acquired a 74 percent stake in Milestones, a chain of upscale restaurants. In 2013, Cara merged with Fairfax to acquire control of Swiss Chalet and East Side Mario's.

- *Divestiture:* In 2000, Cara sold its Beaver Food Catering business. In 2001, it sold its health care

institutional food services division. In 2006, it sold its airport terminal business as well as Second Cup. It divested the Summit division (distribution company) in 2007. In 2010, it sold its airline catering business, Cara Airline Solutions, to Gategroup, in order to focus its operation on restaurants.

- *Growth:* Cara has divested its noncore businesses and is focused on its restaurants. The divestitures resulted in cash that will be used to expand the number of restaurants. The growth strategy will see an increase in restaurants and revenues in the years ahead.

- *Business strategy:* Arjen Melis, president of corporate development at Cara, describes Cara's business strategy as "pursuing a portfolio of distinct brands, each of which targets a differentiated consumer segment."

Sources: Adapted from www.cara.com, retrieved October 7, 2011; "Case Study: Cara Operations Ltd.," *National Post Business*, October 2002, pp. 47–50; interview with Arjen Melis, president of Corporate Development, Cara Operations Limited, May 27, 2008; "Cara Operations Selling Airline Catering Business to Swiss Company Gategroup," *The Canadian Press*, September 15, 2010; "Cara Operations Ltd. Financial Profile," Report on Business Financial Profile, *The Globe and Mail*, April 21, 2011, p. B1.

BUSINESS STRATEGIES

We discussed corporate strategy as corporate-wide plans used to manage and control the various units that exist within an organization. But many large organizations operate several businesses under the same or different names, and each of these might have its own strategy. For example, Alcan Aluminum operates two "divisions" or businesses, one that focuses on primary metals and one that focuses on fabrication. Each has a different business strategy, although the overall corporate strategy is growth.

Business strategy focuses on one line of business (in a diversified company or public organization), while corporate strategy examines questions about which competitive strategy to choose as a multi-business corporation. Corporate strategies focus on long-term survival and growth. Business strategy concerns itself with how to build a strong competitive position. As Thompson and colleagues note, business strategy is the action plan for a single line of business to gain competitive advantage.[10]

Corporate strategies and business strategies are differentiated in the following ways. Corporate strategies are concerned with questions such as these: Should we be in business? What business should we be in? Business strategies are concerned with questions such as these: How should we compete? Should we compete by offering products at prices lower than those of the competition or by offering the best service? Business strategy is concerned with how to build a competitive position, and with the best way to compete in that line of business. Air Canada was struggling with its business strategy when it attempted to segment the market by creating a series of subbrands—discount, high end, and charter. The discount airline Zip and then Rouge, were created to compete directly with WestJet. Businesses try to demonstrate to the customer that their product or service is better than their rivals' because they have lower prices or more innovative services.

We will spend some time describing the strategic planning process, because HR professionals are expected to understand the language of business and to be able to discuss HR programs using the terminology of strategic planning. By learning the models and terms used by managers in business, HR managers will be able to propose or defend HR programs in ways that other managers will understand.

> **Business strategy**
> Plans to build a competitive focus in one line of business

// THE STRATEGIC PLANNING PROCESS

A strategic plan describes the organization's future direction, performance targets, and approaches to achieve the targets.[11] There are many models or approaches to the development and implementation of strategy. Here is a useful framework of the steps that are involved in strategic planning, which is also illustrated visually in Figure 1.2:[12]

1. Establish the mission, vision, and values.
2. Develop objectives.
3. Analyze the external environment.
4. Identify the competitive advantage.
5. Determine the competitive position.
6. Implement the strategy.
7. Evaluate the performance.

FIGURE 1.2

THE STRATEGIC PLANNING PROCESS

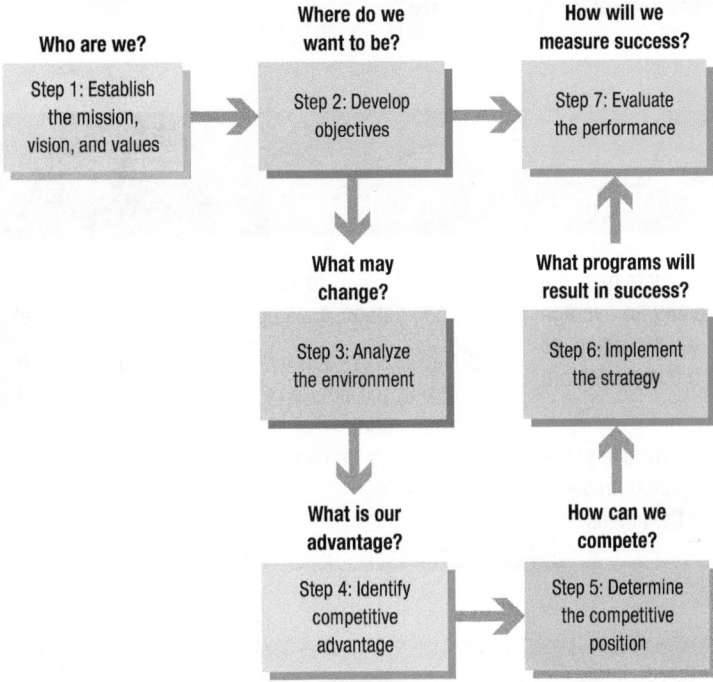

1. ESTABLISH THE MISSION, VISION, AND VALUES

A **mission statement** articulates the purpose for which, or the reason, an organization exists.[13] It also stipulates the value the organization offers for its customers and clients.[14] For example, Alibaba's mission statement is "to make it easy to do business anywhere."

Many believe that conveying a strong sense of mission is the most important role for the CEO. MacMillan Bloedel changed the company's position by articulating this mission statement: "The most respected and environmentally responsible forest company in Canada, and an example for others internationally. The public has granted us a license to operate, and they have a right to expect that we will be responsible guardians of their renewable resource." See HR Planning Today 1.3 to find out if you can recognize some mission statements, and see HR Planning Notebook 1.3 for an exercise to rate your organization's mission statement.

A **vision statement** defines the organization's long-term goals. The distinction between a mission statement and a vision statement is that whereas the mission statement answers the questions "Who are we? What do we do? Why are we here?," the vision statement answers the question "Where are we going?"[15] A good vision statement sets a clear and compelling goal that serves to unite an organization's efforts. For example, the vision of Alibaba is "We aim to build the future infrastructure of commerce. We envision that our customers will meet, work and live at Alibaba, and that we will be a company that lasts at least 102 years.[16]

Mission statement
An articulation of the purpose of the organization and the value it creates for customers

Vision statement
A definition of the organization's long-term goals.

Values
The basic beliefs that govern individual and group behaviour in an organization

Values are the basic beliefs that govern individual and group behaviour in an organization. While vision and mission statements answer the questions about what must be accomplished, values answer the question "How must we behave?" For example, 3M Company states, "We will grow by helping our customers win–through the ingenuity and responsiveness of people who care."

HR PLANNING TODAY　　1.3

THE "PERSON ON A BUS TEST" OF MISSION STATEMENTS

A test of a good mission statement is its ability to pass the "person on a bus test." In other words, could an average person correctly identify the company after reading its mission statement? Can you guess which companies are attached to these mission statements?

1. X will be a world leader in providing innovative physical and electronic delivery solutions, creating value for our customers, employees and all Canadians.

2. Our mission: to inspire and nurture the human spirit— one person, one cup and one neighborhood at a time.

3. To improve the lives of vulnerable people by mobilizing the power of humanity in Canada and around the world.
Answers on page 26.

HR PLANNING NOTEBOOK　　1.3

RATE YOUR ORGANIZATION'S MISSION STATEMENT

On a scale of 0–2, with 0 indicating "no," 1 indicating "somewhat," and 2 indicating "yes," evaluate your organization's mission statement using the following questions:

1. Does the statement describe an inspiring purpose that avoids playing to the self-serving interests of stakeholders?

2. Does the statement describe the organization's responsibilities to stakeholders?

3. Does the statement define a business domain and explain why it is attractive?

4. Does the statement describe the strategic positioning that the company prefers in a way that helps to identify the sort of competitive position that it will look for?

5. Does the statement identify values that link with the organization's purpose and act as beliefs with which employees can feel proud?

6. Do the values resonate with and reinforce the organization's strategy?

7. Does the statement describe important behaviours and standards that serve as beacons of the strategy and values?

8. Are the standards described in a way that enables individual employees to judge when they are behaving correctly?

9. Does the statement give a portrait of the company capturing the culture of the organization?

10. Is the statement easy to read?

11. If the total is ten or less, then work is needed to improve the mission statement. Fifteen or more … great job!

Source: Reprinted from Andrew Campbell, "Mission Statement," *Long Range Planning*, Vol. 30, No. 6, 1997, with permission from Elsevier.

The mission, vision, and value statements of Cara, a leading food service and restaurant business, are presented in HR Planning Today 1.4.

Sometimes values reflect the founders' ethics; sometimes they are just words on a poster on the wall. In order to develop employee buy-in to values, invite employees to participate in the elaboration of the organization values as described in HR Planning Notebook 1.4. Then these values should be part of every orientation workshop and training course, and be modelled by all employees, especially senior management. The articulation of values serves these important purposes:

- Conveys a sense of identity for employees.
- Generates employee commitment to something greater than themselves.
- Adds to the stability of the organization as a social system.
- Serves as a frame of reference for employees to use to make sense of organizational activities and to use as a guide for appropriate behavior.

Strong and clear mission and vision statements enable all employees to work toward common goals.

2. DEVELOP OBJECTIVES

At this stage, the management team develops short-term objectives to realize its high-level mission, vision, and value. Objectives are an expression, in measurable terms, of what an organization intends to achieve.[17] Goals can be classified as hard or soft. Hard goals always include numbers, usually relative to performance last year, or to competition. For example, an organization would not state a goal as "increased profitability"; the statement would be action oriented and specific: "to increase profitability in 2017 by 7 percent over 2016."

HR PLANNING NOTEBOOK 1.4

CREATING ORGANIZATIONAL VALUES

1. Invite all employees to offer ideas about the current and the desired values for the organization.

2. Record these without judgments, criticisms, or comments.

3. Have the group identify common themes.

4. Discuss and debate these themes, until there is consensus on a short list of core values.

5. Have subgroups take one value, and develop a definition of the value and the employee behaviours related to that value.

6. Have groups present their definitions and behaviours, which may be adopted or revised.

7. Appoint one person from each team to incorporate the revisions into a value statement, which is then combined with all the value statements. These then become the company values.

HR Planning Notebook 1.5 offers some examples of typical objectives for corporations. Soft goals usually define the targets for the social conduct of the business, and may not always be quantifiable. Soft goals may include being ethical and environmentally responsible, and providing a working environment free of discrimination with opportunities for professional development. One of the most widely applied frameworks for categorizing objectives is the balanced score card model, which divides organizational strategy into four comprehensive perspectives: financial, customer, learning and growth, and internal business process.[18] An advantage of this framework, discussed more thoroughly in Chapter 14, is that it forces each organizational member to think about how his or her actions can contribute to organizational strategy implementation.

3. ANALYZE THE EXTERNAL ENVIRONMENT

To achieve the company objectives, managers must be aware of threats and opportunities in the external environment. By scanning and monitoring technology, laws and regulations, the economy, sociocultural factors, and changing demographics, managers can make reactive and proactive changes to the strategic plan. These will be discussed in detail in Chapter 3.

4. IDENTIFY THE COMPETITIVE ADVANTAGE

Besides the external environment, managers also need to consider what **competitive advantage** the organization possesses—that is, what characteristics enable it to generate more value for customers at a lower cost, thereby earning higher rates of profit than its competitors.[19] Competitive advantage normally derives from those resources that allow the organization to perform more effectively or efficiently than competitors, which fall into three categories:

> **Competitive advantage**
> The characteristics of a firm that enable it to earn higher rates of profit than its competitors

- *Tangible assets:* These are future economic resources that have substance and form from which an organization will benefit. Examples are land, inventory, building, location, cash, and technology.
- *Intangible assets:* These are future economic resources that have been generated from past organizational events. These assets lack substance and form. Examples are human capital, reputation, goodwill, trust, and copyright.

- *Capabilities:* These are a complex combination of people and processes that represent the firm's capacity to exploit resources to achieve the firm's objectives.[20] Examples are managerial capabilities, innovative capabilities, marketing capabilities, and organizational cultures. These capabilities—the collective skills, abilities, and expertise of an organization—are the outcome of investments in staffing, training, and other HR areas. They are stable over time and are not easy to measure or benchmark; therefore, competitors cannot copy them.[21]

The resource-based view suggests that for these resources and capabilities to provide a sustained competitive advantage, they must meet four criteria:[22]

1. They are *valuable* to the firm's strategy (they help generate value/reduce cost).
2. They are *rare* (competitors don't have them).
3. They are *inimitable* (they cannot easily be copied by competitors).
4. They can be *organized* by the firm (the firm can exploit the resources)

The acronym for this view is VRIO. The culture at Southwest Airlines meets all these characteristics, as can be seen in HR Planning Today 1.5. Besides culture, many

> **Capabilities**
> A complex combination of people and processes that represent the firm's capacity to exploit resources that have been specially integrated to achieve a desired result

HR PLANNING TODAY   1.5

CULTURE AS A COMPETITIVE ADVANTAGE

Southwest Airlines' strategy is that of low cost/low price/no frills flights, a strategy that has resulted in profits every year since 1974. The organization's culture is its competitive advantage, and possesses all the key characteristics.

ATTRIBUTE: VALUABLE

Does the Southwest Airlines culture offer customers something that they value? Yes. The culture results in employees who are productive, flexible, motivated, and willing to accept a low base pay and work long hours. This not only keeps costs down but also improves utilization and on-time delivery performance.

ATTRIBUTE: RARE

Is Southwest Airlines the only one with this type of culture? If not, is the level of its culture higher than that ofcompetitors? Yes. Each airline has its own culture but only the Southwest culture has inspired employees to care so much about their company that they accept very low base salaries, yet are highly productive and flexible; work almost twice as long and are

more motivated than other airline's employees; and would rather support the company than the union. The "family" at Southwest is just not found at other airlines.

ATTRIBUTE: IMITABILITY

Is it easy for other firms to acquire this culture? No. Duplicating this culture is likely to be difficult. Although others may think that they know what makes Southwest employees so motivated, productive, flexible, and dedicated, that may not be the case. Also, building the Southwest culture may have involved a series of events that are impossible for another firm to re-create.

ATTRIBUTE: ORGANIZE

Is the firm organized, ready and able to exploit the resource? Yes. Southwest's good position in relation to suppliers and customers enables it to appropriate the value from its extraordinary culture. Barring a major change that diminishes the culture or reverses the relationship, Southwest should continue to make money.

other forms of resources have a potential to meet all four criteria. For example, the innovative capabilities embedded in employees' specialized expertise, knowledge-sharing routines, and incentive systems for innovation are unique to the organization; and customers' trust in the brand name, created by a cumulated history of ethical behaviours of the business and its employees, is not transferable. Some common reasons for these resources and capabilities being a source of sustained competitive advantage are: they are unique, they must be built up over time, they require large-scale investment, and they are socially complex.[23] As you can see, human resources play a key role in creating most capabilities.

Resources and capabilities become **core competencies** when they serve as a firm's competitive advantage. Core competencies distinguish a company competitively and reflect its personality.[24] In other words, a core competency is a competitively important activity that directly contributes to a company's strategy.[25] The core competency of Southwest Airlines is culture and that of Sony is miniaturization. Walmart's core competency is its cross-docking inventory management system, which helps it reduce costs. Kimberly-Clark is the best in the world at producing paper-based consumer products, choosing to specialize in category-killer brands (where the name of the product is synonymous with the name of the category—for example, Kleenex).[26]

Core competencies can be leveraged. For example, when Amazon.com developed the competency to sell books through the Internet, it leveraged this competency to deliver other consumer products such as CDs. HR managers should be particularly aware of how to contribute to the creation of core competencies.

What if the competencies needed for gaining competitive advantage constantly evolve? In fact, many companies face this difficulty when they continuously compete to seize emerging market opportunity or develop new technology. **Dynamic capabilities**—the ability to adapt and renew competencies in accordance with changing business environment[27]—are particularly important in these situations. Being able to regenerate its competencies responsively, Amazon.com started online bookselling in 1998, more than a decade earlier than Borders. Amazon.com was also the first to pioneer digital books with the Kindle e-reader in 2007, three years earlier than Borders. Borders' lack of dynamic capabilities to regenerate itself, in contrast, was one of the main reasons for its bankruptcy.[28]

With the information from external environment and internal competence analysis, managers can summarize the conclusions using a SWOT analysis, which is a tool for analyzing a company's resource capabilities and deficiencies, its market opportunities, and the external threats to its future.[29] SWOT is an acronym for **S**trengths, **W**eaknesses, **O**pportunities, and **T**hreats. A *strength* is something that a company does well or an attribute that makes it more competitive. A *weakness* is something that an organization does poorly, or a condition, such as location, that puts it at a disadvantage relative to competitors.[30] *Opportunities* and *threats* are environmental conditions external to the firm that may be beneficial or harmful. But an organizational strength can be used to combat an external threat. For example, the very capable legal department (a strength) of Texas Instruments was able to collect nearly $700 million in damages and royalties from Korean and Japanese firms that were infringing on its copyright (a threat). Sometimes an external indicator, such as a rising concern with personal health, may be beneficial for one sector (health clubs) and harmful to others (tobacco companies).[31]

5. DETERMINE THE COMPETITIVE POSITION

On the basis of the external environment and internal competence, managers then decide the competitive position the company wants to achieve. A company cannot usually compete by being ready to offer any product or service at various prices through multiple channels of distribution. The senior managers must determine who the customers are, where they are located, and what product or service characteristics these customers value. Thus the organization has to create a **value proposition**—a statement of the fundamental benefits it has chosen to offer in the marketplace. The value proposition of TD Bank's Green Line Investor services was very simple: lower-cost transactions than through traditional brokerage channels.

Michael Porter made a major contribution to the field of strategic management by grouping the many ways in which organizations can compete into five generic competitive strategies:[32]

Value proposition
A statement of the fundamental benefits of the products or services being offered in the marketplace

1. *Low-cost provider strategy:* The goal here is to provide a product or service at a price lower than that of competitors while appealing to a broad range of customers. Fast-food businesses use this strategy almost exclusively. A range of customers from toddlers to seniors consumes the cheap hamburger, a good but basic product with few frills. A company competing on this basis searches continually for ways to reduce costs.

2. *Broad differentiation strategy:* An organization employing this strategy seeks to differentiate its products from competitors' products in ways that will appeal to a broad range of buyers. It searches for features that will make its product or service different from that of competitors and that will encourage customers to pay a premium. Thus, Burger King will introduce the Whopper with "frills," for which people will pay an extra dollar. The goal is to provide a unique or superior value to the buyer in terms of product quality, product features, or service.

3. *Best-cost provider strategy:* The goal here is to give customers more value for their money by emphasizing a low-cost product or service and an upscale differentiation. The product has excellent features, including several upscale features that are offered at low cost. East Side Mario's offers hamburgers but presents them on a plate, with extras such as potato salad, served by a waiter in an attractive setting featuring focused lights and art on the walls.

4. *Focused or market niche strategy based on lower cost:* The goal here is to offer a low-cost product to a select group of customers. Red Lobster uses this approach, selling fish and seafood at reasonable prices to a narrow market segment.

5. *Focused or market niche strategy based on differentiation:* Here, the organization tries to offer a niche product or service customized to the tastes and requirements of a very narrow market segment. For example, Bymark Restaurant in Toronto sells a $35 hamburger that uses sirloin meat and truffles.

Under Porter's schema, business strategy concerns itself with the product and market scope. What particular goods and services are to be provided? What distinguishing features or attractive attributes will characterize these products and services? Typical product characteristics are cost, quality, optional features, durability, and reliability. Market dimensions refer to the characteristics of the target market—size, diversity, buying patterns, and geographic regions. The model has been criticized for its overlapping categories. Most textbooks on strategy suggest that there are really only three competitive positions: cost, differentiation, and focus.

6. IMPLEMENT THE STRATEGY

Strategy implementation is the process of establishing the programs, budgets, and procedures for facilitating the achievement of the strategic goals. If the goal is growth, what are the techniques for achieving this goal? Should a company expand its distribution channels to other regions? Should it attempt to change its culture? **Strategy implementation** is the process by which the strategy is put into action. This process is sometimes called *operational planning*. It consists of programs, budgets, and procedures, such as those for HR. The **program** outlines the steps or activities necessary to accomplish the goal. If the goal is innovation, how can HR recruit, select, train, and create a supportive culture to accomplish it? The role of the HR function in enabling the execution of strategy is discussed in Chapter 2. The budget lists the detailed costs of each program, and defines how the organization is going to allocate its financial resources. Most organizations establish a *hurdle rate*, the percentage of return on investment necessary before a program is implemented. As you will see in Chapter 14 on evaluation, most HR managers are very skilled at preparing a budget for the implementation of a new program, but unable to discuss, in dollars, the rate of return for the program. **Procedures** list the steps required to get the job done. Most HR professionals use procedures—for example, the procedure to recruit a university student—based on experience. But other functional areas would have these procedures established as standard operating practice; these would be applied uniformly across the company, in every site.

<aside>
Strategic implementation
The process by which a strategy is put into action

Program
The steps or activities necessary to accomplish a goal

Procedures
The steps required to get a job done
</aside>

7. EVALUATE THE PERFORMANCE

Developing a strategy is easy; making it happen is not. The ability to execute strategy is becoming a more important criterion for assessing not only managers but also the

There are many benefits to formulating and evaluating organizational strategy.

whole organization. The successful implementation of a strategy is judged by the ability to meet financial targets such as profits, and the ability to meet benchmarked ratios of efficiency and effectiveness such as R&D expenses to sales, or sales to assets. As you will see in Chapter 14, companies are using the balanced scorecard approach to evaluate other important indicators of success, such as customer satisfaction or employee engagement. These measures are becoming increasingly valuable for their ability to predict financial and operational performance.

BENEFITS OF STRATEGY FORMULATION

Working through the strategic planning process has these benefits:

- *Clarity:* There is focused and guided decision making about resource allocations.
- *Coordination:* Everyone is working toward the same goals.
- *Efficiency:* Daily decision making is guided toward the question "Does it fit with our strategy?"
- *Incentives:* Employees understand the behaviours and performance that will be rewarded.
- *Adjustment to change:* If a major change is under consideration, understanding the current strategy is essential.
- *Career development:* Helps potential employees decide if they want to work for the company, if there is a skills fit, and what training and development they will need to undergo.

Organizations that do not see the benefits of strategic planning have succumbed to these errors:

- Relegating the process to official planners, and not involving executives and managers (and even employees), resulting in no buy-in.
- Failing to use the plan as the guide to making decisions and evaluating performance.
- Failing to align incentives and other HR policies to the achievement of the strategy.

An understanding of the strategic planning process is the essential first step to creating an HR strategy that makes sense for the organization. Strategic HR planning complements the traditional approach to HR planning (forecasting supply and demand) but adds more strategic choices. Thus, at the most senior levels of the corporation, HR professionals move from an administrative role to the role of strategic partner. They understand strategies and business needs and create the kind of HR competencies that build competitive advantage.

The strategic planning model has dictated the structure of this text. We emphasize aligning HR strategy with business strategy (Chapter 2); monitoring and analyzing external factors (Chapter 3); assessing the strengths and weaknesses of organizations' human resources (Chapters 4–8); the ways to implement an organizational change (Chapter 9), which will help with the following chapters that deal with determining the HR implications of corporate strategies such as restructuring (Chapter 10), going international (Chapter 11), mergers and acquisitions (Chapter 12), outsourcing (Chapter 13), and assessing the effectiveness of these efforts (Chapter 14). Figure 1.3 graphically summarizes the organization of this book.

FIGURE 1.3

AN OVERVIEW OF THE ORGANIZATION OF THE TEXTBOOK

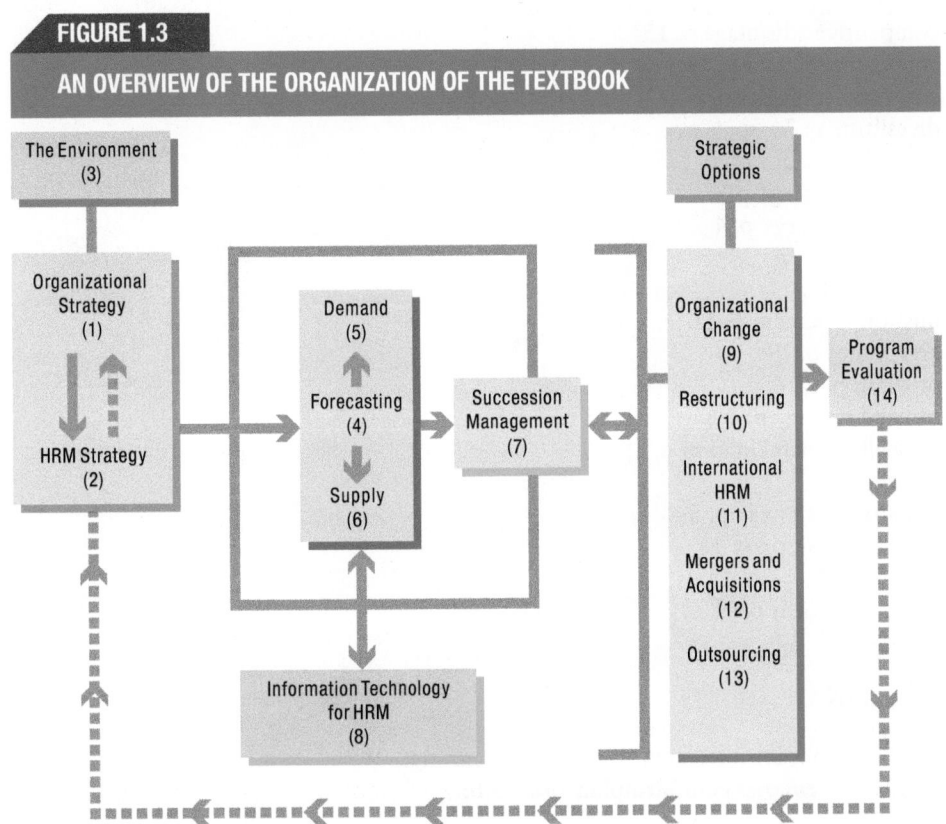

Note: Chapter numbers in parentheses

// SUMMARY

It is important that HR professionals appreciate the role of strategic planning in their organizations and understand the language and terminology of strategic planning. A strategy is a planned process whereby organizations can map out a set of objectives and methods of meeting those objectives. A strategy may be *intended*–formulated at the beginning of the process–or *realized*–what actually happens. The strategy may also be *emergent*; that is, it is changing as necessary to deal with environmental changes. Corporate or company-wide strategies are concerned with the long-term view of the organization. Business strategies focus on one line of business, building a strong competitive position. One useful framework is a seven-step approach (see Figure 1.2). By understanding strategy language and models, the HR professional can work with other executives to implement HR practices that enable strategy.

KEY TERMS

acquisition p. 8
bankruptcy p. 7
business strategy p. 10
capabilities p. 16

WEB LINKS

Excellent links for references on strategic planning:
http://www.entarga.com/stratplan/index.htm

A publication that provides articles, interviews, and case studies focused on strategic management and general business issues:
http://www.strategy-business.com

DISCUSSION QUESTIONS

1. Identify companies currently operating under these corporate strategies: restructuring–turnaround, divestiture, liquidation, and bankruptcy; and growth–incremental, international, and mergers and acquisitions.

2. Review these three mission statements and assess whether they meet the "person on a bus" test.

   - To provide book lovers and those they care about with the most inspiring retail and online environments in the world for books and life-enriching products and services.

   - X is dedicated to building a world-class national resource enabling Canadians to know their country and themselves through their published heritage, and to providing an effective gateway to national and international sources of information.

   - X is an independent campaigning organization that uses nonviolent, creative confrontation to expose global environmental problems and to force the solutions essential to a green and peaceful future.

3. The focus in this chapter (and in strategy literature) is on private companies. Check the websites of government departments and identify at least ten strategies (often called *plans* or *mission statements*). Can you identify any that correspond to some of

the models of business strategies? Can you create a model or typology for public-sector organizations? To start, consult J. Tomkins, "Strategic Human Resources Management in Government: Unresolved Issues," *Public Personnel Management*, Vol. 31, No. 1 (2002): 95–110.

EXERCISES

1. Identify two companies working in the same sector (hotels, restaurants, and post-secondary institutions are good choices), one using a low-cost provider strategy and one using a differentiation strategy.

2. Research these two companies' mission, vision, and value statements.

3. Discuss their differences in resources, capabilities, and core competencies.

4. Compare and contrast the practices of the two companies.

CASE STUDY   LOBLAW COMPANIES LTD.

The Canadian food retailing sector had been growing at less than 1 percent a year, and in 2012 it was a $86 billion business. There are a number of competitors in this sector, including Sobeys, Metro, Costco Canada, Canada Safeway, and Walmart Canada. Loblaw Companies is Canada's largest food distributor with sales of more than $32 billion, 1,000 stores, and 136,000 employees. The organizational objectives were to control costs through efficiencies and differentiate its products (through private-label brands such as President's Choice, No Name, Organics PC, and Joe Fresh) and its stores (through 22 different brand banners such as Loblaw, Fortinos, No Frills, Provigo, Zehrs, Wholesale Club, and Atlantic Superstore). In 2009, it acquired T&T, the largest Asian foods chain, to capitalize on the growing ethnic food market. Loblaw wants to see sales growth of 5 percent a year. In 2013, it acquired Shoppers Drug Mart.

The largest threat to Loblaw's strategy is Walmart, the world's largest retailer. The latter has a growth strategy, opening hundreds of stores every year. Walmart arrived in Canada in 1994, by acquiring 122 Woolco stores. Walmart not only used size and scale to compete (as did other retailers) but also mastered the use of technology to drive costs down. For example, its centralized information system tracked the operations of 5000 stores worldwide, and linked them with about 30 000 suppliers, all in real time.

Sources: www.loblaws.com; "Loblaw Companies Limited: Company Profile," www.datamonitor.com; Z. Olyjnk, "Look Who's Eating Loblaw's Lunch," *Canadian Business*, vol. 80, no. 5 (February 26, 2007): 44; http://www.canadiangrocer.com/top-stories/state-of-the-canadian-grocery-industry-31101, retrieved November 28, 2014.

QUESTION

1. Conduct a SWOT analysis for Loblaw. As a group, assess the company against the strengths, weaknesses, threats, and opportunities contained in the SWOT matrix below.

SWOT ANALYSIS

Potential Resource Strengths and Competitive Capabilities

• A powerful strategy	• Superior intellectual capital relative to key rivals
• Core competencies in _____	• Cost advantages over rivals
• A distinctive competence in _____	• Strong advertising and promotion
• A product that is strongly differentiated from those of rivals	• Product innovation capabilities
• Competencies and capabilities that are well matched to industry key success factors	• Proven capabilities in improving production processes
• A strong financial condition; ample financial resources to grow the business	• Good supply-chain management capabilities
• Strong brand-name image/company reputation	• Good customer service capabilities
• An attractive customer base	• Better product quality relative to rivals
• Economy of scale and/or learning and experience curve advantages over rivals	• Wide geographic coverage and/or strong global distribution capacity
• Proprietary technology/superior technological skills/important patents	• Alliances/joint ventures with other firms that provide access to valuable technology, competencies, and/or attractive geographic markets

POTENTIAL MARKET OPPORTUNITIES

• Openings to win market share from rivals	• Expanding the company's product line to meet a broader range of customer needs
• Sharply rising buyer demand for the industry's product	• Utilizing existing company skills or technological know-how to enter new product lines or new businesses
• Serving additional customer groups or market segments	• Online sales

• Expanding into new geographic markets	• Integrating forward or backward
• Falling trade barriers in attractive foreign markets	• Entering into alliances or joint ventures that can expand the firm's market coverage or boost its competitive capacity
• Acquiring rival firms or companies with attractive technological expertise or capabilities	• Openings to exploit emerging new technologies

POTENTIAL RESOURCE WEAKNESSES AND COMPETITIVE DEFICIENCIES

• No clear strategic direction	• Behind on product quality, R&D, and/or technological know-how
• Resources that are not well matched to industry key success factors	• In the wrong strategic group
• No well-developed or proven core competencies	• Losing market share because _____
• A weak balance sheet; too much debt	• Lack of management depth
• Higher overall unit costs relative to key competitors	• Inferior intellectual capital relative to leading rivals
• Weak or unproven product innovation capabilities	• Subpar profitability because _____
• A product/service with ho-hum attributes or features inferior to those of rivals	• Plagued with internal operating problems or obsolete facilities
• Too narrow a product line relative to rivals	• Behind rivals in e-commerce capabilities
• Weak brand image or reputation	• Short on financial resources to grow the business and pursue promising initiatives
• Weaker dealer network than key rivals and/or lack of adequate global distribution capability	• Too much underutilized plant capacity

(Analysis continues)

POTENTIAL EXTERNAL THREATS TO COMPANY'S WELL-BEING

• Increasing intensity of competition among industry rivals may squeeze profit margins	• Likely entry to potent new competitors
• Slowdowns in market growth	• Loss of sales to substitute products
• Growing bargaining power of customers or supplies	• Restrictive trade policies on the part of foreign governments
• A shift in buyer needs and tastes away from the industry's product	• Costly new regulatory requirements
• Vulnerability to industry driving forces	• Increased costs relating to utilities

Source: Thompson, Strickland, and Gamble, *Crafting and Executing Strategy*, 14/e © 2005. Reprinted with the permission of the McGraw-Hill Companies, Inc.

ANSWERS TO HR PLANNING TODAY 1.3

1. Canada Post
2. Starbucks, and
3. Canadian Red Cross

// REFERENCES

1. HBC. "Our History." http://www.hbcheritage.ca/hbcheritage/history/overview.asp. Retrieved October 17, 2014

2. Collis, D.J., and M.F. Rukstad. 2008. "Can You Say What Your Strategy Is?" *Harvard Business Review*, Vol. 86: 82–90.

3. Anthony, W.P., P.L. Perrewe, and K.M. Kacmar. 1993. *Strategic Human Resources Management*. Fort Worth, TX: Harcourt Brace Jovanovich.

4. Quinn, J.B. 1980. *Strategies for Change: Logical Incrementalism*. Homewood, IL: Richard D. Irwin.

5. Collins, J. 2001. *Good to Great*. New York: Harper Business.

6. Lengnick-Hall, C., and M. Lengnick-Hall. 1990. *Interactive Human Resource Management and Strategic Planning*. New York: Quorum Books.

7. Duane, M.J. 1996. *Customized Human Resource Planning*. Westport, CT: Quorum Books.

8. Thompson, A.A., M.A. Peteraf, J.E. Gamble, and A.J. Strickland. 2010. *Crafting and Executing Strategy: The Quest for Competitive Advantage*, 18th ed. New York: McGraw-Hill Companies.

9. http://www.theglobeandmail.com/globe-investor/target-heads-north-in-zellers-deal/article1868308, retrieved March 28, 2011.

10. Thompson et al., 2010.

11. Thompson et al., 2010.

12. Woodcock, C.P., and P.W. Beamish. 2003. *Concepts in Strategic Management*, 6th ed. Toronto: McGraw-Hill Ryerson.

13. Certo, S.C., and J.P. Peter. 1993. *Strategic Management: A Focus on Process*, 2nd ed. Boston: Irwin.

14. Kaplan, R.S., and D.P. Norton. 2008. "Mastering the Management System." *Harvard Business Review*, January: 64–77.

15. Certo and Peter, 1993.

16. http://www.alibabagroup.com/en/about/overview. Retrieved November 17, 2014.

17. Crossan, M.M., J.N. Fry, and J.P. Killing. 2002. *Strategic Analysis and Action*, 5th ed. Toronto: Prentice Hall.

18. Kaplan, R.S., and D.P. Norton. 2007. "Using the Balanced Scorecard as a Strategic Management System." *Harvard Business Review*, July/August: 150–161.

19. Peteraf, M.A., and J.B. Barney. 2003. "Unraveling the Resource-Based Tangle." *Managerial & Decision Economics*, Vol. 24: 309–323.

20. Hitt, M.A., R.D. Ireland, R.E. Hoskisson, W.G. Rowe, and J.P. Sheppard. 2002. *Strategic Management, Competitiveness and Globalization Concepts.* Toronto: Nelson Thomson Learning.

21. Ulrich, D., and N. Smallwood. 2004. "Capitalizing on Capabilities." *Harvard Business Review*, June: 119–127.

22. Barney, J.B. 1995. "Looking Inside for Competitive Advantage." *Academy of Management Executive*, Vol. 9: 49–61; Collis, J., and C.A. Montgomery. 1995. "Competing on Resources: Strategy in the 1990s," *Harvard Business Review*, Vol. 73, No. 4 (July/August 1995): 118–128.

23. Collis, D.J., and C.A. Montgomery. 2008. "Competing on Resources." *Harvard Business Review*, Vol. 86: 140–150.

24. Hoskisson, R.E., M.A. Hitt, and R.D. Ireland. 2004. *Competing for Advantage.* Mason, OH: Thompson South-Western.

25. Thompson et al., 2010.

26. Collins, 2001.

27. Teece, D.J., G. Pisan, and A. Shuen. 1997. "Dynamic Capabilities and Strategic Management." *Strategic Management Journal*, Vol. 18: 509–533.

28. Kary, T., and L. Sandler. "Borders Files Bankruptcy, Is Closing Up to 275 Stores." http://www.bloomberg.com/news/2011-02-16/borders-book-chain-files-for-bankruptcy-protection-with-1-29-billion-debt.html , retrieved March 28, 2011.

29. Thompson et al., 2010.

30. Thompson et al., 2010.

31. Dess, G.G., and G.T. Lumpkin. 2003. *Strategic Management: Creating Competitive Advantages.* Boston: McGraw-Hill.

32. Porter, M.E. 1985. *Competitive Advantage.* New York: Free Press.

CHAPTER

ALIGNING HR WITH STRATEGY

CHAPTER LEARNING OUTCOMES

AFTER READING THIS CHAPTER, YOU SHOULD BE ABLE TO:

- Understand the importance of strategic HR planning.
- Identify the risks associated with not planning.
- Discuss approaches to linking strategy and HR, including the barriers to becoming a strategic partner.
- List the characteristics of an effective HR strategy.

Google grew within a decade from a startup to a global company with a $180 billion market capitalization. Google's core business is its web search engine, which generates 99 percent of its revenue through advertising. Thanks to this cash cow, Google has been able to sponsor many innovative and competitive services, including its Gmail service, which was the first to have one-gigabyte storage, and Google Talk, which allowed free phone calls in North America. It also entered the smartphone industry, in which its free Android operating system quickly gained a 30 percent market share within two years.[1]

Google's success was in part due to its economies of scale in its financial, information, and technology resources. To keep growing, Google needs to continuously sense market opportunities and take action faster than others. Google knows that such dynamic capability cannot be generated from financial or physical resources alone, but also must come from the analytical, decision-making, and innovative capabilities of its human resources. Consequently, a software engineer at Google can receive up to $151,000 starting salary (excluding options, bonuses etc.), compared to Apple ($149,000), Facebook ($138,000), and Microsoft ($128,000).[2] Google is also famous for its extraordinary benefits for employees such as free food, varied recreational activities, and free services such as tax advice, on-site child care, and doctors. Even at 2010 year-end, when the U.S. economy was still in recession, Google gave all employees a 10% raise plus a $1000 bonus to retain valuable talents. It is not surprising that annually, the company ranked among the top five on *Fortune* magazine's list of the best companies to work for.[3]

Google has strategically aligned its HR practices with the company's needs as well. To encourage innovation, it allows employees to spend 20 percent of their paid time doing anything they want. To help employees work better, the company has designed a course called "Managing Your Energy for Your Sustained Performance" for 2000 first-year employees.[4] It has also established a talent analytics function consisting of 30 researchers, analysts, and consultants who have scientifically studied what types of human capital were strategic to the company's performance, what types of managers were effective or ineffective, and what types of HR practices enabled the recruitment and retention of the best talent.

As Google's vice-president of people operations has commented, "It's not the company-provided lunch that keeps people here. Googlers tell us that there are three reasons they stay: the mission, the quality of the people, and the chance to build the skill set of a better leader or entrepreneur. And all our analytics are built around these reasons."[5]

// STRATEGIC HRM

Human resources management (HRM) can be viewed as an umbrella term that encompasses the following:

- Overarching HR *philosophies* that specify the values put on HR that inform an organization's policies and practices
- Formal HR *policies* that direct and partially constrain the development of specific practices, such as to increase workforce diversity
- Specific HR *practices*, such as recruitment, selection, and appraisal

Strategic HRM is the management of HR philosophies, policies, and practices to enable the achievement of the organizational strategy. Ideally, these philosophies, policies, and practices form a system that attracts, develops, motivates, and trains employees who ensure the survival and effective functioning of the organization and its members.[6] There is an emerging view that the discipline of HRM should be split into two areas, much like accounting and finance or sales and marketing.[7]

> **Strategic HRM**
> Interrelated philosophies, policies, and practices that facilitate the attainment of organizational strategy

One area would deal with transactional activities, such as payroll, which are routine but necessary, just like accounting. The second area would function like a decision science, concerned with the effective utilization of human capital, much like finance. In this model, strategic HRM would be concerned with decisions about HR practices, the composition and behaviours of employees, and the effectiveness of these decisions given various business strategies.[8] These strategic activities are comprehensive, are planned, and in their contribution to organizational success are considered high-long-term-value-added.[9]

While managers recognize implicitly that the marketing strategy must support the business strategy, there is not the same sense among managers that HR programs can be designed to support the organizational strategy. And yet human capital issues are at the top of the CEO agenda, with more than half of the top priorities (attraction, retention, innovation) needing HR input.[10] According to recent surveys, three-quarters of Canadian organizations believe that HR is more influential now than five years ago; the reorganization of HR importance is especially higher among CEOs and senior managers (about three-quarters believe so) than other managers (about half).[11]

// THEORIES OF THE STRATEGIC MANAGEMENT OF HUMAN RESOURCES

HR practitioners themselves do not seem to value theory. HR is seen as atheoretical and problem driven.[12] But the field is young, and perspectives are indeed emerging that can be seen as providing the theoretical underpinnings.

HRM MAKING STRATEGIC CONTRIBUTIONS

Human resources management, formerly called "personnel management," started as an administrative function and has traditionally been associated with costs in organizations. Its contributions were often measured by the number of disputes resolved, applicants recruited, total hours spent on training, etc. It is no wonder that many organizations attempted to minimize the size of the HR department by outsourcing administrative tasks to external vendors.

During the 1980s, strategic HR researchers and practitioners started to wonder whether HRM could make strategic contributions to organizations. Certain "high-performance" HR practices, such as selective hiring, extensive training, and competitive pay, came to be considered "best practices," because they were often found in the most successful organizations.[13] Cumulated research showed consistent evidence that the implementation of high-performance HR systems significantly predicted various organizational performance indicators, ranging from reduced employee turnover to improved quality and organizational performance.[14]

This perspective stimulated a broad implementation of high-performance HR systems in many businesses, as managers began to believe that investment in HR would eventually lead to higher financial performance. The term *human resources* was adopted, reflecting the recognition of personnel as valuable "resources" that create competitive advantage, an idea that can be traced back to the resource-based view.

RESOURCE-BASED VIEW

The resource-based view was introduced in Chapter 1, in which the culture of Southwest Airlines was described as a resource that provided a sustained competitive advantage, because its culture is valuable, rare, and very difficult to imitate or substitute. The less a resource can be imitated, the more durable the source of competitive advantage. In addition to culture, a firm's human resources can create sustained competitive advantage if they meet all four criteria suggested by the resource-based view. First, employees who have superior performance because of their skills, commitment, or flexibility are *valuable*—they help the company beat out competitors by offering better service/unique products or reducing costs. The employee loyalty of Marks & Spencer, for example, helped reduce its labour costs to 8.7 percent, as against an industry average of 10 to 20 percent. This dramatically added value to the company.[15]

Second, human resources can be *difficult for competitors to imitate*. If IBM introduces a new software package in January, Microsoft can probably imitate or duplicate this package by February of the same year. However, if IBM technical support people are trained and motivated to provide "knock-your-socks-off service," Microsoft will have a difficult time imitating this workforce within a month. Indeed, Porter estimates that it takes approximately seven years to duplicate a competitive edge in human resources. The competition can't just "buy" these employees, because their effectiveness is embedded in the HR systems of training, compensation, performance appraisal, and culture that allow them to work productively.[16]

Third, the best human resources are *rare*. "Talent war" describes the fierce competition among firms, especially in the high-technology industry, for the best talent. Almost 80 percent of Canadian organizations indicated that they had difficulty recruiting quality candidates with skills that were important to the organization or in high demand.[17] More reputable employers known for their advantage in attracting, developing, and keeping good talent are more likely to gain access to the best talent on the market. "Canada's Top 100 Employers" is an annual competition among Canadian businesses on their offerings to employees. Research In Motion was included for five consecutive years from 2007 to 2011, for its practices such as planning for retirement, providing a BlackBerry on the first day, offering tuition subsidies, and giving on-site child care, etc.[18] However, as its share price plummeted, its cumulative reputation as a best employer was ruined by its recent reshuffling of the boardroom and across-the-board layoffs of nearly a quarter of its workforce, which will damage its future ability to attract and retain top talent.

Finally, the value of human resources can be *hard to substitute*. As discussed in Chapter 1, dynamic capabilities are critical for today's businesses to continuously lead the competition. Dynamic capabilities allow businesses to be the first to discover new opportunities, to act faster than others to seize opportunities, and to quickly create the internal processes needed to realize these opportunities.[19] Other resources such as technology and physical resources do not have free will, and thus cannot substitute for decisions and changes made by human resources.[20] Take, for example, the competition between Apple and Nokia. Nokia was once known for its superior technology in producing the most reliable hardware. However, technology and resources do not regenerate by themselves. Yesterday's cutting-edge technology can become inadequate today. Apple bested Nokia in accurately sensing the potential market for smartphones, swiftly entering the business, and successfully regenerating its technology to become competitive in the market, largely due to the dynamic capabilities created by its human resources. The HR department's role, then, is to develop a system that will facilitate and stimulate innovative thinking processes.

Therefore, a firm's human resources are more valuable for sustained competitive advantage than technological and physical resources, particularly in today's competitive and fast-changing environment, because human resources are less visible, more complex, and can initiate change.[21] For these reasons, human resources are increasingly perceived as strategic resources. Given the unlimited potential of HR, how to exploit it is explained by the contingency perspective.

THE CONTINGENCY PERSPECTIVE

In Chapter 1 we learned that business strategies ranged from low cost to high differentiation. Although high-performance HR practices in general contribute to high performance, they may be more cost effective for businesses that pursue a differentiation strategy than for those implementing a low-cost strategy. This is called the *contingency perspective* of HRM. It is not difficult to imagine that employees working at Ritz Carlton would be very different from those working at Comfort Inn: they vary in their human capital (e.g., communication skills), as well as in the behaviours (e.g., customer orientation) that they display to customers. Such employee differences are largely shaped by the HR practices in place, and can be explained by the human capital and behavioural theories.

HUMAN CAPITAL THEORY

Human capital
The sum of employees' knowledge, skills, experience, and commitment invested in the organization

Classical economists describe three types of resources or inputs used in the production of goods and services: land, capital, and labour. Labour, or **human capital**, refers to the collective sum of the attributes, experience, knowledge, and commitment that employees choose to invest in their work. This intangible asset comprises the knowledge, education, vocational qualifications, professional certifications, work-related experience, and competence of an organization's employees.[22] As researchers have noted, "In the new economic paradigm, as the demands for continuous change make innovation, adaptability, speed and efficiency essential features of the business landscape, the strategic importance of intellectual capital and intangible assets [has] increased substantially. While these assets are largely invisible ... the sources are not. They are found in the human capital of the firm's employees."[23] From the perspective of human capital, employees are viewed as a capital resource that requires investment.[24]

Employees are of value to the organization to the extent that they work toward accomplishing organizational objectives. Costs incurred in training, motivating, compensating, and monitoring employees can be viewed as investments in human capital, just as maintenance of equipment is an investment in the capital of the firm.[25] Thus, human capital's value added can be estimated by:

$$\frac{\text{Total revenue} - (\text{operating expenses} - \text{total compensation costs})}{\text{Total compensation costs}}$$

Using this formula, it was estimated that the median human capital return on investment for Canadian organizations was $2.26, meaning that each dollar organizations invested on human capital generated $2.26 in return. Human capital return on investment also varied by industry, with finance, insurance, and real estate having the highest median return ($6.89), followed by manufacturing and construction ($2.19), and

These scientists represent the human capital of their organization.

wholesale and retail trade ($2.02).[26] It is reasonable to expect that human capital return on investment would also vary by strategy, with differentiated organizations generating a higher return than low-cost organizations.

The advantages of an organization with effective HR practices may come not only from having better resources but also from making better use of these resources by achieving higher productivity per worker and matching the capabilities of employees with the strategy.[27] Organizations that compete on service excellence, for example, would invest on service-related human capital. Banks that invested in HR systems for service quality, such as selecting, training, and rewarding employees' service-related skills, had superior service-related human capital and subsequently higher customer evaluation of service quality.[28] To simplify, having a stock of human capital is similar to having a team of talented players. Knowing how to leverage their talents is like having skills in managing and coaching this team. So, too, without the right HR systems, the employees are less effective.

BEHAVIOURAL THEORY

The behavioural perspective suggests that different strategies require not only different human capital, but also different behaviours of employees. HR Planning Today 2.1 describes how employee behaviour can influence organizational outcomes.

An effective HR system first accurately identifies the behaviours needed to implement a strategy. For example, what kinds of employee behaviours are needed for Google to produce innovative ideas? This question may not sound difficult for HR managers; providing

expert opinion on human behaviour might be where the HR profession adds the most unique value. Most HR managers have a clear understanding of whether the company needs risk taking or rule following, competition or teamwork. HR's role is to tactfully challenge and refocus baseless ideas of human behaviour.[29] How to design the HR system to ensure that employees have the skills and opportunities to exhibit desired behaviours and are motivated to do so is more complex and requires deep thinking and systematic analysis.[30] In general, researchers considered performance appraisal, pay for performance, incentive plans, advancement opportunities, and benefits to enhance employee motivation to behave. Concomitantly, practices such as employee involvement, participation in decision making, voice and grievance, performance feedback, teamwork, and job enrichment operate to provide opportunities for employees to behave. Both practice bundles have shown significant impact on organizational outcomes.[31]

Behavioural perspective suggests that these HR practices should be further linked to a particular behavioural objective. For example, what kinds of HR practices will produce innovative behaviours? We learn from the opening vignette that Google encouraged innovative behaviours by selecting people with high creativity, providing them with time and freedom to innovate, and motivating them to innovate through various incentive programs. But this is only one of many ways of encouraging creativity; each method may be specific to each organization's culture and traditions. We will discuss the alignment of HR system with business strategy in more detail later in the chapter.

The behavioural perspective is particularly important as the HR department is asked to define and develop the behaviours necessary to achieve organizational capabilities of innovation, speed, and accountability.[32]

STRATEGIC HR PLANNING

Despite the potential of HRM to make strategic contributions, HRM issues are often cited as a threat to an organization's ability to execute strategy. The free will, complex

behaviours, and human capital make effectively planning and managing human resources extremely difficult.

A more traditional perspective of the HR planning concept implied that the organization was concerned only with possible problems of labour surpluses and shortages. The goal was to determine the knowledge, skills, and abilities (KSAs) required within broad organizational outcomes such as growth or decline. Much emphasis was put on the statistical techniques for analyzing resource supply and demand forecasting while ignoring managerial realities and support for the process.[33] This is now regarded as a narrow, linear approach to HR planning.

There is some concern that the narrow approach of HR planning has been preoccupied with resource supply and demand forecasting without considering the different HR practices required by fundamentally different strategies. For example, a company that decides to grow through the introduction of innovative products needs employees with different kinds of skills from a company that will grow through great customer service. Under traditional HR planning models, both strategies would require the acquisition and absorption of large numbers of employees, but the HR prescriptions for selection, training, and performance management, for example, would differ radically.

In this book, we are suggesting both an approach of forecasting supply and demand of human resources and an approach that calls for tailoring HR policies and practices to the organizational needs of the future. The proliferation of bankruptcies, mergers, and restructuring has affected our view of employees profoundly and highlighted the need for the input of HR professionals in formulating policy.

THE IMPORTANCE OF STRATEGIC HR PLANNING

Executives are demanding that the HR department move from articulating perceived value ("training builds employee skills") to demonstrating real value (the training results in fewer errors or more sales). As a member of the corporate team, the focus of HR must be on scoring points, not just coaching, training, or counting the number of players. The value of HR will be seen in its ability to deliver the behaviours needed to enable the organization's strategy. There are at least two reasons strategic HR planning is so important: (1) employees help an organization achieve success because they are strategic resources, and (2) the planning process itself results in improved goal attainment.

The value of employees as a resource must be placed within a strategic framework. In other words, a strategy itself can become obsolete, making current employee skills obsolete. Suppose, for example, that the current workforce may be valuable because of manual skills, but the market for the company's manufactured products is declining. Environmental analyses suggest that the corporation enter the high-tech field, with its demand for flexible, knowledgeable workers. By changing the strategy, the "value" of the current workforce is diminished. This requires HR planners to be forward looking; when there is a vacancy, HR managers might not look for replacements for current skills, but rather consider what skills will enable the organization to implement its strategy a few years from now. A corollary is that employees can expect to face different HRM practices throughout their lifetimes, and even within a single organization. Employees might be asked to exhibit different behaviours, depending on strategic goals, and these behaviours will be motivated by different HRM practices.[34] HR planning ensures that human

assets are managed and matched to the organizational strategy. Readers are invited to assess the HR planning efforts led by Billy Beane at the Oakland Athletics in the end-of-chapter exercises.

IMPROVED GOAL ATTAINMENT

Strategic HRM can improve an organization's performance. The goals of these HRM strategies are to shape employee behaviour so that it is consistent with the direction the organization identifies in its strategic plans. Organizations with clear strategies provide direction and meaning to employees and mitigate the need for control by substituting a consistency of purpose—in other words, a mission. This articulated vision for the future may result in a more effective organization through increased motivation and performance, lowered absenteeism and turnover, and heightened stability, satisfaction, and involvement.[35] HR Planning Today 2.2 illustrates how HSBC Canada used HR planning to facilitate a strategic change.

To summarize, strategy formulation is important to the attainment of organizational goals in order to align all HR functional strategies with overall strategy and to focus employees on important missions and goals of the organization. Research and observations have demonstrated that developing HR practices that support the strategy leads to improved strategy implementation.[36]

HR PLANNING TODAY 2.2

HSBC CANADA: UPFRONT PLANNING

HSBC Canada is a subsidiary of the London-based HSBC Holdings plc with more than 60 000 employees. In 2009, the parent company decided to move all support functions including HR to shared services, in order to lower HR costs and help operational partners become more independent in HR services. In addition, HSBC launched a multiyear enterprise resource planning initiative to ensure that employees across the corporation use a consistent version of PeopleSoft HR application developed by Oracle. The subsidiaries were fully empowered to determine how to launch the change.

To lead this change, Pat Brosseau, vice-president of HR for HSBC Canada, emphasized the importance of HR planning. She had to reduce the number of HR generalists working with business-line colleagues. To this end, she and her team invested considerable effort into understanding what the new operating model would look like, defining the HR experience that all HSBC employees would have,

and detailing each HR role. "We went into granular detail using process maps and policy reviews to understand, for example, exactly how the role of an employee relations specialist would differ from an HR generalist in the new operating model," she explained. Three factors helped the change progress:

- Within HR there is a change management unit consisting of three HR generalists with organizational design experience and skills, developed road maps, communication plans, and tactics for HR clients.

- HR professionals collaborate with the HSBC Canada project management team.

- HR professionals work with communications specialists in the corporate communications department to ensure the overall effectiveness of the communication plan.

// THE RISKS

Is there a downside to strategic HR planning? The strategic management of human resources seems beneficial, but some researchers point out that there are costs.[37] Research shows that these include the increased time and energy involved in making decisions, greater potential for information overload, impossible commitments to employees, and an overconcern with employee reactions that may be incompatible with industry conditions. As anyone who has gone through the strategy formulation and implementation process understands, the strategy formulation phase is relatively easy; motivating employees to commit to the strategy and implement it is far more difficult. A further problem is that any HR plan for the future may create employees' expectations that they have jobs for life and will be trained for those jobs, whereas the reality is that conditions change, and the plan may change, resulting in job losses.

Another problem, some would argue, is that organizations that commit to one strategy become blind to changes in the environment and lose their flexibility. However, incremental adjustments based on environmental scanning are part of strategy implementation. The risk of not having a strategy seems greater.

There are risks to not developing a strategy. Organizations that do not actively scan the environment face the danger of being out of touch with reality. Today's operating decisions may be based on yesterday's conditions. Comfortable with past success, the managers in these organizations focus on resolving internal problems, much like those who concentrated on making better horse carriages when automobiles were on the horizon.

One example of a company not in touch with reality was Consumers Distributing. It did not develop a strategy to match or surpass the changing distribution networks and customer-service levels of its competitors. The company, now bankrupt, continued to require customers to come to the stores and stand in line, often for out-of-stock items. Meanwhile, its competitors were offering electronic purchasing or were providing greeters at the door of the store who helped the customers find anything they wanted, all for a competitive price. MacMillan argues that firms that develop strategies gain an advantage and control their own destinies.[38] An apt cliché is "an organization that fails to plan, plans to fail."

// LINKING HR PROCESSES TO STRATEGY

Strategic HRM has to facilitate the formulation and implementation of corporate and business-level strategies. Senior managers must focus on issues such as What are the HR implications of adopting a strategy? What are the internal and external constraints and opportunities? Exactly what policies, practices, and philosophies contribute to the successful implementation of the strategy?

The basic premise is that every HR policy and practice must directly support the organization's strategy and objectives.[39] This does not happen as frequently as it should. Aligning HR strategy with business strategy can be done in one of these ways:

1. Start with organizational strategy and then create HR strategy.
2. Start with HR competencies and then craft corporate strategies based on these competencies.
3. Do a combination of both in a form of reciprocal relationship.

Let us examine each approach.

CORPORATE STRATEGY LEADS TO HR STRATEGY

A traditional perspective of HR planning views HRM programs as flowing from corporate strategy. In other words, personnel needs are based on corporate plans. If a firm decides to compete on the basis of offering low-cost products, HR policies and practices must align and be based on low labour costs. McDonald's is a good example. To illustrate the alignment of HR programs with business strategy, HR Planning Today 2.3 focuses on two strategies under Porter's model: the low-cost-provider strategy and the differentiation strategy. Although Porter recognized the importance of HRM, and even concedes that, in some firms, HRM holds the key to competitive advantage, he did not delineate any specific practices that can be aligned with business strategy. HR Planning Today 2.3 provides one of the few "recipes" for using HR strategies to support a business strategy.

HR Planning

At the entry level, succession planning is minimal, ensuring only the feeder line to the next level. Outside labour markets are monitored to ensure that entry-level people are in adequate supply. The availability and use of fringe workers—those who are retired, temporarily unemployed, students, and so on—is part of the planning strategy, particularly if the employment market is offering better opportunities to the normal supply of low-skilled workers.

At the executive level, succession management assumes the same importance as in other organizations.

Selection

Recruitment is primarily at the entry, or lowest, level and is from the surrounding external labour market. Recruitment is by word of mouth, and application forms are available on-site, thus saving the costs of recruiting in newspapers. Most other positions are staffed internally through promotions. Thus, career paths are narrow.

Compensation

A low-cost-provider strategy includes lower wages and fringe benefits. Beyond the legal minimum pay requirements, firms with this strategy carefully monitor what their competitors are paying in the local labour market. These firms' strategy tends to be a lag strategy, where they attempt to pay wages slightly below industry norms.

One way of achieving these lower costs is to outsource production to sites with lower labour costs. In the United States, this means moving production from high-wage states, such as New York, to low-wage states, such as New Mexico. In Canada, wages are very similar across provinces, so firms analyze wage rates in countries such as India, which pay employees substantially less for similar productivity. Outsourcing has also meant moving the work from highly unionized plants, where workers make $20 or more an hour, to nonunionized smaller sites, where workers are paid slightly more than the minimum wage.

Cost reduction in wages can also be achieved through the use of part-time workers, who receive no fringe benefits. Canadian organizations pay around 30 percent in fringe benefits, so the savings gained by using part-time workers is substantial among large employers. Food franchises employ part-time workers almost exclusively to reduce labour costs.

Pay for performance, such as incentive compensation that is linked to productivity, rewards individual effort. Group rewards are based on explicit, results-oriented criteria and the meeting of short-term performance goals.

Programs designed to reduce labour costs, such as outsourcing or using part-time workers, can easily be imitated by competitors, and so may produce no long-term competitive advantage. However, an innovative compensation scheme that cannot be duplicated by rivals may provide a competitive advantage. For example, in an arrangement between the Great Atlantic and Pacific Tea Company (A&P) and the United Food and Commercial Workers (UFCW), workers took a 25 percent pay cut in exchange for cash bonuses. If the store's employees could keep labour costs at 10 percent of sales by working more efficiently orgenerating more store traffic, they would receive a cash bonus of 1 percent of store sales. This arrangement resulted in an 81 percent increase in operating profits. However, unions were opposed to the spread of this practice, and so A&P's rivals in the low-margin food business were unable to reduce their labour costs in the same way. Any incentives for performance would reward cost savings, or improvements in efficiency, as this example shows.

Training

Training is minimal, as few skills are required. Any training is based on increasing efficiency in the current job, or specialization for the current position. Such training is fast and inexpensive. McDonald's can train a new hamburger flipper or cashier within a few hours. There is little to no investment in the long-term development of the employee, nor in the acquisition of skills for jobs other than the current one.

The training staff is lean, with the organization relying on outside suppliers for its limited training needs. However, most training takes place on the job in the form of direct instruction from or coaching by the supervisor. The jobs are so narrow in scope, so repetitive in nature, that little need for training exists.

Performance Evaluation

Short-term results, with explicit and standardized criteria, are used to evaluate an employee's performance. The feedback is immediate and specific. Individuals are held accountable only for their own behaviour or results, not for

that of the team or the company. Only the supervisor provides input for the performance evaluation. Forms are kept to a minimum, and rating is done against check marks. Feedback, if based on a performance review, tends to be one-way, with little opportunity for the employee to debate the results or receive developmental feedback. Results are used for consideration for promotion.

Labour Relations

Low-cost providers try to prevent the formation of a union because they believe that unions drive up wages. Unions find low-cost providers, such as McDonald's, difficult to unionize. (Employees working part-time hours have little interest in unionization because they believe that this is a part-time job that they will leave in the near future, and they are unlikely to benefit from belonging to a union, to which they have to pay fees. It is also difficult to organize those working night shifts.) Furthermore, employees quit often, and many low-cost providers absorb turnover rates of 300 percent annually as a cost of doing business. High turnover has the primary advantage of keeping compensation levels low.

Now that we have an idea of how HR programs align with a low-cost provider strategy, let us examine what these programs would be like under a differentiation strategy.

Strategy 2: The Differentiation Strategy

In most markets, buyer preferences are too diverse to be satisfied by one undifferentiated product. Firms providing features that appeal to a particular market segment are said to compete on a differentiation strategy. A firm competing on the basis of a differentiation strategy will offer something unique and valuable to its customers. BMW, Polo Ralph Lauren, Rolex, and Hewlett-Packard's scientific instruments divisions are firms that compete successfully by charging a price premium for uniqueness. The primary focus is on the new and different. Observation, experience, and market research will establish what buyers consider important, what has value, and what buyers will pay for these features. Then the firm can offer a product or service that commands a premium price, increase unit sales within this niche, and gain buyer loyalty among those who value these features. The extra price outweighs the extra costs of providing these features.

A firm can differentiate itself from its competitors in many ways:

- Having quality products
- Offering superior customer service
- Having a more convenient location
- Using proprietary technology
- Offering valuable features
- Demonstrating unique styling
- Having a brand-name reputation

These different features can be anything. Common examples show some firms competing on service (Four Seasons Hotels), engineering design (BMW), image (Polo Ralph Lauren), reliability (Bell), a full range of products or services (Procter & Gamble), technological leadership (RIM), and quality (Honda).

Most of the time, these competitive advantages are combined, such as by linking quality products with proprietary technology and superior customer service, thus providing the buyer with more value for money. The key in this strategy is to provide the differentiation that is perceived to be of value to customers while keeping costs down. For example, a slice of lemon in a glass of ice water delivered to the table is an obvious way to differentiate the restaurant, but at low cost. After-dinner mints are less expensive than valet parking, but may be equally appreciated by diners.

A differentiation strategy calls for innovation and creativity among employees. HRM is affected in fundamentally different ways in organizations that want to use employees' brains rather than their limited (mainly manual) skills in the low-cost-provider strategy.

The starting point for aligning HR programming with a differentiation strategy is the employee.

The Employee

Organizations competing on a differentiation strategy require from their employees creative behaviour, a long-term focus, interdependent activity, and some risk taking, as well as an ability to work in an ambiguous and unpredictable environment. Their employees' skills need to be broad, and employees must be highly involved with the firm. Organizations encourage employees to make suggestions, through both informal and formal suggestion systems, for new and improved ways of doing their job. Employees at Corning Canada Inc., for example, submit their suggestions

to their supervisors, who review them formally and give feedback directly to the employee. Contrast this with the traditional suggestion box, which many employees view as a recycling bin because of the lack of timely feedback.

HR Planning

In a company that has a differentiation strategy and that recognizes people are the key to competitive advantage, HR planning is taken very seriously. For example, at Sumitomo Metals in Japan, the business planning group reports to HR because the company understands that identifying what needs to be done is less difficult than planning how to do it.

Succession management is critical as employees have to possess many attributes to move ahead in the organization. Thus, a strong emphasis on developing skills for the future is part of the promotion policy. Investments in career moves, training, and developmental experiences are substantial. Long-term job security and reciprocal loyalty are the norm.

Selection

Companies with a differentiation strategy need employees who have a broad range of skills and the ability to learn from others. An innovative atmosphere requires employees who are self-motivated and do not require a great deal of supervision. Employees are selected for their abilities to think creatively, to be flexible in work attitudes, and to be able to work in teams. However, selection for these characteristics is more difficult and usually involves team interviews and behaviourally based evidence of innovative performance. Employees are normally recruited through reputation (word of mouth) or through graduate schools. Some testing for creative ability may be used.

Compensation

Compensation plans affect employee behaviour more directly than most HR practices. For example, Drucker describes a compensation scheme he implemented at General Electric (GE) in which pay for performance was based only on the previous year's results. As such, for ten years, GE lost its capacity for innovation because investing in innovation affects expenses and decreases profits, so everyone postponed spending on innovation.

However, compensation is carefully designed in firms that have a differentiation strategy. Pay rates may be slightly below average market rates but there are substantial opportunities to increase those base levels through incentive pay. Pay for performance is a large part of the compensation package and will be dependent on individual, group, and corporate results. These results are a combination of process and financial criteria and are set in advance, usually on a yearly basis.

There is a more varied mix of types of compensation; individuals may receive salary, bonus, or stock option incentives. Internal equity is of greater concern than equity with the external market. Egalitarian pay structures are associated with greater product quality. Nonmonetary rewards also play a larger role in HR strategy in these types of firms. At Honda, the team that designs a unique transportation vehicle is awarded a trip to Japan.

Training

Companies with a differentiation strategy have a strong training team. The focus of training is on both skills and attitudes. Process skills, such as decision making, the ability to work in teams, and creative thinking, are emphasized as much as skills needed for the current job. The training itself is seen as an opportunity to generate new ideas and procedures. Indeed, customers and cross-functional teams might be included in the training program. Developmental experiences are encouraged. The value of working in another division or another country is recognized and encouraged. Employees receive promotions or other job opportunities based, partially, on their willingness to undertake training and their track record in learning.

Performance Evaluation

In companies with a differentiation strategy, performance appraisal is based not on short-term results but instead on the long-term implications of behaviour. Processes that are deemed to lead to better results in the long term are rewarded. Thus, companies encourage and appraise attitudes such as empowerment, diversity sensitivity, and teamwork in an effort to build future bottom-line outcomes. Working beyond the job is encouraged, not punished. Failure is tolerated, although management tries to distinguish between bad luck and bad judgment or stupidity.

Evaluation tends to be based on a mixture of individual and group (and sometimes corporate) criteria. Thus, an individual might be evaluated on his or her ability to

achieve results and to work as a member of the team, the group's performance might be measured against established quotas, and the company might be measured in terms of its overall financial performance.

Appraisals that include input from employees, functional experts, peers, and so on—360° evaluations—are the norm. Organizations in the service sector are more likely to include customers as sources of input for performance appraisal.

Labour Relations

Any structure or process that reduces the capacity to be innovative and flexible is difficult to tolerate. Traditional unions, with rigid collective agreements, are encouraged to work collectively toward a new union–management relationship. This relationship is characterized by shared information such as open books, shared decision making about best approaches, and shared responsibility for solving problems as they arise.

Sources: Adapted from R.S. Schuler and S.E. Jackson, "Linking Competitive Strategies with Human Resource Management Practices," *Academy of Management Executive*, Vol. 1, No. 3 (1987), pp. 207–219; D. Ulrich, "Using Human Resources for Competitive Advantage," in R.H. Kilman and I. Kilman, eds., *Making Organizations Competitive*, San Francisco: JosseyBass, 1991; P.F. Drucker, "They're Not Employees, They're People," *The Harvard Business Review*, Vol. 80, No. 2 (2002), pp. 70–77; M. Belcourt and S. Thornhill, "Growing from the Inside Out: Human Resources Practices for Growth Strategies," Proceedings of the Administrative Sciences Association of Canada, 1999.

Four Seasons hotel is an example of a differentiation strategy.

But another perspective reverses this view, suggesting that employee competencies determine the business strategy.

HR COMPETENCIES LEAD TO BUSINESS STRATEGY

A competing view states that an organization cannot implement a strategy if it does not have the human resources necessary. Currently, companies are scrambling to find qualified workers in many fields, as discussed in Chapter 6 on labour supply.

Small businesses seem to be better at this second approach. The owners of very small businesses are nimble and quickly recognize that if an employee has a certain capability, it can be exploited to develop new products or services. Diversity management efforts are currently building on this theme. For example, if the number of employees who speak Mandarin reaches a sufficient number within an organization, the observant executive will start to explore Asian markets.

This "skills determine strategy" outlook relies too heavily on employee capabilities and not enough on environmental analysis; nor is consideration given to changing HR practices in training or compensation to facilitate this change in strategy.

These perspectives represent two extremes on a continuum between organizational strategy and HR practices. The reality is closer to the concept of reciprocal interdependencies.[40]

RECIPROCAL INTERDEPENDENCY BETWEEN HR STRATEGY AND BUSINESS STRATEGY

An emerging perspective sees HR strategy as contributing to business-level strategy and vice versa. Increasingly, in large firms, senior HR vice-presidents are asked not only to review business plans to ensure consistency with HR strategy but also to provide input to this strategy based on HR strengths and weaknesses.

In this context, an organization chooses a business strategy, such as being a leader in innovative products, based on its in-house, highly educated, trained employees who have been socialized to value creativity. Simply phrased, an organization develops its employees and then capitalizes on their skills; the employees then learn new skills, and so it continues. In many ways, HR strategy generates the business strategy, and business strategy determines HR strategy. This concept of reciprocal interdependence is widely accepted in the HR strategy literature.[41]

An emerging view is that HR should build its strategies by starting with the issues facing the business. All HR programs should be created to solve real business problems and add value, thus becoming indistinguishable from the business.[42]

HR BECOMES A BUSINESS PARTNER

The key point here is the concept of *concurrent strategy formulation*. Strategy development is conducted at the same time that HRM issues are considered. The HR senior management team moves from outsider status to insider status. The implications are not trivial; HR managers must understand the numbers language of business or the outcome expectations of nonprofit organizations. They must be able to understand analyses presented by marketing, financial, and operational managers. Cost–benefit assessments of options within the HR domain will have to be prepared and defended. Entrepreneurial instincts will have to be sharpened, as HR managers will be expected to engage in scanning HR capabilities for business opportunities in this two-way approach to strategic HR planning. An example of this occurred when an organization was experiencing a rapid downward spiral in business. The traditional HR response would have been to prepare for downsizing the workforce. Instead the HR manager created a unit to lobby—successfully—the government to support two major contracts.[43]

Alternative solutions to problems have to be generated. For example, if the low-cost strategy depends on hiring personnel at minimum wage, HR managers have to develop strategies to deal with rapid training and high turnover rates. This option will have to be compared with outsourcing, use of robots, or even increasing wages to reduce the costs of turnover. The HR manager is no longer the auditor, but a partner and problem solver. Linkages between the HR manager and other managers, both formal and informal, ensure that this partnership role is enacted.

HR PLANNING NOTEBOOK   2.1

ARE YOU A STRATEGIC PARTNER?

Do you understand the business? What financial indicators are important to the company? Who are your customers, and what is your competitive advantage? What major technological changes will affect your work?

Do you know what the corporate plan is? Can you quickly list the major initiatives of your organization?

Do you align HR programs, policies, and practices with organizational strategies and goals? How can HR position the organization to succeed? Are the people management processes focused and measured on deliverables and not functions? Does HR report on effectiveness (the impact that the training program had on employee behaviour) or just efficiencies (such as the number of people being trained)?

Are major organizational decisions made with your input? Are you on the executive team? Are you part of the strategic planning process?

Count the number of times you answered yes. The higher the number, the greater the likelihood that you are a strategic partner or have the ability to be one.

// STRATEGIC PARTNERING

Human resources professionals recognize the need to play a more strategic role within the organization. Although about 55 percent of HR managers are playing that role now, executive teams expect most of them to be more strategic and to demonstrate added value over the next five years.[44] Why do executives ignore HR's contribution to strategy? Some argue that it is because management is not satisfied with HR services in general; that "people" issues belong only to HR, and HR can take care of any problems in executing the strategy. Surveys have found that CEOs want HR to be business people first, then HR leaders. CEOs wish that HR executives would be less concerned with narrow HR policies and processes and focus on answering the question, "Do we have the organization design and people to achieve our plan?"[45]

These attitudes are changing, as organizations realize the impact that HRM strategy can have on organizational effectiveness and as HR managers develop the internal relationships to ensure that the strategy is effective. However, you cannot just ask to be on the executive team; you have to prove yourself. HR Planning Notebook 2.1 poses the question, "Are you a strategic partner?"

// BECOMING MORE STRATEGIC

HR departments are restructuring in order to be able to do the basics right (payroll, safety training, and so on) while enhancing the performance of business units and supporting strategic moves. Traditionally, HR has been organized into functional units (training, compensation, and so on). However, there are some more innovative practices, where the unit is organized according to the services provided, as outlined in HR Planning Notebook 2.2.

It seems feasible to design HR policies to match strategy, but what happens when an organization has more than one business strategy and more than one HR strategy? We attempt to answer that question in the next section.

// HR STRATEGY DIFFERENTIATION

Firms with more than one business strategy are likely to have more than one approach to HR strategy. As different divisions are responsible for realizing different aspects of the strategy, employees in different divisions may be encouraged to display different behaviours through appropriate HR practices. The challenge is to treat employees across divisions in an equitable fashion while motivating different behaviours that align with the divisions' strategies or functions. For example, 3M adopted HR practices that support innovation in the research and development branch while adopting policies that support low costs in the manufacturing branch. But to achieve equity, the company cultivated a culture of trust by implementing a series of HR practices such as educating employees on company's mission and objectives, ensuring compensation fairness, and facilitating communication to enhance employee engagement and perception of fairness.[46]

Recently researchers have suggested that HR strategy can be further differentiated based on jobs/positions within divisions. From a strategic perspective, different

Corporate HR

The key officer functions as a practice director, similar to what is found in consulting companies, and is on the executive team. Studies in the United Kingdom and Australia show that companies that included the HR director on the executive team experienced twice the growth in earnings per share compared to those who did not.[47]

Services Inc.

The part of HR that is administrative, estimated to be 60 percent to 70 percent of HR work, is located in a separate unit called Services Inc. The administrative burden is reduced through call centres and use of the Internet and intranet. The type of HR work done in Services Inc. includes compensation and benefits administration, training and education administration, staffing administration, and records management. There are three levels of service: Tier one is accessed by computer or telephone, and deals with minor things such as changes in addresses; everything is processed without human intervention. Tier two directs HR requests for information not listed on Tier-one sites—such as questions about retirement eligibility or finding a course on innovation—to a call centre that can provide a quick response or explanation. Tier three comprises case workers—highly skilled professionals—who provide extensive and comprehensive assistance to complex issues such as employee relations or employee assistance.

Services Inc. is driven by cost reduction—it has to be the lowest cost and most efficient provider of service, whether outsourced or provided in-house. It may be located in Information Services or wherever appropriate as part of an organization-wide effort to provide services through the centralization of technology and call centres.

Solutions Inc.

This branch of corporate HR consists of HR subject-matter experts—all of whom possess professional credentials acquired through advanced study and extensive experience. Their role is to transform the organization through training and development, labour relations, compensation design, strategic staffing, and organizational development. They are responsible for creating solutions to organizational problems and for preparing the organization to achieve its strategic intents. These experts act like consultants to the organization and operate on a for-profit basis—that is, their efforts are measurable and must result in an increase in performance measures. The consultants are on the cutting edge of research and put innovative, state-of-the-art theories into practice.

Organization Capability Consultants

Operating as the third branch of corporate HR, the HR professionals in this unit are dispersed throughout the organization, providing guidance and assistance to operating units, with the goal of improving the effectiveness of the organization. If asked questions about changing benefits or dealing with a potential unionization threat, they hand out cards with the contact numbers for Services Inc. or Solutions Inc. They build organizational capabilities by aligning HR strategies, processes, and practices with the needs of the business. Their HR solutions should change existing processes to create "better-faster-cheaper" approaches.

Source: From MELLO, *Strategic Human Resource Management*, 1E. © 2002 South-Western, a part of Cengage Learning, Inc. Reproduced by permission. www.cengage.com/permissions.

positions assume different roles in strategy implementation. Two considerations are (1) when a position is directly responsible for creating the strategic capabilities of the business, and (2) when different job holders may vary substantially in their job performance, then the position is considered a strategic position.[48] For example, at Big Pharma, the strategic capability of the business is new product development, thus the R&D scientists would assume the most strategic role. Walmart's strategic capability is its distribution

and logistics systems that allow it to achieve high efficiency at low costs, thus the distribution and logistics specialists should be considered strategic positions. Organizations should have a special HR strategy for these strategic positions to ensure that they can attract, motivate, and retain top players in these positions.[49]

From a human capital perspective, even within the same positions, some individuals may deserve differential HR strategy than others for two reasons—because their human capital is (1) valuable to the business strategy and (2) unique (hard to replace).[50] For example, R&D scientists who have desirable skills in new product development in a particular domain, or founding members who have extensive experience within the company, may deserve differential HR management. Recent surveys showed that up to 67 and 58 percent of Canadian organizations had differential treatment (such as additional compensation, enhanced development opportunities, and career planning) for employees with rare skills and valuable skills, respectively.[51] Human capital was found to be significantly related to organizational performance, particularly when the human capital was unique to the organization.[52] The basic prescription is to design HR programs that support the business strategy.

CHARACTERISTICS OF AN EFFECTIVE HRM STRATEGY

The purpose of HR strategy is to capitalize on the distinctive competencies of the organization and add value through the effective use of human resources.[53] Effective HRM strategies include external and internal fit, and a focus on results.

Fit is an important consideration when designing HR programs. We look at two important types of fit: external fit and internal fit.

These workers are trained to provide excellent customer service in support of a marketing promise of 24-hour support.

EXTERNAL FIT

HR programs must align with or fit the overall strategy of the organization. If the business strategy is to differentiate from competitors based on superior service, then selection and training programs should be developed to hire and train people in the skills and behaviours necessary to deliver superior service. Fit with other functional strategies is as important as fit with business strategies. HR senior management must be included in strategy discussions to be sure this happens. This is sometimes called the "best fit" approach to strategic HR, where HR strategies match organizational strategies.

INTERNAL FIT

We look at two types of internal fit: a fit with other functional areas, such as marketing, and a fit among all HR programs. Fit with other functional areas is important. If the marketing department is developing an advertising plan that promises 24-hour access to customer service representatives but the HR plan does not include compensation differentials for shift work, the overall marketing strategy might fail.

HR programs must also be consistent with each other. That is, training, selection, and appraisal must work together to support a strategy. If the training department decides to teach employees to use the Internet to handle customer service, the staffing department must hire people who either are computer literate or who have the kinds of intelligence that enable them to learn computer skills rapidly. This working together is commonly referred to as "bundling" HR practices. The "best practices" approach, in which bundles of HR practices are internally consistent, suggests that there is a direct relationship between an internally consistent bundle of HR practices and firm performance.[54] If an organization adopts one best practice, such as structured interviewing, without adopting bundles of best practices that align with it, it will not increase the impact in a synergistic manner. However, there is disagreement as to what, exactly, these best practices are.[55]

FOCUS ON RESULTS

The hard work of deciding on strategy is not its formulation but its implementation and the tracking of results. Many HR managers do not have the resources or skills to measure results to see if the goals have been achieved. Unless the strategy contains performance measures—that is, is results oriented—it will be difficult to know how successfully the strategy was implemented. Chapter 14 presents various methods for evaluating programs.

Many HR programs are described as solutions looking for problems. Although HR managers insert the word "strategic" in front of HR programs, they fail to demonstrate the link to results. Before any HR program is introduced, the following chain needs to be developed.

HR program → employee human capital and behaviours
→ organizational strategy → organizational outcome

So, if the overall corporate outcome for a retailer is "growth in sales," and the strategy to do this is through customer service (a differentiation strategy), then what employee human capital and behaviours are required? If, for example, product knowledge and sales skills are needed, then HR programs could be designed to select and/or develop these skills.

// SUMMARY

Strategic HRM is a set of distinct but interrelated philosophies, policies, and practices with the goal of enabling the organization to achieve its strategy. HR strategy is embedded in theories of the resource-based view of the firm, the behavioural perspective, and the human capital approach. By involving HR in discussions of strategic policies, an organization has a better chance of being effective in the implementation of these policies. There are various approaches to linking HRM strategies to organizational strategies. We can start with the corporate strategy that leads to the HR strategy, or start with the HR competencies that lead to the business strategy, or use a blend of the interrelationship of the HR strategy and the corporate strategy. Aligning HR strategy with the corporate strategy and with other functional strategies is important.

KEY TERMS

human capital p. 32
strategic HRM p. 29

WEB LINKS

The *Canadian HR Reporter* website, with articles on strategic HRM:
http://www.hrreporter.com/articlesearch?keywords=hr%20strategies

The HR strategy of the Department of Health and Social Services of the government of the Northwest Territories:
http://pubs.aina.ucalgary.ca/health/62245.pdf

DISCUSSION QUESTIONS

1. "Employees are our biggest asset." "Yes, but they can walk out the door any time and all your investment in them will be lost." Explain why investments in human capital are important. Using the example of a great coach, explain why all is not lost if some of the team members quit.

2. Your family has experience in the restaurant business in the country from which they immigrated. They decide to open a large restaurant (with about 30 waiters, several chefs, etc.) specializing in your regional cuisine. These different types of foods may appeal to people in the neighbourhood, but you will need to differentiate this restaurant from others, and offer great service, with explanations, customization, etc. Describe the ways in which you would use HRM programs to train the waiters.

3. Research recent corporate bankruptcies in North America. Why do you think many of the once most successful companies no longer exist? Discuss how the most successful companies today manage their human resources to be innovative.

EXERCISES

This chapter outlined how organizations must align HR programs (and therefore employee behaviours) with corporate strategy, using predominantly businesses as

examples. But here are two mini-cases about how sports (tennis and baseball) can use the same principles of HR planning to achieve goals.

1. Canada had never had a tennis player in the top ten rankings of the best players in the world. And yet, in 2014 Milos Raonic was ranked 6, Eugenie Bouchard was ranked 7, and Vasek Popsipil won doubles at Wimbledon. Was this just a lucky streak of talented players emerging? Not at all. It was a plan, started ten years ago. First, Tennis Canada built two excellent tournament facilities: The Rexall Centre in Toronto and the Uniprix Stadium in Montreal, generating more revenue and more sponsorships. Money available for player (talent) development soared from $4 million to $12 million. But other countries had even more money to spend on player development. So the next steps were critical to the success. Tennis Canada established a national training centre in Montreal, recruited a coach who had coached top players in Europe, and selected only 10–12 adolescents who had demonstrated exceptional skills and motivation, who go to school in the morning, and then spend 5 hours training in the afternoon. They are supported extensively, with coaching sessions in Europe, and travel to tournaments around the world. And this new plan worked!

   What are the important behaviours for sports players in individual (not team) sports? What (HR) programs can be used to generate these behaviours?

2. Traditionally, Major League Baseball scouts chose players for their future potential, and selection decisions were made on gut instinct. Bill James studied baseball statistics for three decades and developed a method called Sabermetrics (based on rigorous statistical analysis) to determine a player's true value to the team. Sabermetrics is a process that analyzes past performance statistics (such as batting averages, earned run averages, bunting, stealing, getting on base, etc.) and links these to winning scores. These findings were not accepted until Billy Beane of the Oakland Athletics put Sabermetrics into practice. Watch the biographical sports movie Moneyball (2011) and learn about this approach. Identify the key competencies/capabilities of players that Billy Beane sought. Did they support the competing strategy of the Oakland Athletics?

CASE STUDY   LINKING HR PRACTICES TO PERFORMANCE

Five Star, a luxury hotel in Auckland, New Zealand, was established in the early 1980s, renovated in the mid-1990s, and basically had not changed since. Competition was increasing as three more luxury hotels had opened in the area. The owners reacted by trying to upgrade the hotel and improve the customer service. In the hotel sector, customer service is the only differentiator from other hotels.

The owners created a vision statement that included a strategy for achieving their vision:

> Five Star is to be recognized as the **finest five-star property** in Auckland and a business leader in the hospitality industry. We will achieve this vision by recruiting and developing **customer-focused employees** who provide the highest level of guest service and by providing the **highest amenity level** of any hotel in Auckland (emphasis in original).

By improving customer service, the owners hope to increase customer satisfaction and impact financial performance—the value chain, as demonstrated below:

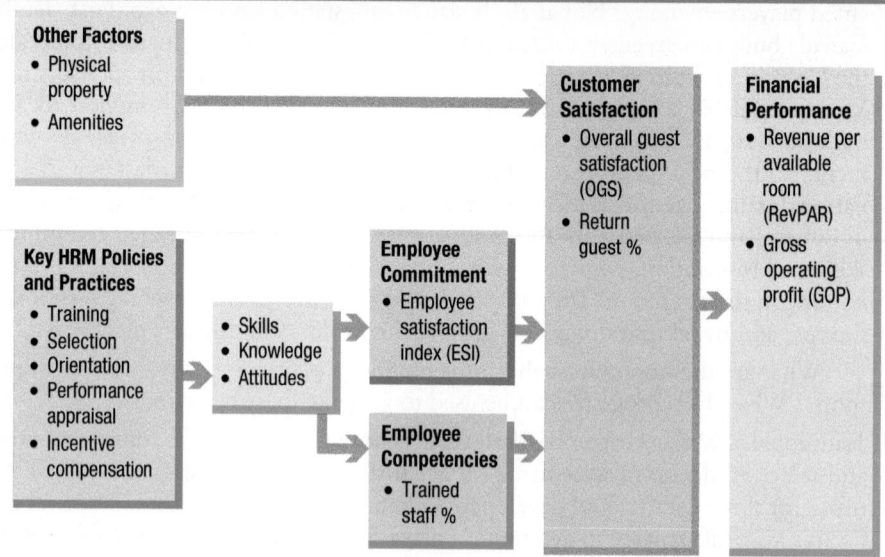

FIGURE 2.1

MANAGEMENT POLICIES AND PRACTICES IN A QUALITY-FOCUSED HOSPITALITY INDUSTRY STRATEGY

Source: P. Haynes and G. Fryer 2000 "Human Resources, Service Quality and Performance: A Case Study," *International Journal of Contemporary Hospitality Management*, Vol. 12, No. 4, pp. 240–248. © Emerald Group Publishing Limited. All rights reserved.

QUESTIONS

1. Develop a list of the competencies (skills, knowledge, and attitudes) that employees of this hotel need to demonstrate in order to become excellent at customer service.

2. Design the HRM selection, orientation, training, performance management, and incentive compensation program that will develop these competencies.

// REFERENCES

1. http://www.economist.com/node/17633138?story_id=17633138. Retrieved March 29, 2011.

2. http://www.economist.com/node/21528436. Retrieved September 9, 2011.

3. Money.cnn.com/magazines/fortune/bestcompanies/2011/index.html. Retrieved March 29, 2011.

4. http://www.economist.com/node/21528436. Retrieved September 9, 2011.

5. Davenport, T. H., Harris, J., and Shapiro, J. 2010. "Competing on Talent Analytics." *Harvard Business Review*, Vol. 88: 52–58.

6. Jackson, S.E., and R.S. Schuler. 1995. "Understanding Human Resource Management in the Context of Organizations and their Environments." *Annual Review of Psychology*, Vol. 46: 237–264.

7. Lawler, E.E., A.R. Levenson, and J.W. Boudreau. 2004. "HR Metrics and Analytics: Use and Impact." *Human Resource Planning*, Vol. 27, No. 4: 27–36.

8. Roos, G., L. Fernstrom, and S. Pike. 2004. "Human Resource Management and Business Performance Measurement." *Measuring Business Excellence*, Vol. 8, No. 1: 28–37.

9. Ruona, W.E.A., and S. K. Gibson. 2004. "The Making of Twenty-First Century HR: An Analysis of the Convergence of HRM, HRD and OD." *Human Resource Management*, Vol. 42, No. 1: 49–66.

10. "The New HR Executive." Corporate Leadership Council, September 2000.

11. Conference Board of Canada. June 2010. "Valuing Your Talent: Human Resources Trends and Metrics."

12. Ferris, G.R., A.T. Hall, M.T. Royle, and J.J. Martocchio. 2004. "Theoretical Development in the Field of Human Resources Management: Issues and Challenges for the Future." *Organizational Analysis*, Vol. 12, No. 3: 231–254.

13. Pfeffer, J. 1995. "Producing Sustainable Competitive Advantage through the Effective Management of People." *Academy of Management Executive*, Vol. 9: 55–72.

14. Combs, J., Liu, Y., Hall, A., and Ketchen, D. 2006. "How Much Do High Performance Work Practices Matter? A Meta-analysis of Their Effects on Organizational Performance." *Personnel Psychology*, Vol. 59: 501–528.

15. Collis, D.J., and Montgomery, C.A. 2008. "Competing on Resources." *Harvard Business Review*, Vol. 86: 140–150.

16. Amit, R., and M. Belcourt. 1999. "Human Resources Processes as a Source of Competitive Advantage." *European Management Journal*, Vol. 17, No. 2 (April).

17. Conference Board of Canada, June 2010.

18. http://www.canadastop100.com/national. Retrieved July 28, 2011.

19. Teece, D.J. 2007. "Explicating Dynamic Capabilities: The Nature and Microfoundations of (Sustainable) Enterprise Performance." *Strategic Management Journal*, Vol. 28: 1319–1350.

20. Chadwick, C., and Dabu, A. 2009. "Human Resources, Human Resource Management, and the Competitive Advantage of Firms: Toward a More Comprehensive Model of Causal Linkages." *Organization Science*, Vol. 20: 253–272.

21. Paauwe, J., and P. Boselie. 2003. "Challenging Strategic HRM and the Relevance of the Institutional Setting." *Human Resource Management Journal*, Vol. 13, No. 3: 56–70.

22. Weatherly, L. 2003. "Human Capital: The Elusive Asset." *SHRM Research Quarterly* (Society for Human Resources Management).

23. Becker, B.E., and M.A. Huselid. 1999. "Overview: Strategic Human Resources Management in Five Leading Firms." *Human Resource Management*, Vol. 38, No. 4 (Winter): 287–301.

24. Hoskisson, R.E., M.A. Hitt, and R.D. Ireland. 2004. *Competing for Advantage*. Mason, OH: Thomson South-Western.

25. Schuller, R.S., and S.E. Jackson 2005. "A Quarter-Century Review of Human Resource Management in the U.S: The Growth in Importance of the International Perspective," *Management Review*, 16, 1, 11–35.

26. Conference Board of Canada, June 2010.

27. Wright, P.M., D.L. Smart, and G.C. McMahan. 1995. "Matches between Human Resources and Strategy among NCAA Basketball Teams," *Academy of Management Journal*, Vol. 38, No. 4: 1052–1074.

28. Liao, H., Toya, K., Lepak, D. P., and Hong, Y. 2009. "Do They See Eye to Eye? Management and Employee Perspectives of High-Performance Work Systems and Influence Processes on Service Quality." *Journal of Applied Psychology*, 94: 371–391.

29. Malley, M.O., and E. Lawler 2003. "What Is HR Good for Anyway?" *Across the Board*, 40, 4, 33–38.

30. Schuller and Jackson, 2005.

31. Subramony, M. 2009. "A Meta-analytic Investigation of the Relationship Between HRM Bundles and Firm Performance." *Human Resource Management*, Vol. 48: 745–768.

32. Ulrich, D., and N. Smallwood. 2004. "Capitalizing on Capabilities." *Harvard Business Review*, June: 119–127.

33. Zedeck, S., and W.F. Cascio. 1984. "Psychological Issues in Personnel Decisions." *Annual Review of Psychology*, Vol. 35: 461–518.

34. Schuler, R.S., and S.E. Jackson. 1989. "Determinants of Human Resources Management Priorities and Implications for Industrial Relations." *Journal of Management*, Vol. 15, No. 1: 89–99.

35. King, A.S. 1995. "Multi-Phase Progression of Organizational Ideology: Commitment." *Mid Atlantic Journal*, Vol. 31, No. 2: 143–160.

36. Lengnick-Hall, C., and M. Lengnick-Hall. 1990. *Interactive Human Resource Management and Strategic Planning*. New York: Quorum Books.

37. Lengnick-Hall, C., and M. Lengnick-Hall. 1988. "Strategic Human Resources Management: A Review of the Literature and a Proposed Typology," *Academy of Management Review*, Vol. 13, No. 3: 454–470.

38. MacMillan, I.C. 1983. "Seizing Competitive Advantage." *Journal of Business Strategy*: 43–57.

39. Anderson, W. 1997. "The Future of Human Resources: Forging Ahead or Falling Behind?" *Human Resources Management*, Vol. 36, No. 1 (Spring): 17–22.

40. Lengnick-Hall and Lengnick-Hall, 1988.

41. Bamberger, P., and A. Feigenbaum. 1996. "The Role of Strategic Reference Points in Explaining the Nature and Consequences of Human Resources Strategy." *Academy of Management Review*, Vol. 21, No. 4 (October): 926–958.

42. Wright, P.M., S.S. Snell, and P.H.H. Jacobsen. 2004. "Current Approaches to HR Strategies: Inside-Out Versus Outside-In." *Human Resource Planning*, Vol. 27, No. 4: 36–47.

43. Quinn, R.W., and W. Brockbank. 2006. "The Development of Strategic Human Resource Professionals." *Human Resource Management*, Vol. 45. No. 3: 477–494.

44. "CEO Perspectives: How HR Can Take on a Bigger Role in Driving Growth." *Economist Intelligence Unit; The Economist* 2012.

45. HRPA/Knightsbridge. 2011. "The Role and Future of HR: The CEO's Perspective" *2011 Research Highlight*, page 3.

46. Schneider, B., and Paul, K.B. 2011. "In the Company We Trust." *HR Magazine*, Vol. 56: 40–43.

47. http://www.accenture.com. Retrieved April 5, 2006.

48. Becker, B.E., M.A. Huselid, and R.W. Beatty. 2009. *The Differentiated Workforce: Translating Talent into Strategic Action*. Boston: Harvard Business Press; Huselid, M.A., R.W. Beatty, and B.E. Becker. 2005. "'A' Players or 'A' Positions? The Strategic Logic of Workforce Management." *Harvard Business Review*, December: 110–117.

49. Becker, Huselid, and Beatty, 2009; Huselid, Beatty, and Becker, 2005.

50. Lepak, D.P., and S.A. Snell. 1999. "The Human Resource Architecture: Toward a Theory of Human Capital Allocation and Development." *Academy of Management Review*, Vol. 24: 31–48.

51. Conference Board of Canada, June 2010.

52. Crook, T.R., J.G. Combs, S.Y. Todd, D.J. Woehr, and D.J. Ketchen Jr. 2011. "Does Human Capital Matter? A Meta-analysis of the Relationship Between Human Capital and Firm Performance." *Journal of Applied Psychology*, Vol. 96: 443–456.

53. Cooke, R., and M. Armstrong. 1990. "The Search for Strategic HR." *Personnel Management*, December: 30–33.

54. Buyens, D., and A.D. Vos. 2001. "Perception of the Value of HR." *Human Resource Management Journal*, Vol. 11, No. 3: 70–90.

55. Panayotopoulour, L., and N. Papalexandris. 2004. "Examining the Link Between Human Resource Management and Firm Performance." *Personnel Review*, Vol. 33, No. 5/6: 499–520.

CHAPTER

ENVIRONMENTAL INFLUENCES ON HRM

CHAPTER LEARNING OUTCOMES

AFTER READING THIS CHAPTER, YOU SHOULD BE ABLE TO:

- Identify the sources that HR planners use to keep current with business and HR trends.
- Understand how environmental scanning is practised.
- Discuss the challenges in scanning the environment.
- Delineate the environmental factors, such as the economic climate, the political and regulatory context, and the social and cultural climate, that influence the practice of HRM.
- Describe the role of the stakeholder, and list several examples.

General Motors (GM) was, for some business experts, associated with the birth of American capitalism. Back in 1955, the chairman of GM conceitedly stated that "What is good for General Motors is good for America." But in 2009 GM filed for bankruptcy and then was revitalized through $50 billion in government bailout funds.[1] How is it possible that a corporation with money and expertise ended up with just 21 percent market share in 2008, from a position of 50 percent market share 50 years earlier?

Some experts feel that the failure was the myopic views held by management. GM's managers refused to adjust to a changing world for more than 30 years. GM managers thought that they understood that North American motorists loved big cars. They did not see or did not realize that the rising costs of fuel and increasing environmental awareness of consumers would demolish their core business of gas-guzzling SUVs. Ironically, GM was among the first to introduce the electric car, EV1, in 1996 but abandoned it in 2002 due to its high cost.

GM studied the competition, but in the wrong way. It appreciated the fact that the Japanese had cost and quality advantages, but did not seem to understand how to adapt these techniques to their own plants. To understand the cost advantages, GM purchased Japanese cars and disassembled them, looking for clues that explained their efficiencies. But while GM was studying these cars, the Japanese were already at the drawing board designing the next generation of cars. To rationalize the Japanese quality advantages, GM blamed the workforce and suppliers for quality and tried to "inspect quality" into the final product. They believed that the Japanese were able to produce superior products because their workers were docile and worked ten hours a day.

GM was myopic and did not seem to understand how factors can interact. Take, for instance, the interaction between the volume of cars sold and the price of fuel. In 1995, Jack Smith, CEO of GM, told investors to see the potential of the global market, because the North American market was saturated. He forecasted that GM would sell 10 million cars in China alone. When asked by an analyst, "Do you think that there will be an impact on fuel prices, if millions and millions of cars are purchased in developing countries?" the reply was, "We think that gas supplies will be adequate and gas prices will rise just at the rate of inflation."

In a reactive way, GM cut fixed operating costs by 22 percent and offloaded its extremely costly health benefits for retirees. (GM management had not foreseen the huge costs of these agreements to care for aging retirees, who were more numerous than employees, which added about $1,400 to the cost of every vehicle.) But it was too late for GM. Toyota overtook GM as the world's largest car maker in 2008. When the demand for cars plummeted due to the economic crisis coupled with rising fuel prices, GM could not sustain its cash flow and filed for Chapter 11 reorganization in the United States in 2009. After receiving government bailout, GM was profitable again.

The auto sector today is transforming rapidly. There are changes in how transportation is viewed in response to erratic fuel prices, energy risks, vehicle safety, and climate change, and consumers are making adjustments through carpooling, biking, and public transportation. Out of GM's mess may emerge entrepreneurial ideas from those outside the auto industry, those who are scanning the environment, reading the trends, and responding innovatively.[2]

To understand strategic HR planning, we must understand how HRM is affected by the environment in which it operates. Just consider the past decade. Was your life touched by any of these events: the 2014 harassment scandals; the 2014 rise of terrorism; the 2013 floods in Alberta, the 2013 ice storm in Ontario; or the 2008 economic meltdown? HR planners want to track trends that influence the way in which employees can be managed. As a result of 9/11 and SARS, most large organizations now have emergency plans in place for the safety of their employees and buildings.

Photographer: Lorraine Hjalte/*The Calgary Herald*. Reprinted with permission of *The Calgary Herald*.

Environmental factors, such as the Calgary flood impact organizational plans.

HR strategists need information about their environment in order to exploit the opportunities or cope with the threats. Environmental factors may influence different industries and businesses in a different way and to a different extent. The opening example shows that gas price and environmental concerns of customers influenced the strategic planning at GM; similarly, customers' attitudes toward nutrition and health may influence the business strategy of restaurants and food retailing chains. Being responsive to environmental changes is a prerequisite for building dynamic capabilities and gaining a first-mover advantage. It is important to note that following environmental changes is not only general managers' responsibility, but also the responsibility of HR managers. Fear over pandemics, costs of fuels, technology development, and the demographics of the workforce all directly influence how work should be designed and how HR should be managed.[3] Being aware of knowledge workers' increasing preference for work–life balance and challenges, Google was among the first to create work–life balance programs as well as flexible job design to attract and motivate top talent. This created a competitive advantage in the company's human resources competency and engagement, which enabled the company to continuously grow and outperform others.

We will look first at the sources and methods HR planners use to track these trends.

// ENVIRONMENTAL SCANNING SOURCES AND METHODS

Environmental scanning
Systematic monitoring of trends affecting the organization

Managers have to develop strategies and keep a keen eye on what is happening in the world outside the organization. **Environmental scanning** is the systematic monitoring of the major factors influencing the organization to identify trends that might affect the formulation and implementation of both organizational and HR strategies.

Environment is a fuzzy term; it covers factors as broad as national and multinational contexts that influence an organization. For example, managers are influenced by the culture in which they operate. A manager in Vancouver will treat her employees differently than a manager in New Delhi, and the employees in each city would have expectations about how managers should supervise. Environment also includes industrial environment, such as Porter's Five Competitive Forces.[4] HR practitioners who understand the competitive environment and its implications for their organizations can then develop practices that create competitive advantage.[5]

The analysis of the external environment consists of these stages:

- *Scanning:* An attempt to identify early signals of changes and trends in the environment. This information is ambiguous, incomplete, and unconnected.

- *Monitoring:* A systematic approach to following some key indicators that may affect the organization, such as legislative changes.

- *Forecasting:* After monitoring a trend, an attempt to project the possible impact on the organization.
- *Assessing:* An attempt to describe the impact of the monitored trend on the organization, and make a judgment of the probability of each of several possible outcomes.[6] For example, what would be the impact of a trend in the increase of social networking sites?

In the past, HR managers monitored changes that might affect their programs and policies by reading newspapers or trade publications. They kept informed of issues regarding employment laws by subscribing to particular news services, and by being a member of the provincial HR association. The next section describes the sources that HR professionals might use to monitor trends in the environment.

SOURCES OF INFORMATION

When developing strategies and determining their likely impact on an organization, HR professionals rely on many sources of information. These include publications, professional associations, conferences and seminars, and professional consultants.

PUBLICATIONS

HR professionals actively scan Canadian newspapers, business publications, and HR magazines, journals, and newsletters. We are fortunate enough to have access to not only a wide range of Canadian sources of information but also the extensive publication network originating in the United States. The authors' experience suggests that Canadian HR trends lag behind U.S. trends by a year or two. For example, workplace violence and employee retention were hot issues in the United States three years before they became important in Canada. Thus, reading U.S. publications acts as an early warning signal for Canadian HR professionals. HR practitioners monitor many of the publications and websites listed in HR Planning Notebook 3.1.

PROFESSIONAL ASSOCIATIONS

Canadian HR professionals and executives belong to a number of organizations that publish newsletters and updates on current events. Many of these, such as the Human Resources Professionals Association, have committees that actively scan the regulatory scene for upcoming changes. Some, like the Conference Board of Canada, conduct research with their members to track trends. Relevant associations are listed in HR Planning Notebook 3.2.

CONFERENCES AND SEMINARS

Most professionals keep current with and even ahead of emerging trends by attending conferences, seminars, and workshops in Canada and the United States. The Human Resource Professionals Association, for example, attracts over 3,000 participants to its conference each year. Such events, including those sponsored by private organizations, are widely publicized in HR publications.

PUBLICATIONS OF INTEREST TO HR PROFESSIONALS

Canadian

Canadian Business (http://www.canadianbusiness.com)

Canadian HR Reporter (http://www.hrreporter.com)

Canadian Journal of Learning and Technology (http://www.cjlt.ca)

The Financial Post Career & HR (http://business.financialpost.com/category/executive/careers)

The Globe and Mail Report on Business (http://www.theglobeandmail.com/report-on-business)

HR Professional (http://www.hrpromag.com)

Ivey Business Journal (http://www.iveybusinessjournal.com)

Profit (http://www.profitguide.com)

Workplace Today (http://www.workplace.ca/magazine)

U.S. and International

Bloomberg Business Week (http://www.businessweek.com)

Economist (http://www.economist.com)

Fortune (http://www.fortune.com)

HR Focus (http://www.hrfocusmagazine.com)

HR Magazine (http://www.shrm.org/publications/hrmagazine)

People Management (http://www.peoplemanagement.co.uk/pm)

Training (http://www.trainingmag.com)

Research Journals—available through Institutional Libraries

Academy of Management Perspectives

Academy of Management Review

Benefits Canada

Business Horizons

Business Quarterly

California Management Review

Canadian Journal of Administrative Studies

Canadian Labour Law Reporter

Compensation

Compensation & Benefits Review

European Management Journal

Harvard Business Review

Human Resource Management

Journal of Applied Psychology

Journal of Business Ethics

Journal of Labor Research

Journal of Management

Journal of Staffing and Recruitment

Labor Studies Journal

Management Review

Occupational Outlook Quarterly

Organizational Behavior and Human Performance

Personnel

Personnel Journal

Personnel Psychology

Public Personnel Management

Training and Development Journal

ASSOCIATIONS OF INTEREST TO HR PROFESSIONALS

Administrative Sciences Association of Canada (HR Division)

Canadian Association of Management Consultants

Canadian Council of Human Resource Associations (links to all provincial HR associations)

Canadian Human Resource Planners

Canadian Industrial Relations Association

Canadian Payroll Association

Canadian Public Personnel Managers Association

Canadian Society for Training and Development

Conference Board of Canada

Human Resource Planning Society

International Association for Human Resources Information Management Association

North American Human Resources Management Association

Society for Human Resources Management

Society for Industrial and Organizational Psychology

World at Work

PROFESSIONAL CONSULTANTS

Organizations that have an active interest in understanding the influence of potential trends often hire consultants to research or interpret these trends for them. The Hudson Institute is an example of a firm that specializes in this form of consulting. Most organizations have a person on staff, often the librarian, whose job is to bring information to the consultants' attention by actively scanning multiple sources.

THE EXPERTS PREDICT THE FUTURE OF HRM

The Society for Human Resources Management attempts to forecast the workplace through the use of environmental scanning. The Society collects data from human resources professionals every two years, and then uses teams of individuals to filter the information in order to target that which is truly critical. The Society also solicits opinions from HR expert panels and opinion leaders. Although some trends, such as rising cost of health care for employers are not relevant for Canadian employers, the following trends are relevant to Canadian employers:

- a shortage of skilled workers
- a large number of boomers retiring at the same time
- lack of STEM (Science, Technology, Engineering and Math) graduates

Facing these environmental trends, the most common actions taken by organizations include updating recruiting, development, and retention methods. They are putting more emphasis on succession planning, and investing more in HR technology.

Sources: Schramm, J., Coombs, J., and Victor, J. (2011, February). SHRM Workplace Forecast: The top workforce trends according to HR professionals, http://www.shrm.org/Research/FutureWorkplaceTrends/Documents/13-0146%20Workplace_Forecast_FULL_FNL.pdf.

// METHODS OF FORECASTING

HR professionals can use several methods to generate predictions about the future or extrapolate from current events to determine their impact on HR practices. These methods include trend analysis, the Delphi technique, nominal group technique, impact analysis, and scenario planning, which are discussed in detail in Chapter 6. An excellent evaluation of all these approaches can be found in Rothwell and Kazanas.[7] The steps of conducting a scenario-based HR planning are outlined in HR Planning Notebook 3.3. Readers are invited to experience a scenario-based technique as part of a group exercise at the end of this chapter.

COMPETITIVE INTELLIGENCE

Competitive intelligence (or business intelligence) is a formal approach to obtain information about your competitors. Learning about competitors' moves early is critical for organizations to respond before the new offering materializes. However, surveys showed that only 23 percent of companies were able to do so.[8] The simplest method is to study their websites for information about their strategies and plans for product launches. Other companies train their employees to ask questions from vendors about the purchasing decisions of their competitors. Some organizations hire competitors' employees to obtain insider information about future plans. Other practices border on illegal or unethical. For example, Avon Products once allegedly hired private detectives to search through the dumpsters outside the Mary Kay corporate offices. Information gathered through all these competitive intelligence methods must be subjected to two evaluation questions: Is the source reliable, and what is the likelihood of the information being correct?[9]

HR PLANNING NOTEBOOK   **3.3**

SCENARIO-BASED HR PLANNING

Step one: Identify three business scenarios that might be played out over the next five years (most desirable case, most likely case, and least desirable case).

Step two: For each scenario, assess the firm's HR readiness. What are the challenges faced under each scenario (e.g., labour shortages, safety concerns). Then identify the HR department's strengths and weaknesses in relation to these challenges.

Step three: Over the next five years, what are the likely trends with rivals, employees, and candidates?

What are the threats posed by rivals? What are the predicted needs and motivations of key employees? What changes do we forecast in the quality and the quantity of our labour pool?

Step four: For each scenario, identify HR initiatives and programs that must be undertaken to deal with the threats and opportunities. For example, to meet a labour shortage of skilled mechanics, a joint program with a community college might be established.

Source: Adapted from P. Boxall and J. Purcell, *Strategy and Human Resource Management*, 2nd ed. (New York: Palgrave Macmillan, 2008), Figure 11.1, p. 294.

// CHALLENGES IN ENVIRONMENTAL SCANNING

There are problems in scanning the environment. These include our inability to accurately predict the future and to isolate what really is important to HR. Can we say what the world will look like in 2050? In 1900, could those working in HRM have predicted what it would look like in 2000? Not likely, because the field of HRM did not exist then. One hundred years ago, there were no payroll and benefits clerks. Even 20 years ago, it would have been difficult to forecast the flattening of organizations; downsizing; the impact of technology, outsourcing, and telecommuting; and a range of other changes we now experience. Most HR strategists limit themselves to a two- to three-year time frame and extrapolate from current trends.

ISOLATING THE CRITICAL FROM THE INSIGNIFICANT

So much change is happening in so many arenas that scanners have trouble picking out the truly important events. For example, which of these HR issues, taken from headlines in HR publications as this text is being written, are critical and which will prove insignificant: War for talent? Outsourcing all HR functions? Workplace harassment?

Four criteria have been suggested for identifying significant trends:[10]

1. Are there ripple effects (change in one aspect impacts another, such as social networking sites affecting both friendships and professional relationships)?

2. How profound are the impacts on people's priorities, roles, and expectations?

3. How large is the impact scope (number of people impacted)?

4. Will the changes endure over time?

One difficulty is that few trends exist in isolation—no issue is an island. Take the issue of the difficulty of finding employees where labour shortages exist. There is a growing concern that companies will be unable to find enough tradespeople. If this problem is addressed in isolation, two solutions might be to (1) increase the number of spaces for apprentices in trade programs and/or (2) recruit tradespeople from other countries. But other trends may influence the ability to fill these jobs. The use of robots may change the need for skilled workers. The abolishment of mandatory retirement may encourage more tradespeople to continue working.

Just as there is a reaction for every action, for every trend there is a countertrend, and countertrends seem to develop in tandem with the trends. As globalization increases, so does "localization," and ethnic pride in customs and culture rises. This is not the same as the idea that the pendulum will always swing back. The current focus on work–life balance cannot be viewed just as a fad, with the resultant expectation that there will be another, replacement fad within a few years. The concepts underlying work–life balance will be embedded in our view of work, just as safety and labour laws are now permanently embedded in the culture of work.

We will now examine the major areas that strategists typically scan.

// ENVIRONMENTAL FACTORS

HR strategists monitor a number of factors more closely because they are more closely related to HRM. Following this tradition, we have included factors such as the economic climate, the political and regulatory context, and issues related to technology,

demographics, and social values and norms. For each factor we have provided some current examples, keeping in mind that such examples quickly lose their relevance. In scanning each factor, we want to consider its potential impact on the organization and strategy in the near and the distant future, and how HRM can be adapted in response to the environmental changes.

ECONOMIC CLIMATE

The economic indices we are so familiar with from the media are also important to HR strategists. Let us look at a few examples of how these indices influence HR managers who are:

- Concerned with the unemployment rate because it affects their ability to recruit
- Worried about the cost of fuel and the employees' willingness to commute
- Worried about the value of the Canadian dollar because it affects the company's ability to sell products internationally, and thus affects employment levels
- Troubled by the amount of public debt because it affects business taxes, and therefore a company's ability to survive and grow
- Anxious about interest rates because they affect how much a company is willing to borrow to grow its business and invest in employees

The recent economic recession, for example, has imposed many changes on HR management in businesses. Many employers try to reduce fixed costs by replacing permanent jobs with contingent jobs. Surprisingly, this trend applies not only to low-paid, low-skilled workers, but also to high-paid, high-skilled professionals and leaders. Deeper and longer recessions may result in permanent job losses as businesses close operations and do not rehire laid-off workers, as would happen in a quicker economic recovery.[11]

An important role of HR managers will thus become outsourcing managers. Interestingly, a drop in demand for contingent, temporary, and contract employees (as reported by search and placement firms) can also predict an economic slowdown before these changes are reported by firms in their financial statements.

Other actions that were taken by HR managers to cope with economic uncertainty include linking employee performance with organizational goals, increasing expectations of employee productivity, putting emphasis on succession planning and readiness, investing in leadership development, using noncash rewards such as time off, time flexibility, and learning opportunities, and retraining employees for new jobs.[12]

GLOBALIZATION

Another trend to watch is increasing globalization. Globalization is the growth in flows of trade and financial capital across borders. Globalization affects sovereignty, prosperity, jobs, wages, and social legislation. In North America, the North American Free Trade Agreement (NAFTA) was established in 1994 among Canada, the United States, and Mexico to gradually remove tariffs and other trade barriers in the region. It has almost tripled the trilateral merchandise trade since 1994 to over $1 trillion in 2012, which has significantly impacted businesses in these three countries. The labour market in Canada is also affected—it has been estimated that one in five jobs in Canada is related

to international trade.[13] This has implications for recruiting and managing international human resources. Compared to the United States in particular, employees in lower-level jobs in Canada on average receive higher pay than their counterparts in the United States, while professionals and those in higher-level positions earn less than those in the United States. As NAFTA makes the workforce more mobile across the border, Canadian businesses need to work hard to retain the best knowledge workers.

The shift in the global economy has also been marked by the rapid growth of emerging economies such as India and China. These countries had workers who were willing to work longer hours for less money than workers in more developed countries. McDonald's has a great deal of experience in globalization, and when the company launches a restaurant in a new country, it works closely with all disciplines to "McDonaldize" a team so that they know the business inside out. Eighteen to 24 months before the restaurant is opened, the company starts with HR. Some of the HR challenges McDonald's has faced in other countries include the fact that part-time employment and multifunctional jobs simply did not exist.[14]

Globalization issues now include crisis management and evacuation in cases of terrorism, civil war, and the outbreak of infectious diseases, such as Ebola. HR managers will need to develop international competencies, as discussed in Chapter 11.

POLITICAL AND LEGISLATIVE FACTORS

Governments, both provincial and federal, can influence the business environment through political programs that result in changes to laws and regulations. For example, governments that wish to improve the climate for job creation emphasize tax cuts, provide tax incentives to develop jobs, increase job-training opportunities, and create balanced labour legislation. Governments can spur economic growth by reducing the public debt, balancing the budget, and cutting taxes. Such measures encourage businesses to invest in that province (or in Canada as a whole) and encourage consumers to spend, resulting in more jobs.

The employer–employee relationship is governed by a legal framework that includes common law (judicial precedents that do not derive from specific laws), constitutional law (e.g., the *Charter of Rights and Freedoms*, acts of federal and provincial parliaments), and contract law (e.g., collective agreements). You are probably familiar with some of these laws. For example, each province has employment standards that establish the maximum number of hours to be worked each day and human rights legislation that prohibits discrimination on the basis of sex, race, and so on. Additionally, governments often enact legislation that affects HR practices directly. For example, the government of Quebec mandates that every organization has to spend 2 percent of its payroll on employee training.

HR professionals need to continuously monitor legislative changes and ensure compliance with legal requirements. For example, Bill 168, an amendment to Ontario's *Occupational Health and Safety Act*, requires that businesses that employ more than five workers develop written policies to regulate workplace violence and harassment. Organizations need to develop and maintain procedures to allow workers to report incidents of threats, as well as to educate workers about the risk and communicate the policy and programs in place.[15]

The decisions not governed by law are usually governed by morals or an ethical code. The concept of ethics is not as clear as laws are. Ethical and moral decisions and

practices go beyond the law, from "you must" to "you should." An employer can require an employee to work overtime and not pay him or her overtime rates (as required by the law). How? The employer gives the employee the title of "manager" (a category exempted from overtime regulations), even when the employee has no managerial responsibilities. Legal? Maybe, but not ethical.

Ethical issues are sometimes raised and resolved by employees, and sometimes organizations have official policies on ethics. For example, most organizations have explicit guidelines on the kinds of "gifts" (kickbacks) that employees may accept from suppliers. But most HRM ethical decisions are much more complicated. Should a company produce goods in a country that employs child labour? Should an organization eliminate one unit (laying off the staff in the process) only to subcontract the work to an outside supplier that employs workers at one-half the compensation rates? Before government steps in with regulations, one important role of HR is to discourage risky behaviours of executives.[16]

TECHNOLOGICAL FACTORS

Technology is the process by which inputs from an organization's environment are transformed into outputs. Technology includes tools, machinery, equipment, and software. Technology has already had a large impact on HR and is predicted to continue to do so at an even faster pace—it took 75 years for telephones to reach an audience of 50 million people, 13 years for television to reach the same number, and only 4 years for the World Wide Web.[17] Computer networks and cloud computing make it possible to store and manage unlimited amounts of data. Social media has impacted how organizations recruit; check references and manage the off-site conduct of their employees. HR Planning Notebook 3.4 outlines the impact of technology.

Every HR function has the potential to become managed electronically. The trend started with payroll and benefits; now software is used to manage training data and succession management information. Online counselling for managers is available, and managers can complete performance appraisals interactively. E-learning is the single most used application on the web.[18] As the hardware becomes smaller and the software becomes smarter, we can expect most HR functions to be managed electronically. HR professionals will need to become technology savvy and/or learn skills of managing vendors of technology solutions.

As well, HR professionals will need to follow trends in the automation of jobs. For example, the Iron Ore Company of Canada uses automatic driverless trains to move ore from the mines, thus reducing the need to hire drivers. IOC states that if they had not adopted automation and new technology, their vacancy rate would be 2000 positions, not the current 200 positions.[19]

© Wavebreak Media/Thinkstock

HR professionals can analyze data to track trends and predict employee behaviour.

See Chapter 8 for a complete review of HR and IT.

In addition, there continue to be concerns about identity theft of employees' personal information and the vulnerability of technology to attack or disaster. According to a panel of technology experts, there will be heightened awareness of HR data privacy.[20] The line is blurring between personal and professional lives as employees use social media. Issues of the protection of intellectual property and the safeguarding of company secrets are made more difficult because of the ease of transferring information using technology. Employee privacy is at risk, as organizations can use Global Positioning Systems (GPS) to track employee locations, including the amount of time spent on breaks, etc. As these trends develop, there will a proliferation of policies about employee monitoring and privacy.

DEMOGRAPHIC FACTORS

Demographics, the study of population statistics, affect HR profoundly. The increasing number of working women, the greying of the workforce, and the arrival of "Gen X's" and "Gen Y's" all influence HR policies.

> **Demographics**
> The study of population statistics

THE LABOUR MARKET

The labour market is the most important demographic factor that should be monitored by HR professionals. A labour market is the area from which an organization

---

HR PLANNING NOTEBOOK 3.4

IMPACT OF TECHNOLOGY ON ORGANIZATIONS

- *Requires changes in skills and work habits of employees:* Employees have to be provided with constant training, and skills are no longer viable for decades.

- *Elimination of some lower-level positions and layers of management:* Routine tasks, normally done by those lowest in the organization hierarchy, are automated, and the surviving employees need more advanced skills. Fewer managers and fewer layers of management are needed.

- *Less hierarchy, more collaboration:* The adoption of technology decreases the need for management as a supervisory control technique.

Power has shifted from management to technical workers, who hold the knowledge about system processes.

- *Telecommuting options:* Telecommuting allows employees to locate farther from their offices, and allows employers to choose office facilities farther from major cities.

- *Electronic monitoring and employee privacy:* Employers monitor e-mail, social media etc. for several reasons, including legal compliance and liability, performance assessment and productivity measures; and security concerns

Sources: Jeffrey A. Mello, *Strategic Human Resource Management*, 1st ed., © 2002; SHRM, Workplace Forecast: A Strategic Outlook, 2004–2005, SHRM 2004.

recruits its employees. Such an area may be metropolitan, regional, provincial, national, or international. The number of people available for work depends on factors such as the unemployment rate, geographic migration, graduation rates from educational institutions, and so on. Demographic issues facing Canadian employers include the underutilization of designated groups, especially those with disabilities and Aboriginal people, the impact of the baby boomers retiring and the rethinking of what it means to retire, and the educational choices of young students.

However, labour markets in the 21st century will become international. Ford, General Motors, and Nestlé already employ more people outside their countries than within. Because of India's huge population of English-speaking software engineers, companies such as Microsoft have employment centres in India.

Any introductory HR textbook will outline the nature of Canada's labour market.

The labour market influences an organization's ability to implement strategy. An organization may decide to enter the high-tech field, only to discover itself unable to recruit enough electrical engineers to meet its personnel requirements, and so must abandon this particular strategy. Companies wishing to grow are facing problems in recruiting and retaining qualified scientists and technologists. There is a growing concern with the division of labour in Canada: the *shortage* of people with the right skills who can earn good money and expect benefits, and the *surplus* of people available to work in "McJobs." Human Resources and Skills Development Canada (HRSDC), the government department concerned with employment issues, is addressing this concern through its National Skills agenda, which will encourage companies to increase their training budgets by one-third (to be in line with other countries), and by requiring that 65 percent of adult immigrants have postsecondary education.[21]

DIVERSITY

There is increasing diversity in the workforce. Terms such as *minority* and *majority* have lost their meaning. People may object to overly broad classifications such as *Asian*, preferring, for example, *Japanese-Canadian* or *Korean-Canadian*.[22] The increasingly diverse workforce demographics present challenges as well as opportunities for organizations to meet their talent needs. The ability of businesses to tap into underutilized pools of highly educated minority groups and effectively manage the diverse workforce will be an important source of competitive advantage in the future. Organizations that tracked representation of diversity groups were more likely to do so for new hires (50 percent) than for a leadership succession pool (17 percent). As a result, although visible minorities represented 16.3 percent of the overall workforce, only 3.3 percent of senior executives were minorities.[23] Given the competition for critical skills, organizations that are able to exploit diverse talent will gain competitive advantage. Organizations may take advantage of inclusion programs, such as catering to communication styles and offering customizable benefits programs to engage different groups.[24]

GENERATIONAL DIFFERENCES

The supply of baby boomers (those born between 1946 and 1964) exceeds the demand for them in middle management and senior ranks. The combination of the surge of workers in their 50s and the flattening of organizations has created a cadre of plateaued workers who are approaching retirement. If a person starts working at 21, retires at 55,

and dies at 89, this person will have spent 34 years at work and 34 years in retirement. Most boomers don't think their money will last that long. Surveys showed that of the 6 percent of the Canadian workforce who were eligible to retire in the next 12 months, only 1 percent expected to retire.[25] The *Income Tax Act* may have to be changed to allow phased-in retirement, and HR planners will have to make work adjustments to accommodate these requests.[26]

"Baby busters" (those born between 1965 and the mid-1970s) follow the boomers, who have created a bottleneck in the organization. There are far fewer baby busters, and most are very well educated and trained, so can command significant incomes.

Gen X employees (those born between 1965 and 1980) have lived with technology all their lives. They have fewer expectations of organizations and perceive themselves as independent agents. Members of Gen Y, born after 1981, are completely comfortable with technology and have a more global and tolerant outlook than people older than they. Gen Y employees are not very interested in climbing a career ladder; indeed, they assume that they will change jobs frequently. For HR managers, an important consideration is how to vary HR practices to engage and motivate these different generations of workers who also have different work values and preferences. HR managers also need to consider how to capitalize on Gen Y employees' knowledge and skills during the short period when they are hired by the company. Instead of continuing to employ people "from the shoulder down," HR managers need to unleash individuals' creativity "from the neck up."[27] Some considerations of intergenerational differences in HR management are outlined in HR Planning Today 3.2. The implication for HR managers is the need for employee segmentation, in the same way that marketers segment customers. HR professionals are often preoccupied with "fairness and equity," which is often translated into exactly the same policies and programs for all employees. But in the same way that a gardener will give different types of flowers different amounts of water, sunshine, fertilizer etc. in order to create ideal growing conditions, HR managers will have to segment or customize career management models for different types of employees. Instead of an employee value proposition offered by organizations, a personal value proposition will be created.[28]

SOCIAL AND CULTURAL FACTORS

RIGHT TO PRIVACY

Society can express its intent through laws and regulations, and in less formal ways within organizations through discipline and terminations. One issue getting more and more public attention is the right to privacy. Does the employer have a moral (and legal) right to monitor employee activities through video surveillance cameras or reading e-mail? Dow Chemical Co. terminated 50 employees and disciplined another 200 because these employees downloaded, saved, or distributed offensive material using the company's e-mail system. (Those who merely opened and deleted the material were not reprimanded.)[29]

WORK–LIFE BALANCE

Another issue is the employee's attempt to balance a personal life with an ever-more-encompassing work life. Research on hours worked indicates that Canadians are spending more time at work. Many employees face the challenge of trying to spend

WORKFORCE STRATEGIES FOR DIFFERENT GENERATIONS

	BABY BOOMERS	GENERATION X	GENERATION Y
Communication	Show respect Choose face-to-face	Get to the point Use e-mail generally, but face-to-face to deal with issues	Orient them quickly E-mail and instant messaging are preferred
Development and job design	Acknowledge accomplishments Create an open work environment	Give them space to explore and find solutions Lighten up! Work can be fun	Provide feedback quickly Challenge them Outline the end game for each task
Recruitment	Use headhunters Advertise in newspapers	Go through social networks Create employee referral programs	Utilize technology (Facebook etc.) Allow space for parental input
Retention	Develop solutions to postpone retirement Highlight value and contributions to the company	Get over the notion of having to pay one's dues Provide flexible work solutions Set up clear steps for advancement	Find them a mentor Allow them to contribute to the community Introduce new opportunities frequently

Source: Adapted from: Tapia, A. (2009). "The Emerging Diverse Workforce: Implications of a Global Demographic Tsunami for Organizations in Canada." Copyright Andrés T. Tapia 2009.

quality time with their families while vigorously pursuing a career. People are generally most active in moving ahead in their careers between the ages of 25 and 45, exactly the stage at which most people raise their children. Both roles are demanding; both require long hours, during the same period (6 a.m. to 10 p.m.). The demographics of the aging workforce mean that working adults will be stressed by the extra demands of caring for their elderly relatives, estimated to consume about 23 hours each month.[30] Organizations have responded to this issue by increasing workplace flexibility. Some options include flextime, part-time work, job sharing, telecommuting, elder care, and child care. The issue of employee well-being is also on the collective bargaining table, with unions asking for family support benefits such as subsidies for child and elder care, and access to wellness facilities. Although the unionized workforce is changing to include more women and older workers, many of the traditional union members, such as low-wage and hourly workers, factory and service workers, and outside workers, cannot take advantage of benefits such as flexible work hours, telecommuting, or on-site gyms.

CONTINGENT WORKERS

Another significant trend in Canada is the continuing growth of contingency workers (part-time, temporary, seasonal, and contract workers). These workers may or may not voluntarily choose to pursue contingency employment and experience different work–life challenges than traditional workers.[31] For example, research shows that seasonal workers experience fewer developmental opportunities at work and are often treated as "costs" rather than "assets" in organizations. Not surprisingly, they report lower commitment to the organization and focus only on completing their assigned tasks.[32] As these contingent modes of employment continue to increase, HR needs to reconsider how to strategically manage these employees to gain competitive advantage. If the organization cannot promise long-term employment, benefits, or developmental opportunities, what other practices can be equally effective in engaging these employees?

STAKEHOLDERS

In addition to general environment, organizations also need to consider the industrial and organizational environment, particularly the relevant groups in this context. Many groups have an influence on the organization's strategy. These groups, referred to as the *stakeholders*, hold expectations of the HR function that can influence HR strategy and practices.

Stakeholders are groups of people who have an interest in the projects, policies, or outcomes of an organization's decisions. Sometimes called constituent groups, they follow the actions of the organization and lobby to have their interests satisfied. These stakeholders affect strategy formulation. Employees want higher wages and job security, suppliers want longer-term relationships, customers want faster service, and shareholders want more dividends and higher stock prices. Organizations will often adapt their strategies to accommodate powerful stakeholders such as unions, regulatory agencies, or customers. Let us look at some of these organizational stakeholders and their interest in HR.

> **Stakeholders**
> Groups of people who have vested interests in an organization's decisions

THE BOARD OF DIRECTORS AND SENIOR EXECUTIVES

This group develops the vision, mission, strategy, and objectives for the organization. As a group, the HR issues that interest them the most include the workforce implications of strategic options such as restructuring, outsourcing, mergers and acquisitions, and going international (all these HR implications are discussed in separate chapters in this text). They have a particular interest in succession management (Chapter 7) and leadership development.

Much of the research on HR planning recognizes the powerful influence of the CEO on the organization's ability to attain its goals. The concept of the rational manager is well embedded in our business psyche. We assume that the head of an organization carefully analyzes the environment–looking at competitors' actions and technological changes–and then decides the best strategy to exploit opportunities and corporate strengths. But hearts may be as influential as heads. Managers are more than rational actors; they have personal values, ethics, attitudes toward risk, and ambition.[33]

Research has shown that different types of strategies require different types of managers and executives. Studies of these managerial elites have found that managers with certain personalities–for example, those with a tolerance for ambiguity–managed firms with a growth strategy more successfully than those with a harvest strategy.[34]

SENIOR MANAGEMENT

Senior managers are typically responsible to the executives for the execution of the strategy and organizational performance. Therefore, they are most interested in the HR programs and practices that affect performance: workforce planning and utilization, incentive compensation, training and development, and performance management systems. They want metrics that spotlight performance indicators such as employee commitment scores, absenteeism, and turnover rate—all discussed in Chapter 14.

SUPERVISORS

This group is responsible for the management of employees and their role in meeting organizational goals. As a group, they want HR to help them with recruitment, selection, compensation, training and development, coaching, and policy development. Their needs are often based on individual employee issues such as poor performance (and the need to terminate an employee) or difficulties in recruiting specialists.

EMPLOYEES

Employees want the HR department to expedite their requests efficiently, confidentially, and fairly. They want HR policies that enable them to be satisfied at work, and to develop skills to be able to do their jobs, now and in the future. They are concerned with HR policies on compensation, training and development, health and safety, and overall working conditions.

The board of directors develop the vision, mission and strategy of the organization.

© Bob Daemmrich/Alamy

As has been indicated earlier, sometimes an organization's strategy is influenced by the kinds of competencies it already possesses. Likewise, strengths can reside in the HR department itself. If the HR department has excelled in its ability to grow rapidly by attracting, hiring, and orienting highly qualified candidates, corporate venturing or a joint venture becomes an attainable goal. If culture management is the HR department's strength, mergers and acquisitions can be considered a strategic option.

UNIONS

The presence of unions in the environment will affect HRM strategy for firms entering new sectors with high unionization rates. Employees who are currently unionized within an organization can influence strategy in two ways. One is a restrictive way, in which the collective agreement limits an organization's ability to make drastic changes in working methods or jobs to accommodate changes in strategic direction. A second way is that unions now play a larger role and are more cooperative than adversarial with regard to HR practices such as profit sharing, plant locations, selection procedures, and quality improvement. Savvy HR planners keep track of the policies of key unions such as the Canadian Auto Workers (CAW), because they set the benchmark for hourly workers in Canada. Any innovative benefit will filter through the economy and affect other organizations' negotiations. The key issues for unions are job security, income security, working hours, and inflation protection.[35] Unionized employees receive higher wages and have better working conditions than their nonunionized counterparts.[36]

RESPONDING TO EXTERNAL FACTORS

While it is interesting to attempt to assess all the changing factors that might affect your organization, the reality is that managers have limited time and resources to monitor everything. Most organizations use an issues priority matrix to determine which are the important trends that may affect them. Using the table below, managers can then rate, from high to low:

1. The probability of these trends actually occurring
2. The likely impact of each of these trends on the organization

A PROACTIVE APPROACH

Some HR managers do not like passively observing the game through their windows; they want to participate and influence how the game is played. Thus, we find most professional associations have a group that lobbies for legislation that will favour the association membership. Most have public relations firms that try to shape the perception of the profession and its goals (thus influencing public opinion favourably toward regulations).

After the environmental scanning, companies can analyze the business environment to determine the impact on the organization and the actions that the organization needs to take. Organizations can use a SWOT analysis to determine the impact on the organization. HR Planning Today 3.3 describes in detail how the Global Wood Group company scans the external environment to identify threats and opportunities.

Figure 3.1 summarizes the environmental and industrial factors that organizations need to scan and monitor to determine the impact on organizational strategy and HR management. On the basis of these analyses, organizations then further reposition the business competitive strategy and develop competitive advantage, as discussed in Chapter 1.

TABLE 3.1

ISSUES PRIORITY MATRIX

		PROBABLE IMPACT ON ORGANIZATION		
		HIGH	MEDIUM	LOW
PROBABILITY OF OCCURRENCE	High	High priority	High priority	High priority
	Medium	High priority	Medium priority	Low priority
	Low	Medium priority	Low priority	Low priority

Source: Reprinted from *Long Range Planning*, Vol. 17, No. 3, Campbell, J., "Foresight Activities in the USA: Time for a Re-assessment," 1984, with permission from Elsevier.

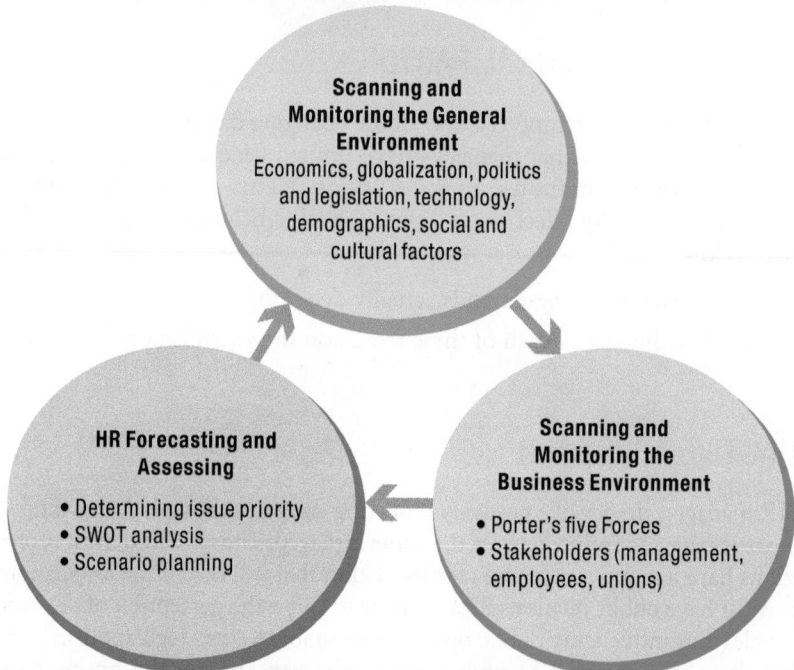

FIGURE 3.1

THE ENVIRONMENTAL ANALYSIS PROCESS

Scanning and Monitoring the General Environment
Economics, globalization, politics and legislation, technology, demographics, social and cultural factors

Scanning and Monitoring the Business Environment
- Porter's five Forces
- Stakeholders (management, employees, unions)

HR Forecasting and Assessing
- Determining issue priority
- SWOT analysis
- Scenario planning

HR PLANNING TODAY   3.3

THE GLOBAL WOOD GROUP

The Global Group of Companies (http://www.globaltotal-office.com), with over 5,000 employees, is perhaps the largest manufacturing interest still operating in the Toronto area. Global Wood, which has developed over the past few years into the Global Wood Group, an autonomous division of the Global Group of Companies, designs and manufactures wood-laminate office furniture. On average, over 75 percent of its production is exported to and sold in the United States. Staff within the Global Wood Group continually scan the external environment through access to:

- *Professional associations:* Organizations such as the Wood Manufacturing Council and the Ontario Furniture Manufacturers Alliance lobby governments on behalf of manufacturers. Liaising with these groups provides the Global Wood Group with information; for example, that the only restrictions

that the United States would have on the importation of Chinese-manufactured wood furniture would apply to bedroom sets.

- *Trade publications:* Publications such as *Offcuts*, *Wood Industry*, *Woodworking*, *Materials Management & Distribution*, and *Wood & Wood Products* revealed information about new products coming onto the market and the offerings of new manufacturers entering North America.

- *Professional conferences and seminars:* At conferences hosted by organizations such as the Woodworking Council and the American Home Furnishings Alliance, Global Wood Group representatives were able to visit the displays of organizations selling machinery and equipment to furniture manufacturers and to ascertain which

companies were purchasing machinery and what production techniques they were using.

- *External consultants and trainers:* ISO auditors visit Global Wood Group facilities for one week every year to review their processes. These auditors have international experience and provide recommendations regarding quality, safety, and environmental management, as well as production techniques, training, and logistics based on best practices from around the world. The Global Wood Group also utilizes outside training organizations to provide additional expert training for staff. This includes allowing employees to attend postsecondary courses.

- *Regular management meetings:* Senior management of the Global Wood Group meets on a weekly basis to review events and to discuss threats and opportunities and formulate strategies to address them.

Through these scanning activities, GW was able to assess threats and opportunities.

Threats

After extensive government reviews, including an investigation under the auspices of the International Trade Commission, the U.S. government decided to eliminate tariffs and restrictions on the importation of all wood furniture products with the exception of bedroom furniture. Manufacturers in China targeted first the residential market and by 2003 had control of the majority of this market in the United States. Using production and quality control techniques developed while manufacturing residential furniture, and the logistics and sales connections that went with it, these manufacturers then targeted the highly profitable commercial furniture market. The Global Wood Group increased their research, using government and industry documents to monitor lumber shipments, equipment purchases, traffic through ports of entry, sales figures, and the marketing efforts of the Chinese manufacturers' representatives. At the same time, the Canadian dollar began its rise from just over 60 cents U.S. to par, which resulted in the loss of the price advantage that Canadian goods had held in the United States. In addition, the announced incremental increases in the minimum wage in Ontario, from $6.85 (as of 2003) to $10.25 (starting on March 31, 2010), created an inflationary impetus on wages. A number of

furniture companies closed their manufacturing facilities in North America and in particular Ontario due to these complications.

Opportunities

But there were opportunities:

1. *Proximity to customers, which enabled a rapid response to order fulfillment:* The Global Wood Group decreased average turnaround time for orders from 30 days between receipt of the order and shipment to 5 days. Recent sharp increases in petroleum prices have increased the cost of shipping a 40-foot [about 12.2 metres] container from China to the United States by up to 30 percent. Rail prices in North America have remained relatively stable in comparison.

2. *The implementation of an internationally recognized quality management system (ISO 9001), which Global Wood combined with the introduction of environmental (ISO 14001) and occupational health and safety (OHSAS 18001) programs:* These require external auditing on a regular basis and conformance with internationally set standards. Adherence to these programs significantly improved quality, while reducing raw material use and lost time due to injuries and improving the work environment, thereby decreasing unwanted turnover. Every piece can be tracked to identify every worker who has handled it. Quality inspectors were eliminated and replaced with an internal responsibility system.

3. *A well-trained workforce:* Global Wood Group increased training phenomenally, both to improve production techniques and to implement and maintain the ISO programs. Beginning with the first day on the job, employees undergo intensive training following a prescribed checklist for each function and duty. The ISO/OHSAS programs require training on a quarterly basis, as well as the monitoring, documentation, and assessment of this training. Employees are empowered, and their roles have expanded beyond physical skills to mental skills such as inspection and quality control. This educated and trained workforce enabled the Global Wood Group to move from mass production to customized production. Rather than 1,000 identical units being manufactured, each unit can now be custom-ordered, with the workers responsible for

matching the hardware, components, and colours with the size specified in the order.

4. *Access to raw material (wood laminate, which is manufactured in Northern Ontario and Quebec), allowing for delivery within one day:* This enabled Global Wood to expand the lines without increasing facility size, so storage areas to stockpile raw material were no longer required. Rather than pay for the removal of scrap wood, Global Wood workers were provided with bonuses for implementing ways and means to reduce the use of raw materials, waste, or scrap material. Eventually, a way was found to grind any remaining wood-based scrap and use it as a source of renewable energy, resulting in a reduction in material costs, waste costs, and energy costs.

5. *Access to latest trends in ergonomics and technology:* By changing the lines to be more ergonomic, Global Wood's lost-time claims were reduced to 0.02 percent of the industry average. By improving the work environment, the employee turnover rate was reduced from 24 percent to 6 percent. Implementing new techniques, such as the use of polyurethane glue and vacuum-assisted materials-handling devices, have improved production speed.

By successfully tracking changes in the operating and competitive environment and proactively making the necessary organization adjustment, Global Wood was able to track the following benefits over a three-year period:

- Increase in production (and orders) of 29 percent
- Increase in revenue of 30 percent, despite the rise of the Canadian dollar
- Reduction in scrap and waste materials of 26 percent
- Reduction in turnover of 18 percent
- Reduction in injuries of 81 percent
- Reduction in defects of 73 percent

As a result, the Global Wood Group has grown to become the most profitable part of the Global Group of Companies, and it now encompasses 12 separate corporations operating in Ontario and Alberta.

Source: Interview with Dan McGarry, Senior Divisional Manager HR (Consulting), Global Wood Group, July 10, 2008.

// SUMMARY

HRM strategy is determined primarily by organizational strategy. However, environmental factors also shape HRM strategy, so HR managers and planners have to continually monitor the environment. Typically, they scan by reading publications, retaining memberships in professional associations, attending conferences, or using professional scanners. A number of methods, such as trend and impact analysis and the Delphi technique, are used to identify future trends. The environmental factors monitored include the economic climate, the political and regulatory climate, and social norms. Stakeholders such as shareholders, unions, customers, and executives contribute strongly to the formulation and implementation of strategy.

KEY TERMS

competitive intelligence p. 60
demographics p. 65
environmental scanning p. 56
stakeholders p. 69

NEL

WEB LINKS

The website of Employment and Social Development Canada is a good place to look for well-researched articles on trends in collective agreements, work–life balance, and other topics of interest to students and employers:
http://www.hrsdc.gc.ca

A Health Canada website that offers trends in workplace health and wellness:
http://www.hc-sc.gc.ca/ewh-semt/index_e.html

DISCUSSION QUESTIONS

1. Search for workplace trends affecting Canadian employers. Using the issues priority matrix (Table 3.1), rate the probability of these issues impacting your career.

2. Using your school as an example, find one trend in each of the areas (economics, globalization, political/legislative, technology, demographic and social/cultural) that will impact enrollment in your school.

3. One trend to watch is the technology development. Discuss how this has impacted your life, as a student and as an employee. Can you predict how it will impact the working patterns of employees? What policies should the HR department develop in anticipation of the continuing use of technology?

EXERCISES: SCENARIO PLANNING

Practise the scenario planning technique for Amazon using the steps below.

1. Form a group of four to six people. Discuss what Amazon will experience, taking into consideration the changes that may occur in the general environment (economics, globalization, political/legislative, technology, demographics, and socio-cultural factors, etc.) and Amazon business environment (suppliers, competitors, especially Alibaba; customers, senior management, employees, etc.). Identify three business scenarios that might play out in the next five years (most desirable case, most likely case, and least desirable case).

2. For each scenario, assess the firm's readiness. What are the challenges faced under each scenario? Identify HR's strengths and weaknesses in relation to these challenges.

3. For each scenario, identify HR initiatives and programs that must be undertaken to deal with the changes.

4. Prepare a group report on the future of the job.

5. Present this report to the class.

After the presentations, discuss the challenges of predicting the future in this manner. Should HR planners not scan the environment because of these problems? Is there a better way?

Magda Hyshka, manager of HR policies for TelPlus, the largest telecommunications company in Canada, had been asked by her director of HR to develop an innovative policy to address the work–family issues facing the company. As part of her research, Magda uncovered the following facts:

- Workers spend an average of 50 hours a week on job-related activities and more than half bring work home.
- Canadian workers are feeling more stress, caused by an insufficient salary, work overload, and a negative work environment.
- About half of Canadian workers spend 22 hours a week in child care, and about 25 percent spend 9 hours a week on elder care.
- Work–life conflict negatively impacts performance, causing employees to be absent from work, reduce productivity, and increase use of benefits.
- Technology enabled employees to work seven days a week and at any time during the day or night, and many felt that they were expected to be available (online) all the time.
- While Canadians are insisting on more work–life balance, Asian workers with equivalent qualifications were willing to work long hours, for less than half the pay.

Sources: Duxbury L. & Higgins, C., "Revisiting work life issues in Canada: the 2012 National Study of Balancing Work and Caregiving in Canada," http://www.healthyworkplaces.info/wp-content/uploads/2012/11/2012-National-Work-Long-Summary.pdf, retrieved December 1, 2014; Y.A. Laroche, *Fine Balance*, Ottawa: Canadian Centre for Management Development, 2000; J. Schramm, J. Coombs, and J. Victor, *Workplace Forecast*, Alexandria, Virginia: SHRM, February 2011; Morrow, J. "Studies stress economic cost of depression in the workplace," http://www.cos-mag.com/health-page/health-page-stories/studies-stress-economic-cost-of-depression-in-the-workplace.html, retrieved December 10, 2014.

QUESTIONS

Continue the research started by Magda. Prepare a report summarizing your findings and recommending policies that will help your employees cope with work–family balance issues.

// REFERENCES

1. http://www.economist.com/node/16846494. Retrieved August 26, 2011.

2. Adapted from a July 13, 2008 broadcast of *The Michael Enright Show*, CBC Radio, available as a podcast; and Taylor, Alex, III. "Gentlemen, Start Your Engines." *Fortune*, January 21, 2008: 70.

3. Young, L. 2010. "The New Normal." *HR Professional*, February: 24–28.

4. Porter, M.E. 2008. "The Five Competitive Forces That Shape Strategy." *Harvard Business Review*, January 2008.

5. Schuler, R.S., and S.E. Jackson. 2005. "A Quarter-Century Review of Human Resource Management in the U.S.: The Growth in the International Perspective." *Management Review*, Vol. 16, No. 1: 11–35.

6. Certo, S.C., and J.P. Peter. 1993. *Strategic Management: A Focus on Process.* Boston: Irwin.

7. Rothwell, W.J., and H.C. Kazanas. 1988. *Strategic Human Resources Planning and Management.* Englewood Cliffs, NJ: Prentice Hall.

8. Coyne, K.P., and J. Horn. 2009. "Predicting Your Competitor's Reaction." *Harvard Business Review*, April: 90–97.

9. Wheelen, T.L., and J.D. Hunger. 2008. *Concepts in Strategic Management and Business Policy*, 11th ed. Saddle River, NJ: Pearson Prentice Hall.

10. Ofek, E., and L. Wathieu. 2010. "Are You Ignoring Trends That Could Shake Up Your Business?" *Harvard Business Review*, July/August: 124–131.

11. Ragan, C. "How to Heal the Deep Scars from the Financial Crisis." *The Globe and Mail*, November 18, 2014: B2.

12. Schramm, J.J., J. Coombs, and J. Victor. 2011. "Workplace Forecast: The Top Workplace Trends According to HR Professions." SHRM.

13. http://www.international.gc.ca/trade-agreements-accords-commerciaux/agr-acc/nafta-alena/index.aspx?view=d. Retrieved August 26, 2011.

14. Overman, S. 2002. "HR Is Partner in McDonaldizing Employees in New Countries." *HR News*, May: 7.

15. http://www.labour.gov.on.ca/english/hs/sawo/pubs/fs_workplaceviolence.php. Retrieved March 31, 2011.

16. Young, 2010.

17. Patel, D. 2002–2003. *Workplace Forecast.* Alexandria, VA: SHRM; and Schramm, J. 2005. "HR's Tech Challenges." *HR Magazine*, Vol. 50, No. 3: 152.

18. http://www.corporateleadershipcouncil.com, June 2002. Retrieved April 5, 2006.

19. Silliker, A. "Big Role for Automation in Tight Labour Market." *Canadian HR Reporter*, 24, 22, 2011: 1–2.

20. Schramm, 2005.

21. Brown, D. 2002. "Ottawa Unveils National Training and Development Strategy." *Canadian HR Reporter*, Vol. 15, No. 5 (March 11): 3, 6.

22. Jamrog, J.J. 2002. "Current Practices: The Coming Decade of the Employee." *Human Resource Planning*, Vol. 25, No. 3: 5–12.

23. Conference Board of Canada. June 2010. "Valuing Your Talent: Human Resources Trends and Metrics."

24. http://www.hewittassociates.com/Lib/assets/NA/en-CA/pdf/DiversityTapia.pdf. Retrieved March 31, 2011.

25. Conference Board of Canada, June 2010.

26. Langton, J. 2005. "Accountants Offer Two Cents on Aging Workforce." *Canadian HR Reporter*, Vol. 18, No. 4: 3.

27. Adams, A. 2010. "Changing Role of HR." *Human Resources*, June: 45–48.

28. Boudrea, J. W. and I. Ziskin. "The Future of HR and Effective Organizations." *Organizational Dynamics,"* 2011, 40: 255–266.

29. Currie, M.B., and D. Black. 2001. "Emerging Issues in the Electronic Workplace." *Ivey Business Journal*, Vol. 65, No. 3 (January/February): 18–29.

30. Tomlinson, A. 2002. "Trickle Down Effects of Retiring Boomers." *Canadian HR Reporter*, Vol. 15, No. 11 (June 3): 1, 12.

31. Connelly, C.E., and D.G. Gallagher. 2004. "Emerging Trends in Contingent Work Research." *Journal of Management*, Vol. 30: 959–983.

32. Ainsworth, S., and A. Purss. 2009. "Same Time, Next Year? Human Resource Management and Seasonal Workers." *Personnel Review*, Vol. 38: 217–235.

33. Guth, W.D., and R. Tagiuri. 1965. "Personal Values and Corporate Strategy." *Harvard Business Review*, Vol. 43, No. 5 (September/October): 123–132.

34. Gupta, A., and V. Govindarajan. 1984. "Business Unit Strategy Managerial Characteristics, and Business Unit Effectiveness at Strategy Implementation." *Academy of Management Journal*, Vol. 27: 25–41.

35. Brown, D. 2002. "CAW–Big Three Negotiations Set the Mark." *Canadian HR Reporter*, Vol. 15, No. 12 (June 17): 3, 12.

36. Lawler, E.E., and S.A. Mohram. 1987. "Unions and the New Management." *Academy of Management Executives*, Vol. 26, No. 1: 293–300.

Monica Belcourt, Parbudyal Singh, Scott A. Snell, Shad S. Morris, George Bohlander, Managing Human Resources, Eighth Canadian Edition, 2017

CHAPTER

Performance Management

After studying this chapter, you should be able to

OUTCOME 1   Explain what performance management is and how the establishment of goals, ongoing performance feedback, and the evaluation process are part of it.

OUTCOME 2   Describe the different sources of performance management information.

OUTCOME 3   Explain the various methods used to evaluate the performance of employees.

OUTCOME 4   Outline the characteristics of effective performance evaluation meetings and feedback sessions and ways in which the performance of employees can be improved.

We have discussed some of the ways that you as a manager can acquire top-notch employees and train and develop them. But how do you know if your efforts are really paying off in terms of what the employees are contributing once they are on the job?

PERFORMANCE MANAGEMENT SYSTEMS

performance management
The process of creating a work environment in which people can perform to the best of their abilities

performance evaluations
The result of an annual or biannual process in which a manager evaluates an employee's performance relative to the requirements of his or her job and uses the information to show the person where improvements are needed and why

Performance management is the process of creating a work environment in which people can perform to the best of their abilities in order to meet a company's goals. It is an entire work system that emanates from a company's goals. Figure 8.1 shows the elements of a performance management process.

Performance evaluations, which are also referred to as performance appraisals and performance reviews, are the result of a process by which a manager evaluates an employee's performance relative to the requirements of his or her job and uses the information to show the person where improvements are needed and why. Evaluations are a tool organizations can use to maintain and enhance their productivity and facilitate progress toward their strategic goals.

Typically, performance evaluations are delivered annually or biannually. In a recent survey of 1,350 HR managers, 76 percent of them said their firms conduct them annually; 12 percent said they conduct them biannually.[1] Some organizations find value in conducting them on a quarterly basis. In many firms, new employees are often put on probationary status for a period of time and evaluated 30, 60, or 90 days after their start dates, with their continued employment contingent upon their performing satisfactorily. However, as you can see from Figure 8.1, the performance appraisal is just part of the performance management process. Aligning the goals of employees with those of the firm, providing workers with continual on-the-job feedback, and providing them with encouragement and rewarding them for a job done well are critical too.

FIGURE 8.1

STEPS IN THE PERFORMANCE MANAGEMENT PROCESS

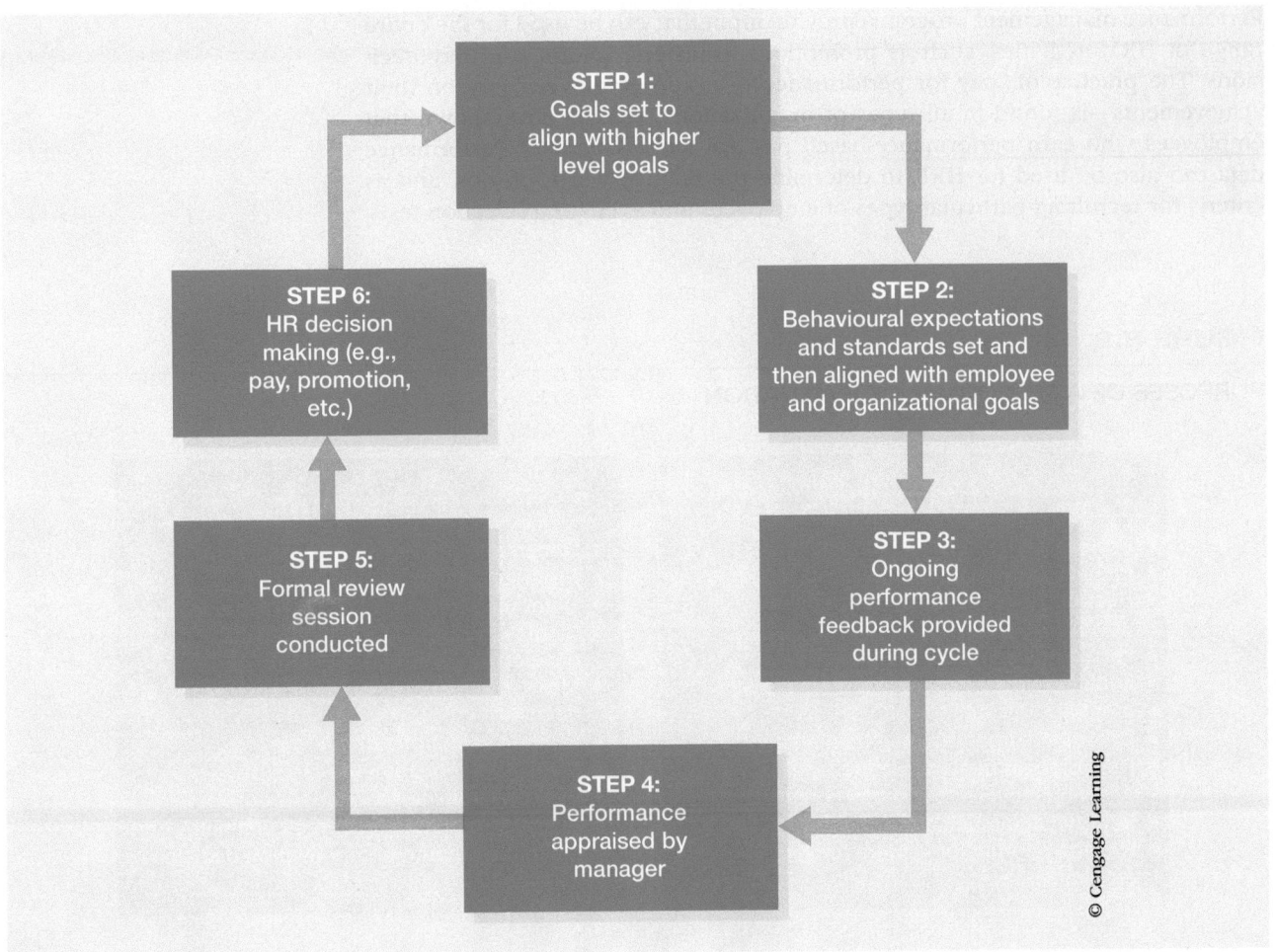

STEP 1: Goals set to align with higher level goals

STEP 2: Behavioural expectations and standards set and then aligned with employee and organizational goals

STEP 3: Ongoing performance feedback provided during cycle

STEP 4: Performance appraised by manager

STEP 5: Formal review session conducted

STEP 6: HR decision making (e.g., pay, promotion, etc.)

© Cengage Learning

You might compare a performance evaluation to taking a test in college. Do tests motivate you? Do they make you want to truly excel, or do you just want to get through them? Now compare your test-taking experience with an experience in which your instructor talked to you about your career plans, complimented you on your performance, and offered you suggestions for improving it. That probably had a greater motivating effect on you.

We hope you can see the analogy we are making. Employers have to appraise you, just as your university has to test you to be sure you graduate with the qualifications people in society expect. But your performance in either scenario consists of so much more than that. That is why organizations need to look at the performance management system as a whole rather than just evaluations. Evaluations are simply a logical extension of the day-to-day performance management process.[2]

THE PURPOSES OF PERFORMANCE MANAGEMENT

It has been said that "what gets measured gets done." Good performance management systems have the capability to influence employee behaviour and improve an organization's performance. One study showed that organizations with strong performance management systems are 40 to 50 percent more likely to outperform their competitors in the areas of revenue growth, productivity, profitability, and market value.[3] In addition to improving a firm's overall performance and profitability, Figure 8.2 shows the other two most common purposes of performance management programs, which are administrative and developmental.

Administrative Purposes

Performance management programs provide input that can be used for the entire range of HRM activities, such as promotions, transfers, layoffs, and pay decisions. The practice of "pay for performance"—basing employees' pay on their achievements—is found in all types of organizations. Studies have shown that employees who earn performance-based pay are more satisfied.[4] Performance data can also be used for HRP, to determine the relative worth of jobs, and as criteria for recruiting particular types of employees and validating selection tests.

FIGURE 8.2

PURPOSES OF A PERFORMANCE EVALUATION

DEVELOPMENTAL	ADMINISTRATIVE
• Provide performance feedback	• Document personnel decisions
• Identify individual strengths and weaknesses	• Promote employees
• Recognize individual performance achievements	• Determine transfers and assignments
• Help employees identify goals	• Identify performance problems and develop ways to correct them
• Evaluate goal achievement of employees	• Make retention, termination, and layoff decisions
• Identify individual training needs	• Validate selection criteria
• Determine organizational training needs	• Meet legal requirements
• Reinforce authority structure	• Evaluate training programs/progress
• Allow employees to discuss concerns	• Assist with human resources planning
• Improve communication	• Make reward and compensation decisions
• Provide a forum for leaders to help employees	

Yet another purpose of having a performance management system in place along with performance evaluations is to document HRM actions that can result in legal action. Because of the government's equal employment opportunity directives, employers need to maintain accurate, objective employee performance records in order to defend themselves against possible charges of discrimination when it comes to promotions, salaries, and terminations. Finally, the success of the entire HR program depends on knowing how the performance of employees compares to the goals established for them.

Developmental Purposes

A performance management system gives managers a concrete framework they can use to gather information about an employee's performance, provide employees with feedback, and discuss an employee's goals and how they align with the organization's goals. The goal is to build on a person's strengths, eliminate potential weaknesses, and further his or her career while improving the performance of the organization as well. By taking a developmental approach to the performance management process, managers help employees understand that the feedback they are getting is designed to improve their future competencies and further their careers and are not being conducted simply to judge them.

Companies such as EDS, a business unit of Hewlett-Packard, are among the firms that have redesigned their performance management programs to focus more on employee development and learning. EDS, for example, integrated its system to work in concert with the company's learning and career management objectives. For each position in the firm, the system includes a detailed job description, performance review information, and a career planner to track employees' long-term goals as well as access to the company's automated career library. The system is ultimately linked to the company's succession policies. By creating this overall system, EDS hopes to shift the role of manager from that of "judge" to one of "coach."[5]

WHY PERFORMANCE MANAGEMENT SYSTEMS SOMETIMES FAIL

Performance appraisals often fall short of their potential. In an ongoing survey of employee attitudes by the HR consulting firm Watson Wyatt, only 30 percent of employees said they thought their company's performance management process actually improved employee performance. Only one in five thought it helped poorly performing employees do better.[6]

Many people fault the formal evaluation process. They believe it discourages teamwork by focusing on workers' individual achievements rather than what their teams or firms accomplish. (Who gets the best rating and the biggest raise? Who does not?) Others contend that evaluations are useful only at the extremes—for highly effective or highly ineffective employees—and are not as useful for the majority of employees in the middle. Other people point out that evaluations often focus on short-term achievements rather than long-term improvement and learning. Still others complain that the only feedback they get is during formal evaluations, or they aren't done at all. This can especially be a problem in small businesses, as this chapter's small business feature shows. It's not uncommon for managers to show new employees to their workstations and leave them on their own or to assign tasks to employees on a routine basis with little or no feedback on the tasks they have already completed. A more complete list of the reasons why formal evaluations fail is shown in Figure 8.3.

For reasons such as these, a substantial number of organizations no longer conduct formal evaluations but use ongoing coaching, individual development plans, or other feedback systems instead. Other organizations, including Xerox, Motorola, and Procter & Gamble, have modified their performance evaluations to try to improve them.[7] At RoundPegg, a hiring startup that develops social

FIGURE 8.3

LET ME COUNT THE WAYS . . . REASONS WHY PERFORMANCE EVALUATIONS CAN FAIL

- The manager is inadequately prepared.
- The employee is not given clear objectives at the beginning of the performance period.
- The manager may not be able to observe performance or have all the information.
- The performance standards may not be clear.
- Ratings are inconsistent among supervisors or other raters.
- The manager rates the employee's personality rather than performance.
- Raters may be subject to perceptual biases such as the halo and/or contrast effect.
- The time span for evaluation is inappropriate (either too short or too long).

- There is an overemphasis on uncharacteristic performance.
- Ratings are inflated because managers do not want to deal with "bad news."
- The language in written evaluations is subjective or vague.
- Organizational politics or personal relationships cloud judgments.
- There is no thorough discussion of the causes of performance problems.
- The manager may not be trained in evaluation or giving feedback.
- There is no follow-up and coaching after the evaluation.

Sources: Patricia Evres, "Problems to Avoid during Performance Evaluations," *Air Conditioning, Heating & Refrigeration News* 216, no. 16 (August 19, 2002): 24–26; Clinton Longnecker and Dennis Gioia, "The Politics of Executive Appraisals," *Journal of Compensation and Benefits* 10, no. 2 (1994): 5–11; "Seven Deadly Sins of Performance Appraisals," *Supervisory Management* 39, no. 1 (1994): 7–8.

applications, all employees have quarterly reviews, or "feedback sessions," that last just 20 minutes. "Our job is to make sure our employees are being successful, and if they're not, we're doing something wrong," say Brent Daily, RoundPegg's co-founder and chief operating officer. "My job here isn't just to make sure everyone is crossing their T's and dotting their I's—my job is to remove the obstacles and allow them to do what they do best."[8]

Because teamwork is so important in organizations today, other companies are starting to use *crowdsourcing* as part of their performance management systems. In an HR context, crowdsourcing involves continually gathering feedback, compliments, and suggestions from the different people who work with an employee using "social recognition" applications installed on a company's computers and mobile devices. Achievers and Globoforce are two such brands. (You can think of the applications as being somewhat analogous to "liking" something someone does on Facebook.) When they are recognized by other workers, employees get points that translate into monetary and other rewards. 3M, the Marriott and Starwood hotel chains, and the pharmaceutical company Eli Lilly are using this type of software. Starwood Hotels believes it keeps all of its employees focused on the important drivers of the firm's performance, builds teamwork, and helps the company identify and reward top performers.[9]

DEVELOPING AN EFFECTIVE PERFORMANCE MANAGEMENT SYSTEM

A firm's HR department ordinarily has the primary responsibility for overseeing and coordinating its performance management system. However, managers from the company's operating departments must also be actively involved, particularly when it comes to helping establish the objectives for the program, to ensure that they are aligned with a company's strategic goals and translate to on-the-job efforts and behaviours. Employees are also more likely to accept and be satisfied with a performance management system when they have the chance to participate in its development. Asking experienced employees to help identify important job

OUTCOME 2

As an employee, do you think you would be in a good position to appraise your boss? What aspects of his or her performance might you be in a good position to appraise?

behaviours also helps ensure that the system takes into account all of the tasks that need to be done in an organization, especially when major changes in the firm and its jobs are taking place.[10]

Performance standards should be based on job-related requirements derived from a job analysis and reflected in an employee's job description and job specifications. Realistic and specific performance standards that are measurable and written down communicate precise information to employees. For example, "the ability and willingness to handle customer orders" is not as good a performance standard as "all customer orders will be filled in 4 hours with a 98 percent accuracy rate." When the standard is expressed in specific, measurable terms, comparing an employee's performance against it results in more accurate feedback. As Figure 8.4 shows, there are four basic elements that must be considered when establishing performance standards: strategic relevance, criterion deficiency, criterion contamination, and reliability.

Strategic Relevance

Strategic relevance refers to the extent to which the performance standards relate to the strategic objectives of the organization in which they are applied. For example, if an organization has established a standard that "95 percent of all customer complaints are to be resolved in one day," then it is relevant for the customer service representatives to be held to this standard when they are evaluated. Companies such as 3M have strategic objectives to the effect that a certain percentage of their sales is to be generated from products developed within the past five years. These objectives are then translated into performance standards for their employees. General Motors and Whirlpool's strategic objectives include cost, quality, and speed, and the two companies have developed metrics to identify and compare their performance around the world on these measures. A strategy-driven performance evaluation process also provides the documentation HR managers need to justify various training expenses in order to close any gaps between employees' current skills and those they will need in the

FIGURE 8.4

ESTABLISHING PERFORMANCE STANDARDS

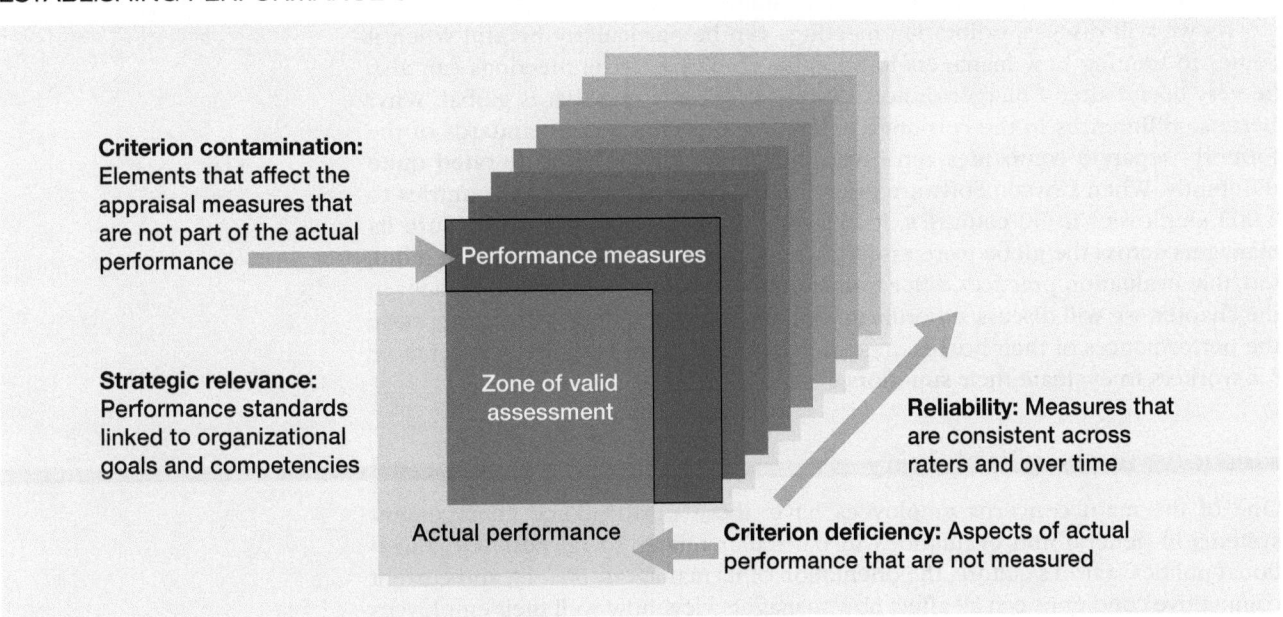

Criterion contamination: Elements that affect the appraisal measures that are not part of the actual performance

Performance measures

Strategic relevance: Performance standards linked to organizational goals and competencies

Zone of valid assessment

Reliability: Measures that are consistent across raters and over time

Actual performance

Criterion deficiency: Aspects of actual performance that are not measured

future to execute the firm's strategy. Moreover, because they provide evidence of a person's performance, evaluation metrics based on a firm's strategy are more defensible in court.[11]

Criterion Deficiency

The performance standards should capture the entire range of an employee's performance. When they focus on a single criterion (such as sales revenues) to the exclusion of other important but less quantifiable performance dimensions (such as customer service), then the performance management system is said to suffer from criterion deficiency.[12]

Criterion Contamination

Just as performance criteria can be deficient, they can also be contaminated. There are factors outside an employee's control that can influence his or her performance. A comparison of performance of production workers, for example, should not be contaminated by the fact that some work with newer machines than others do. A comparison of the performance of travelling salespeople should not be contaminated by the fact that territories differ in terms of their sales potential.[13]

Reliability

As we discussed in Chapter 6, reliability refers to the stability or consistency of a standard or the extent to which individuals tend to maintain a certain level of performance over time. Reliability can be measured by correlating two sets of ratings made by a single rater or by two different raters. For example, two managers would rate the same individual. Their ratings would then be compared to determine interrater reliability.

To make sure managers are rating employees consistently, some companies use a process called **calibration**. During calibration meetings, a group of supervisors, led by their managers and facilitated by an HR professional, discuss the performance of individual employees to ensure that all managers apply similar standards to all of the firm's employees. The supervisors begin the process by rating employees whose performances are especially good or especially poor. They then attempt to rate employees who lie more in the middle and try to achieve a consensus on their performance. Initially, the ratings are likely to vary considerably simply because some managers are hard raters and others are not. Over subsequent evaluation periods and calibration meetings, however, the ratings should begin to converge, or become more similar.

As we will discuss, calibration meetings can be particularly helpful when it comes to training new managers to appraise employees. The meetings can also be very useful after a merger or acquisition—especially one that is global. Why? Because differences in the corporate cultures and performance standards of the formerly separate companies can cause the same employees to be rated quite differently. When Lawson Software grew from 1,400 employees in 3 countries to 4,000 employees in 30 countries, it successfully used calibration to be sure its managers across the globe were assessing employees accurately.[14] Keep in mind, too, that evaluation practices differ from country to country. For example, later in the chapter, we will discuss subordinate evaluations whereby employees appraise the performances of their bosses. In some countries, it's not culturally acceptable for workers to evaluate their superiors.

Fairness and Acceptability

One of the main concerns employees have about performance management systems in general and evaluations in particular relates to fairness. Organizational politics, a firm's culture, the orientation of its managers, history, and current competitive conditions can all affect how managers view how well their employees

calibration
A process whereby managers meet to discuss the performance of individual employees to ensure that their employee evaluations are in line with one another

are doing on the job as well as rate them.[15] Sometimes managers inflate evaluations because they want to obtain higher salaries for their employees or because higher ratings for their subordinates make them look good as supervisors. Alternatively, managers might want to get rid of troublesome employees by inflating their performance and passing them off to another department.

Even when evaluations are supposed to be confidential, employees often have a keen sense about whether the process is fair or not, or at least they think they do. Employees who believe the system is unfair are likely to consider the process a waste of time or feel frustrated and cynical. As we discussed earlier, in the section on developing a performance management system, if employees are allowed input as to what constitutes a good performance and how the performance management system operates, they are more likely to feel reassured that it's fair. As a result, the program is more likely to be successful.

Acceptability relates to how difficult it is to administer and use the performance management system. If using it is time consuming or difficult or if it's hard to see how it's really helping the organization, the system is likely to fail.

LEGAL ISSUES

Because performance evaluations are used to make many personnel decisions, they must meet certain legal requirements. Employers might face legal challenges when evaluations indicate that an employee's performance is acceptable or above average but then the person is later passed over for promotion, disciplined for poor performance, discharged, or laid off from the organization. Companies such as Goodyear and Ford have also faced legal battles in the United States because their performance evaluations were viewed as discriminatory against older workers.[16]

So, from a legal perspective, performance evaluations can be a double-edged sword. You need them to help employees perform better and document your actions as a manager, but if they are poorly done or inaccurate, or you don't make decisions based on them, you can find yourself in legal trouble. To avoid problems such as these, performance evaluations should meet the following legal guidelines:

- Performance ratings must be job related, with performance standards developed through a job analysis. Only evaluate those areas that are necessary for effective job performance.

- Employees must be provided with clear, written job standards in advance of their evaluations so they understand what they need to do to get top ratings.

- Managers who conduct the evaluations must be able to observe the behaviour they are rating. This implies having measurable standards with which to compare employee behaviour.

- Do not allow performance problems to continue unchecked. Document problems when they occur and refer to them in employees' evaluations. This information may prove decisive should an employee take legal action. An employer's credibility is strengthened when it can support performance evaluation ratings by documenting instances of poor performance.

- Supervisors should be trained to use evaluation forms correctly and apply the evaluation standards when making judgments.

- A firm's HR department should review the evaluations to see if minority groups are being adversely impacted.

- The evaluations should be discussed openly with employees and counselling or corrective guidance offered to help poor performers improve their performance. Be open to the possibility that employees could be transferred to other positions that better suit their abilities.

- An appeals procedure should be established to enable employees to express their disagreement with the evaluations.[17] Having evaluations reviewed by a supervisor's superior can also reduce the chance of biased evaluations and evaluations that could be legally problematic.

Specific, measurable job standards help remove vagueness and subjectivity from performance evaluations.

WHO SHOULD APPRAISE AN EMPLOYEE'S PERFORMANCE?

Just as there are multiple standards by which to evaluate performance, there are also multiple people who can evaluate an employee's performance. Given the complexity of today's jobs, it is often unrealistic to presume that one person can fully observe and evaluate an employee's performance. At IBM, employees are regularly reviewed by a broad cross-section of the company's leaders, not just their immediate bosses. As shown in Figure 8.5, the raters can include supervisors, peers, team members, employees themselves, their subordinates, customers, vendors, and suppliers. Each may be more or less useful for the administrative and developmental purposes we discussed earlier.

Manager/Supervisor Evaluations

The **manager and/or supervisor evaluation** has been the traditional approach to evaluating an employee's performance. In most instances, supervisors are in the best position to perform this function, although it may not always be possible for them to do so. Managers with many subordinates often complain that they do not have the time to fully observe the performance of each of them. These managers must then rely on performance records to evaluate an employee's performance. If reliable and valid measures are not available, the evaluation is likely to be less than accurate as a result. (Recall our earlier discussion of criterion deficiency and criterion contamination.) In addition, research has shown that the ratings managers give employees they have known for less than one year are less reliable, which can be a drawback of relying solely on information from managers.[18]

Self-Evaluations

In many firms, employees are asked to evaluate themselves on self-evaluation forms. A **self-evaluation** can increase an employee's involvement in the review process and get the employee thinking about his or her strengths and weaknesses. In other words, they serve as a catalyst for discussion. The employee and his or her manager then discuss the employee's job performance and agree on a final evaluation.

> **manager and/or supervisor evaluation**
> A performance evaluation done by an employee's manager and often reviewed by a manager one level higher
>
> **self-evaluation**
> A performance evaluation done by the employee being evaluated, generally on an evaluation form completed by the employee prior to the evaluation meeting

FIGURE 8.5

ALTERNATIVE SOURCES OF EVALUATION

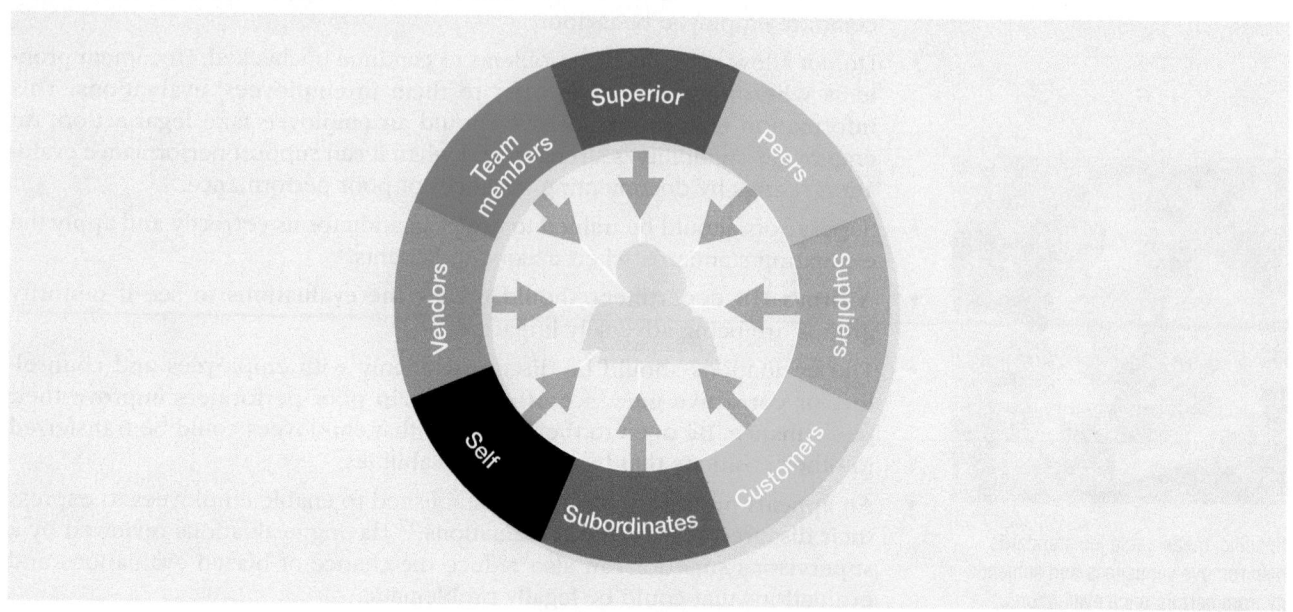

It's not uncommon for employees to present themselves in a highly favourable light in self-evaluations or believe they will have more influence over the outcome of a performance evaluation. If that expectation is not met, the employee can become frustrated. For this reason, self-evaluations are often best used for developmental purposes rather than for administrative decisions.[19]

Subordinate Evaluations

subordinate evaluations have been used by both large and small organizations to give managers feedback on how their subordinates view them.[20] Subordinates are in a good position to evaluate their managers because they are in frequent contact with their superiors and occupy a unique position from which to observe many performance-related behaviours, such as their leadership ability, ability to delegate, employee supportiveness, and so on. Managers are often hesitant to be evaluated by the people they supervise, particularly when it might be used as a basis for compensation decisions. However, when the information is used for developmental purposes, managers tend to be more open to the idea. Evidence suggests that when managers heed the advice of their subordinates, their own performance can improve substantially. To avoid any problems with retaliation, subordinate evaluations should be submitted anonymously and the results of the individuals combined in a single report.[21]

Peer Evaluations

Individuals of equal rank who work together are increasingly asked to evaluate each other using a **peer evaluation**. With peer evaluations, coworkers complete an evaluation on the employee. The forms are then usually compiled into a single profile, which is given to the supervisor for use in the final evaluation. One advantage of peer evaluations is the belief that they furnish more accurate and valid information than evaluations by superiors. Supervisors often see employees putting their best foot forward, whereas those who work with their

subordinate evaluations
A performance evaluation of a superior by an employee, which is more appropriate for developmental than for administrative purposes

peer evaluation
A performance evaluation done by one's fellow employees, generally on forms compiled into a single profile for use in the evaluation meeting conducted by the employee's manager

Some managers give their teams autonomy but hold them accountable for results.

iStockphoto

fellow employees on a regular basis may see a more realistic picture. Peers can readily identify leadership and interpersonal skills along with other strengths and weaknesses of their coworkers. For example, a superior asked to rate a patrol officer on a dimension such as "dealing with the public" might not have had much opportunity to observe it. Fellow officers, on the other hand, likely would have.

For employees who have trouble confronting their coworkers about problems, the reviews provide a forum in which to address issues and resolve conflicts. They also provide an opportunity to hand out praise.[22] However, peer evaluations alone should not be used to make administrative decisions related to salaries, bonuses, promotions, and other major decisions about an employee. They should also be kept confidential so that interpersonal rivalries or hurt feelings don't result among coworkers. Instead of listing individual comments and ratings from an employee's peers, the ratings should be tallied to arrive at a composite score and the comments summarized by the worker's supervisor.

Team Evaluations

An extension of the peer evaluation is the **team evaluation**. In a team setting, it may be nearly impossible to separate an individual's contribution. To address this issue, organizations have used team evaluations to evaluate the performance of their teams as a whole.[23] These companies believe that team evaluations can help break down barriers between individual employees and encourage a joint effort on their part. Frequently, the system is complemented by the use of team incentives or group variable pay (see Chapter 10).

Customer Evaluations

Customer evaluations are another source of performance evaluation information. External customers' evaluations, of course, have been used for some time to appraise restaurant personnel. However, companies such as Federal Express and BMW Canada are among the companies that have utilized external customers as well. To provide feedback to its technicians and see how well they have performed, Sears routinely calls customers after the technicians have serviced their appliances. Other companies survey their vendors and suppliers as part of the evaluation process. By including the firm's business partners in the performance reviews, managers hope to produce more objective evaluations, more effective employees, more satisfied customers, and better business performance.[24]

In contrast to external customers, internal customers include anyone inside the organization who depends on an employee's work output. For example, managers who rely on the HR department for selecting and training employees would be candidates for conducting internal customer evaluations of employees in the department or the department as a whole. For both developmental and administrative purposes, internal customers can provide extremely useful feedback about the value added by an employee or team of employees.

PUTTING IT ALL TOGETHER: 360-DEGREE EVALUATIONS

Companies such as Intel and Disney are among the many organizations that have used a multiple-rater approach—or **360-degree evaluation**—that combines various sources of performance evaluation information.[25] Jobs are multifaceted, and different people see different things. As the name implies, 360-degree feedback is intended to provide employees with as accurate a view of their performance as possible by getting input from all angles: supervisors, peers, subordinates, customers, and the like.

Figure 8.6 shows a list of pros and cons of 360-degree evaluation. When Intel established a 360-degree system, the company observed the following safeguards to ensure its maximum quality and acceptance:

- *Ensure anonymity.* Make certain that no employee ever knows how any evaluation team member responded. (The supervisor's rating is an exception to this rule.)
- *Make respondents accountable.* Supervisors should discuss each evaluation team member's input, letting each member know whether he or she used the rating scales appropriately, whether his or her responses were reliable, and how other participants rated the employee.
- *Prevent "gaming" of the system.* Some individuals may try to help or hurt an employee by giving either too high or too low an evaluation. Team members may try to collude with one another by agreeing to give each other uniformly high ratings. Supervisors should check for obviously invalid responses.
- *Use statistical procedures.* Use weighted averages or other quantitative approaches to combine evaluations. Supervisors should be careful about using subjective combinations of data, which could undermine the system.
- *Identify and quantify biases.* Check for prejudices or preferences related to age, gender, ethnicity, or other group factors.[26]

Based on the experiences of companies such as Canadian Tire, described in the Reality Check, it appears that 360-degree feedback can be a valuable approach to performance appraisal. As with any appraisal technique, its success depends on how managers use the information and how fairly employees are treated.

TRAINING APPRAISERS

A weakness of many performance evaluation programs is that raters are not adequately trained for the task, so the feedback they provide their subordinates is not as accurate or useful as it might be or is actually destructive. Training appraisers can vastly improve the performance evaluation process, however. According to one HR manager: "What's not important is the (evaluation) form

FIGURE 8.6

PROS AND CONS OF 360-DEGREE EVALUATION

PROS	CONS
• The system is more comprehensive because feedback is gathered from multiple perspectives.	• The system is complex in combining all the responses.
• It may lessen bias and prejudice because feedback comes from more people, not one individual.	• The feedback can be intimidating and cause resentment if employees feel the respondents have "ganged up" on them.
• The feedback from peers and others may improve an employee's self-development.	• There may be conflicting opinions, although they may all be accurate from the respective standpoints.
	• Raters must undergo some training.
	• Employees may collude or "game" the system by giving invalid evaluations to one another.
	• Raters may not feel accountable if their evaluations are anonymous.

Sources: Compiled from David A. Waldman, Leanne E. Atwater, and David Antonioni, "Has 360-Degree Feedback Gone Amok?" *Academy of Management Executive* 12, no. 2 (May 1998): 86–94; Bruce Pfau, Ira Kay, Kenneth Nowak, and Jai Ghorpade, "Does 360-Degree Feedback Negatively Affect Company Performance?" *HR Magazine* 47, no. 6 (June 2002): 54–59; Maury Peiperl, "Getting 360-Degree Feedback Right," *Harvard Business Review* 79, no. 1 (January 2001): 142–147; Joyce E. Bono and Amy E. Colbert, "Understanding Responses to Multi-Source Feedback: The Role of Core Self-Evaluations," *Personnel Psychology* 58, no. 1 (Spring 2005): 171–205.

Reality Check

Canadian Tire 360-Degree Matrix

"Accentuate the positive; build on leadership strengths" is the principal theme of leadership performance evaluation and development conducted by the Canadian Tire Corporation as described by Janice Wismer, vice president of HR. Canadian Tire is a network of interrelated businesses with retail, financial, and petroleum interests. About 45,000 employees work in 1,000 retail stores across Canada.

The customized 360-degree feedback process used at Canadian Tire is research based and designed to build a cadre of great leaders. The first step in the design of the 360-degree feedback instrument was to benchmark other organizations that had effective 360-degree feedback processes. Twenty-seven key employees at Canadian Tire were interviewed to identify the attributes of their great leaders as measured by the standards of the organization. These key leadership attributes were then discussed and evaluated in workshops with important stakeholders. A total of 16 competencies were identified. Seven related to "who one is"—characteristics such as *trustworthy*, *passionate*, and *curious*. Nine others focused on "what one can do for the team, business, and enterprise," such as *make strategic choices*, *motivate and celebrate*, and *communicate authentically*.

To date, about 170 managers have been assessed by an average of 9 colleagues, including peers, subordinates, and bosses. Colleagues complete a self-survey, and all feedback assessment is analyzed relative to their own organization and to industry standards, which are maintained in a database. A confidential feedback report is given to each individual.

In addition to the generation of individual reports, an aggregate one-page executive summary is produced. The report, presented as a matrix, provides a visual summary colour-coded under each competency comparing aggregate feedback data for all individuals in a defined business unit. The sample 360-degree matrix shown below lists key attributes across the horizontal axis and the employee's feedback along the vertical axis. To maintain confidentiality, identifiers are assigned to the supervisors and managers so that they can see their relative standing but without knowing the identity of the other employees. In the colour coding, red signifies a weak performance, yellow is an average performance, and green indicates exceptional strengths. By using this 360-degree matrix, HR can identify areas where groups of employees need professional development, thus investing training dollars where

it matters most. In the example, Executives A, B, and C are perceived as generally excellent across most of the eight areas of interest, whereas Executives M, N, and O are experiencing considerable difficulty. In addition, most of the executive team performed well in areas 1, 2, and 3, having the most difficulty in area 8. In this case, individual development plans may work well for executives having problems in areas 1, 2, and 3, whereas a group development solution may be best designed for area 8.

According to Ed Haltrecht, Ph.D., CHRP, who specializes in measurement and organizational leadership development, in most organizations when performance feedback is presented, both the employee and the manager focus on the reds—the weaknesses—and try to work out methods of development to improve this area. What is unique about Canadian Tire is that the focus is on the positive. It has found that improvements in weak areas (provided that they are not fundamental flaws) do not affect overall performance, whereas improvements in areas of strength bring managers from good to extraordinary. The goal is to identify and strengthen attributes so employees will distinguish and present themselves as extraordinary. Individuals first address any "fundamental flaws," either a very weak attribute of the individual or, more importantly, elements regarded as critical to the organization. In the sample 360-degree matrix, Executives I, L, N, and O have potential fundamental flaws in areas 1 and 2. If there are no fundamental flaws, then development focuses on building strengths. This combination has resulted in measurable gains in performance.

This approach is research based. One book, *The Extraordinary Leader: Turning Good Managers into Great Leaders*, by John Zenger and Joseph Folkman (New York: McGraw-Hill, 2002), presents several significant findings based on 225,000 evaluations of 20,000 people. Poor leaders were identified as those scoring in the bottom 10 percent; extraordinary leaders scored in the top 10 percent. Employee turnover in a call centre was 19 percent for the units managed by the poor managers, 14 percent for the middle group, and 9 percent for the extraordinary leaders. In another case that looked at a bank, net incomes for the bank generated by those groups whose managers were extraordinary, average, and poor were $7 million, $3.7 million, and $1.9 million, respectively. Employee satisfaction indices were at the 80th percentile for top managers compared to the 18th percentile for the bottom-scoring managers. Likewise,

continued

union vulnerability indices, which measure how attractive the organization is to a union's membership drive, reflected the 91st percentile for the top-scoring managers compared to the 10th percentile for the poor managers—that is, poorer managers are more likely to attract union interest. Although the pay structure was the same across different departments, those led by the top-scoring managers had employees who were at the 65th percentile in satisfaction with company pay and job security; the employees of average managers were in the 50th percentile; and poor managers' employees scored at the 37th percentile for satisfaction with company pay and job security.

Canadian Tire's leadership development system also recognizes two other significant research findings: first, extraordinary leaders have about three competencies at which they excel, and developing a few strengths to very high performance levels has a greater impact than improving several competencies from poor to average. Second, competencies travel together, and improvement in one leads to significant progress in others. Identifying these companion competencies has proven to be extremely worthwhile. In a nutshell, these are the findings: start with the right set of competencies or attributes, focus on strengths, eliminate any fundamental flaws, and pay attention to companion attributes.

The assessment feedback process at Canadian Tire is seen as a tool for dialogue and for focusing on what makes a great company and what matters in leadership. Those employees who try to improve are given a developmental opportunities guidebook. Canadian Tire has discovered that the best development methods are challenging stretch assignments, coaching and mentoring, personal feedback, talks with consultants, and training programs.

Executive	1. Treats others with respect.	2. Gives credit to others who have contributed or performed well.	3. Shows consistency between words and action.	4. Models the core values of the corporation; leads by example.	5. Treats team members as individuals based on knowledge of their strengths and development needs.	6. Takes actions that build a high level of commitment to work group goals and objectives.	7. Obtains resources so that the team has the knowledge, skills, and experience required to deliver results.	8. Where there is underlying conflict, helps parties involved bring up their issues and get to the heart of the problem.	Mean
A	5.0	4.9	4.9	4.6	4.8	4.6	4.6	4.5	4.7
B	5.0	4.8	4.9	4.9	4.9	4.8	4.3	3.7	4.7
C	5.0	4.7	4.5	4.7	4.7	4.7	4.5	4.2	4.6
D	4.8	4.6	4.2	4.7	4.3	4.3	4.6	4.1	4.4
E	4.7	5.0	4.7	4.0	3.7	4.0	4.3	4.3	4.4
F	4.8	4.3	4.3	4.5	4.4	4.3	4.1	3.2	4.2
G	4.6	4.2	4.2	4.2	4.2	4.1	4.2	3.9	4.2
H	4.5	4.4	4.1	4.2	4.3	3.9	3.9	4.1	4.2
I	4.4	3.8	4.0	4.3	4.0	4.3	4.5	3.7	4.2
J	4.4	4.3	4.5	4.2	4.1	4.2	3.9	4.0	4.2
K	4.6	4.2	4.5	4.0	4.5	4.2	3.6	4.3	4.1
L	3.8	4.4	4.3	4.3	3.7	4.1	4.5	3.9	4.1
M	4.4	4.2	4.4	4.1	4.2	4.0	4.0	4.2	4.1
N	4.3	3.8	4.1	3.9	4.0	4.0	3.5	2.9	3.9
O	3.3	4.1	4.0	3.6	3.8	3.8	3.9	3.3	3.6
Mean	4.5	4.3	4.4	4.2	4.2	4.2	4.1	3.9	4.2

Source: Interview with Janice Wismer and Ed Haltrecht.

or the (measuring) scale. What's important is that managers can objectively observe people's performance and objectively give feedback on that performance." Nonetheless, in a survey of 55 HR managers from medium and large companies, more than half said their companies did either little or no evaluation of how well their supervisors do evaluations.[27] In addition to providing supervisors with training, firms should make accurately evaluating and developing their subordinates a standard by which the supervisors themselves will be evaluated.

Establishing an Evaluation Plan

A training program for raters is most effective when it follows a systematic process that begins by explaining the objectives of the firm's performance management system and its philosophy on evaluations. For example, the rater needs to know the purpose for which the evaluation is to be used. Using the evaluation for compensation decisions rather than development purposes can affect how the rater evaluates the employee and may change the rater's opinion of how the evaluation form should be completed. The mechanics of the rating system should also be explained, including how managers should keep performance records and review them, how frequently the evaluations are to be conducted, who will conduct them, what the standards of performance are, and how to go about preparing for evaluations. In addition, evaluation training should alert raters to the weaknesses and problems of evaluations so that they can be avoided.

Eliminating Rating Errors

Eliminating the subjective errors made by managers in the rating process is an extremely important part of evaluating the performance of an employee. The "halo error" we discussed in Chapter 6, when we looked at selecting employees, can occur during the evaluation process if raters do not have carefully developed descriptions of the employee behaviours being rated. The "horn error" is the opposite of the halo effect. It occurs when a manager focuses on one negative aspect about an employee and generalizes it into an overall poor evaluation rating. A personality conflict between a manager and his or her employees increases the probability of the horn effect, which can lead to a high level of frustration on the employee's part if it is not corrected.[28]

Distributional error. A *distributional rating error* occurs when a single rating is skewed toward an entire group of employees. For example, raters who are reluctant to assign either extremely high or extremely low ratings commit the error of central tendency. In this case, all employees are rated about average. It is also common for some raters to give unusually high or low ratings. For example, a manager might erroneously assert, "All my employees are excellent" or "None of my people are good enough." These beliefs give rise to what is called leniency or strictness error.[29]

One way to reduce distributional errors is to explain to raters that when you are looking at large groups of employees, you should generally expect to find significant differences among them. Using clearly defined characteristics or dimensions of performance and providing meaningful descriptions of behaviour, known as "anchors," on the scale can help raters determine how individual employees should be rated. Another approach is to require ratings to conform to a forced distribution, which is also sometimes referred to as forced ranking. Managers appraising employees under a forced distribution system are required to place a certain percentage of employees into various performance categories. For example, it may be required that 10 percent of ratings be poor (or excellent). This is similar to the requirement in some schools that instructors grade on a curve. A variation of this is peer ranking, whereby employees in a work group are ranked against one another from best to worst.

The Business Case

Rank and Yank

Research shows that performance appraisals can have a positive financial impact, but there is the potential to lose money if the wrong system is chosen. Goodyear Tire & Rubber Co. abandoned a performance rating system for salaried employees just as discrimination attorneys were planning to file a class-action lawsuit over it. Goodyear said it was dropping major parts of its program, including its so-called 10-80-10 feature, which essentially graded all salaried employees on a curve. The top 10 percent were rated A, the middle 80 percent were rated B, and the bottom 10 percent were rated C. Those falling in the bottom 10 percent weren't eligible for raises or bonuses and were warned that they might lose their jobs.

The lawsuit alleged that the workers who got C ratings were humiliated and stigmatized among their peers and managers. The legal arm of the AARP, formerly known as the American Association of Retired Persons, joined the lawsuit as co-counsel. Most of the plaintiffs who got C rankings in the case were Goodyear employees who were over 50 years old. "This case will send a clear message that performance rating schemes that target older workers for unfair treatment are illegal and will not be tolerated," said Laurie McCann of AARP.

Jack McGilvrey, a 59-year-old salaried employee, was one of those named in the suit. He claimed that he always received ratings of at least "good/effective performer" in his formal performance reviews up through the late 1990s. In 2000, he was ranked "highly effective." But in February 2001, he was transferred to a new department and shortly thereafter was given a C rating in his performance review. The suit asserted that Mr. McGilvrey didn't deserve the rating and received it as part of Goodyear's plan to discriminate against older employees. He was later dismissed.

The lawsuit against Goodyear has many parallels to one filed in 2001 against Ford Motor Co. In that case, also joined by AARP, the company modified its plans in the face of a legal challenge. The Ford case was eventually settled.

In modifying its white-collar ranking system, Goodyear said it would replace those A, B, and C rankings with the terms *exceeds expectations*, *meets expectations*, and *unsatisfactory*. There will be no requirement to assign those ratings to set percentages of employees. The company also said it was stepping up training for managers so they learn to do a better job of conducting performance reviews.

Source: Timothy Aeppel, "Goodyear Ends Ratings System Ahead of Discrimination Suit," *The Wall Street Journal Online* (September 12, 2002): B8. Copyright © 2002 Dow Jones & Company, Inc. Reprinted with permission of Dow Jones & Company, Inc. in the format Textbook, via Copyright Clearance Center.

Although forced distribution and peer ranking may solve leniency and strictness errors, they can create other rating errors—particularly if most employees are performing above the standard, in the middle, or below the standard. Similarly, with peer ranking, three employees all performing nearly at the same level would have to be ranked 1, 2, and 3. That creates a misleading picture of how well the individuals are performing, which in turn affects their pay, promotability, and so forth. Companies, including Ford, Goodyear (described in the Business Case), and Microsoft, abandoned their forced ranking systems after lawsuits, lower morale, decreased teamwork, and destructive employee competition ensued following their use. In addition, not all corporate cultures are conducive to forced ranking systems. For example, at Starbucks, which fosters a corporate climate based on teamwork, using a forced ranking system would probably be counterproductive.

Because of the legal issues related to forced ranking, companies that use it obviously need to carefully train their appraisers.[30] Not all companies have abandoned the practice, however. Yahoo recently instituted it. Some people have speculated that the move was an effort to turn the Internet company around by ridding the firm of employers who were merely "punching the clock" but not contributing much to the organization.

Temporal (recency) error. Some rating errors are temporal in that the performance review is biased either favourably or unfavourably depending on the way performance information is selected, evaluated, and organized by the rater over time. For example, when the evaluation is based largely on the employee's recent behaviour, good or bad, the rater has committed the temporal (recency) error. Managers who give higher ratings because they believe an employee is "showing improvement" may unwittingly be committing recency error. Having the rater routinely document employee accomplishments and failures throughout the whole evaluation period can minimize the recency error. One way for managers to do this is by keeping a diary or a log.

Contrast error. Contrast error occurs when an employee's evaluation is biased either upward or downward because of another employee's performance. For example, an average employee may appear very productive when compared with a poor performer. However, that same employee could appear unproductive when compared with a star performer. Contrast errors are most likely when raters are required to rank employees in order from the best to the poorest.[31]

Similar-to-me error. The similar-to-me error occurs when a supervisor inflates the evaluations of people with whom they have something in common. For example, if both the manager and the employee are from the same town or went to the same schools, the manager may unwittingly have a more favourable impression of the employee. The similar-to-me error can be powerful, and when the similarity is based on race, religion, or gender, it can result in discrimination.

Furthermore, raters should be aware of any stereotypes they may hold toward particular groups. For example, one study found that men who experience conflicts between family and work received lower overall performance ratings than men who did not experience such conflicts. Women, on the other hand, were judged no differently whether they experienced family–work conflicts or not.[32]

A host of organizations, such as Avenor, a pulp and paper company based in Montréal, have developed formal training programs to reduce errors such as these. Holding "mock" calibration meetings can help trainers improve the accuracy of their ratings. The training can pay off, particularly when participants have the opportunity to (1) observe other managers making errors, (2) actively participate in discovering their own errors, and (3) practise job-related tasks to reduce the errors they tend to make.[33] Google, which often conducts performance reviews with input from employee groups, has compiled a "cognitive biases" list for employees to refer to as they discuss ratings.[34]

Feedback Training

A training program for raters should provide some pointers managers can use to provide performance feedback to employees on an ongoing basis and during formal evaluations and feedback sessions. During formal evaluations in particular, many managers are as nervous about giving feedback as employees are about receiving it. Often they just want them to be over. When this happens, managers do not engage employees in much of a conversation during the evaluations, which is a major drawback.

Managers need to understand that employees want to know how they are doing and how they can improve. They are less eager to be appraised or judged. This is why it is important for their managers to provide them with ongoing feedback and not just "dump on them" during a formal performance evaluation. If an employee is doing something wrong, waiting for a formal evaluation later in the year to communicate that information is the wrong approach. The person needs to be corrected immediately.

Even when appraising an outstanding employee, managers often are reluctant to evaluate an employee's performance. Sometimes it is as simple as the manager lacks the skills to execute an effective performance review session; sometimes there is never enough money to recognize even the top performer. So reviews are postponed or handled poorly, and the result is that the organization's best performers are left frustrated, angry, disillusioned, and demotivated.

temporal (recency) error
A performance rating error in which the evaluation is based largely on the employee's most recent behaviour rather than on behaviour throughout the evaluation period

contrast error
A performance rating error in which an employee's evaluation is biased either upward or downward because of comparison with another employee just previously evaluated

similar-to-me error
A performance rating error in which an appraiser inflates the evaluation of an employee because of a mutual personal connection

Conflicting purposes of the evaluation can also hamper the effectiveness of the feedback employees receive. For example, if an evaluation program is used to determine an employee's future pay and at the same time to motivate the person to perform better, the two purposes can end up conflicting with one another. Often when salary decisions are discussed during a performance evaluation, they tend to become the dominant topic of conversation, and managers spend a lot of time justifying their pay decisions. As a result, ways to improve the employee's future job performance get less discussion.

Feedback training should cover at least three basic areas: (1) communicating effectively so as to gain the employee's support, (2) diagnosing the root causes of performance problems, and (3) setting goals and objectives for the employee to achieve in conjunction with the feedback. A checklist such as the one in Highlights in HRM 8.1 can be used to help supervisors prepare for performance evaluation meetings so that their subordinates get the best information as possible from the result.

PERFORMANCE EVALUATION METHODS

OUTCOME 3

As an employee, would you rather be evaluated on your personality traits, your on-the-job behaviours, or the results that you get?

Now that you understand more about performance management, the question is how do you go about measuring, or appraising, it? Performance evaluation methods can be broadly classified as measuring traits, behaviours, or results. Trait approaches based on people's characteristics continue to be used despite their subjectivity. Behavioural approaches provide more action-oriented information to employees and therefore may be best for development. The results-oriented approach has become more popular because it focuses on the measurable contributions that employees make to the organization.

Trait approaches are designed to measure the extent to which an employee possesses certain characteristics—such as dependability, reactivity, initiative, and leadership—that are viewed as important for the job and the organization in general. Trait methods became popular because they are easy to develop. However, if not designed carefully on the basis of job analysis, trait evaluations can be notoriously biased and subjective.

graphic rating scale method
A trait approach to performance rating whereby each employee is rated according to a scale of characteristics

Graphic Rating Scales

In the **graphic rating scale method**, each trait or characteristic to be rated is represented by a scale on which a rater indicates the degree to which an employee possesses that trait or characteristic. An example of this type of scale is shown in Highlights in HRM 8.2. There are many variations of the graphic rating scale. The differences are to be found in (1) the characteristics or dimensions on which individuals are rated, (2) the degree to which the performance dimension

Highlights in HRM 8.2

Graphic Rating Scale with Provision for Comments

Appraise employee's performance in PRESENT ASSIGNMENT. Check (✔) most appropriate square. Appraisers are *urged to freely use* the "Remarks" sections for significant comments descriptive of the individual.

1. KNOWLEDGE OF WORK: Understanding of all phases of his/her work and related matters

Needs instruction or guidance	Has required knowledge of own and related work	Has exceptional knowledge of own and related work
☐ ☐	☐	✔ ☐

Remarks: *Is particularly good on gas engines.*

2. INITIATIVE: Ability to originate or develop ideas and to get things started

Lacks imagination	Meets necessary requirements	Unusually resourceful
☐	✔ ☐	☐ ☐

Remarks: *Has good ideas when asked for an opinion, but otherwise will not offer them. Somewhat lacking in self-confidence.*

3. APPLICATION: Attention and application to his/her work

Wastes time Needs close supervision	Steady and willing worker	Exceptionally industrious
☐	✔ ☐	☐ ☐

Remarks: *Accepts new jobs when assigned.*

4. QUALITY OF WORK: Thoroughness, neatness, and accuracy of work

Needs improvement	Regularly meets recognized standards	Consistently maintains highest quality
☐ ☐	☐ ☐	✔

Remarks: *The work he turns out is always of the highest possible quality.*

5. VOLUME OF WORK: Quantity of acceptable work

Should be increased	Regularly meets recognized standards	Unusually high output
☐	✔ ☐	☐ ☐

Remarks: *Would be higher if he did not spend so much time checking and rechecking his work.*

is defined for the rater, and (3) how clearly the points on the scale are defined. In Highlights in HRM 8.2, the dimensions are defined briefly, and some attempt is made to define the points on the scale. Subjectivity bias is reduced somewhat when the dimensions on the scale and the scale points are defined as precisely as possible. This can be achieved by training raters and by including descriptive evaluation guidelines in a performance evaluation reference packet.[35]

Also, the rating form should provide sufficient space for comments on the behaviour associated with each scale. These comments improve the accuracy of the evaluation because they require the rater to think in terms of observable employee behaviours while providing specific examples to discuss with the employee.

Mixed-Standard Scales

The **mixed-standard scale method** is a modification of the basic rating scale method. Rather than evaluating traits according to a single scale, the rater is given three specific descriptions of each trait. These descriptions reflect three levels of performance: superior, average, and inferior. After the three descriptions for each trait are written, they are randomly sequenced to form the mixed-standard scale. As Highlights in HRM 8.3 discusses, supervisors evaluate employees by indicating whether their performance is better than, equal to, or worse than the standard for each behaviour.

Forced-Choice Method

The **forced-choice method** requires the rater to choose from statements, often in pairs, that appear equally favourable or equally unfavourable but are designed to distinguish between successful and unsuccessful performance. For example, forced-choice pairs might include the following:

1. ___ a) Works hard   ___ b) Works quickly
2. ___ a) Shows initiative   ___ b) Is responsive to customers
3. ___ a) Work is reliable   ___ b) Performance is good

Highlights in HRM 8.3

Example of a Mixed-Standard Scale

DIRECTIONS: Indicate whether the individual's performance is above (1), equal to (0), or lower than (2) each of the following standards.

1. _____ Employee uses good judgment when addressing problems and provides workable alternatives; however, at times does not take actions to prevent problems. (medium PROBLEM SOLVING)

2. _____ Employee lacks supervisory skills; frequently handles employees poorly and is at times argumentative. (low LEADERSHIP)

3. _____ Employee is extremely cooperative; can be expected to take the lead in developing cooperation among employees; completes job tasks with a positive attitude. (high COOPERATION)

4. _____ Employee has effective supervision skills; encourages productivity, quality, and employee development. (medium LEADERSHIP)

5. _____ Employee normally displays an argumentative or defensive attitude toward fellow employees and job assignments. (low COOPERATION)

6. _____ Employee is generally agreeable but becomes argumentative at times when given job assignments; cooperates with other employees as expected. (medium COOPERATION)

7. _____ Employee is not good at solving problems; uses poor judgment and does not anticipate potential difficulties. (low PROBLEM SOLVING)

8. _____ Employee anticipates potential problems and provides creative, proactive alternative solutions; has good attention to follow-up. (high PROBLEM SOLVING)

9. _____ Employee displays skilled direction, effectively coordinates unit activities, is generally a dynamic leader, and motivates employees to high performance. (high LEADERSHIP)

NEL

The rater then selects one statement from the pair without knowing *which* statement correctly describes successful job behaviour. Because it's not immediately clear which response results in a higher rating, less bias results.

The forced-choice method is not without limitations, the primary one being the cost of establishing and maintaining its validity. The fact that it has been a source of frustration to many raters has sometimes caused the method to be eliminated from evaluation programs. In addition, it cannot be used as effectively as some of the other methods as a tool for developing employees.

Essay Method

Unlike rating scales, which provide a structured form of evaluation, the **essay method** requires the appraiser to compose a statement that best describes the employee's strengths and weaknesses and make recommendations for his or her development. Often the essay method is combined with other rating methods because it provides additional descriptive information about an employee's performance that cannot be generated with a structured rating scale. Essays also provide an excellent opportunity for supervisors to point out the unique characteristics of the employee being appraised, including specific points about the employee's promotability, special talents, skills, strengths, and weaknesses.

A limitation of the essay method is that composing an essay that attempts to cover all of an employee's essential characteristics is a very time-consuming task (although when combined with other methods, this method does not require a lengthy statement). Another disadvantage of the method is that it tends to be subjective and might not focus on the relevant aspects of a person's job performance. A final drawback of this evaluation method is that the quality of the performance evaluation could be affected by the supervisor's writing skills. Good writers may simply be able to produce more favourable-sounding evaluations.

BEHAVIOURAL METHODS

As we mentioned, one of the potential drawbacks of a trait-oriented performance evaluation is that traits tend to be vague and subjective. We discussed earlier that one way to improve a trait-based method is with a rating scale that describes behaviour along a scale, or continuum. Behavioural methods specifically describe which actions should (or should not) be exhibited on the job.

Critical Incident Method

The critical incident method, described in Chapter 4 in connection with job analysis, is also used as a method of evaluation. Recall that a **critical incident** occurs when employee behaviour results in unusual success or unusual failure in some part of the job. An example of a favourable critical incident occurs when a janitor observes that a file cabinet containing classified documents has been left unlocked at the close of business and calls the firm's security officer to correct the problem. An example of an unfavourable incident occurs when a mail clerk fails to deliver an Express Mail package immediately, instead putting it in with regular mail to be routed two hours later. The manager keeps a log or diary for each employee throughout the evaluation period and notes specific critical incidents related to how well they perform.

When completing the evaluation form, the manager refers to the critical incident log and uses this information to substantiate an employee's rating of outstanding, satisfactory, or unsatisfactory in specific performance areas and overall. This method can also help a manager counsel employees when they are having performance problems while the problem is still minor. It also increases the objectivity of the evaluation by requiring the rater to use job performance criteria to justify the ratings.[36]

essay method
A trait approach to performance rating that requires the rater to compose a statement describing employee behaviour

critical incident
An unusual event that denotes superior or inferior employee performance in some part of the job

Behavioural Checklist Method

The behavioural checklist method requires the rater to check statements on a list that describe characteristics of the employee's behaviour. A checklist developed for salespeople who sell electronic products might include a number of statements, such as the following:

_____ Questions customers about their needs

_____ Identifies products that meet customers' needs

_____ Keeps abreast of new developments in technology

_____ Processes orders correctly

Behaviourally Anchored Rating Scale (BARS)

A **behaviourally anchored rating scale (BARS)** consists of a series of 5 to 10 vertical scales—one for each important dimension of performance identified through job analysis. These dimensions are "anchored" by behaviours identified through a critical incident job analysis. The critical incidents are placed along the scale and are assigned point values according to the opinions of experts. A BARS for the job of firefighter is shown in the upper portion of Highlights in HRM 8.4. Note that this particular scale is for the dimension described as "Firefighting Strategy: Knowledge of Fire Characteristics."

A BARS is typically developed by a committee that includes both subordinates and managers. The committee's task is to identify all the relevant characteristics or dimensions of the job. Behavioural anchors in the form of statements are then established for each job dimension. Several participants are asked to review the anchor statements and indicate which job dimension each anchor illustrates. The only anchors retained are those that at least 70 percent of the group agrees belong with a particular dimension. Finally, the anchors are attached to their job dimensions and are placed on the appropriate scales according to values that the group assigns to them.

At present, there is no strong evidence that a BARS reduces all of the rating errors mentioned previously. However, some studies have shown that scales of this type can yield more accurate ratings. One major advantage of a BARS is that personnel outside the HR department participate with HR staff in its development. Employee participation can lead to greater acceptance of the performance evaluation process and of the performance measures that it uses. The procedures followed in developing a BARS also result in scales that have a high degree of content validity. The main disadvantage of a BARS is that it requires considerable time and effort to develop.

Behaviour Observation Scale (BOS)

A **behaviour observation scale (BOS)** is similar to a BARS in that they are both based on critical incidents. However, the lower portion of Highlights in HRM 8.4 shows that rather than asking the evaluator to choose the most representative behavioural anchor, a BOS is designed to measure how frequently each behaviour has been observed.

A BOS allows the appraiser to play the role of observer rather than of judge, which makes it easier to provide constructive feedback to the employee, who will be more willing to accept it. Research shows that users of the system frequently prefer it over the BARS or trait scales for (1) maintaining objectivity, (2) distinguishing good performers from poor performers, (3) providing feedback, and (4) identifying training needs.[37]

Highlights in HRM 8.4

BARS and BOS Examples

Example of a BARS for Municipal Fire Companies

FIREFIGHTING STRATEGY: Knowledge of Fire Characteristics.

This area of performance concerns the ability of a firefighter to understand fire characteristics to develop the best strategy for fighting a fire.

HIGH
7 — Finds the fire when no one else can
6 — Correctly assesses best point of entry for fighting fire

AVERAGE
5 — Uses type of smoke as indicator of type of fire
4 — Understands basic hydraulics
3 — Cannot tell the type of fire by observing the color of flame
2 — Cannot identify the location of the fire

LOW
1 — Will not change the firefighting strategy in spite of flashbacks and other signs that accelerants present

Sample Items from Behaviour Observation Scales

For each behaviour observed, use the following scale:

5 represents *almost always*   95–100% of the time
4 represents *frequently*   85–94% of the time
3 represents *sometimes*   75–84% of the time
2 represents *seldom*   65–74% of the time
1 represents *almost never*   0–64% of the time

Sales Productivity	Never				Always
1. Reviews individual productivity results with manager	1	2	3	4	5
2. Suggests to peers ways of building sales	1	2	3	4	5
3. Uncovers specific needs for each contact	1	2	3	4	5
4. Keeps account plans updated	1	2	3	4	5
5. Follows up on customer leads	1	2	3	4	5

Source: Adapted from Landy, Jacobs, and Associates. Reprinted with permission.

RESULTS METHODS

Rather than looking at the traits of employees or the behaviours they exhibit on the job, many organizations evaluate employees' accomplishments—the results they achieve through their work. Advocates of results evaluations argue that they are more objective and empowering for employees. Looking at results such as sales figures and production output involves less subjectivity. Results evaluations often give employees responsibility for their outcomes while giving them discretion over the way they accomplish them (within limits). This is employee empowerment and engagement in action.

Productivity Measures

A number of results measures are available to evaluate performance. Salespeople are evaluated on the basis of their sales volume (both the number of units sold and the dollar amount in revenues). Production workers are evaluated on the basis of the number of units they produce and perhaps the scrap rate or number

management by objectives (MBO)

A philosophy of management that rates the performance of employees based on their achievement of goals set mutually by them and their manager

of defects detected in their work. Executives are frequently evaluated on the basis of a company's profits or growth rate. Each of these measures directly links what employees accomplish to results that benefit the organization. In this way, results evaluations can directly align employee and organizational goals.

But there are some problems with results evaluations. First, recall our earlier discussion of criteria contamination. Results evaluations can be contaminated by external factors that employees cannot influence. Sales representatives who have extremely bad sales territories or production employees who cannot get materials due to shipping delays will not be able to perform up to their abilities. Obviously, it is unfair to hold employees accountable for circumstances beyond their control. Furthermore, results evaluations can inadvertently encourage employees to "look good" on a short-term basis while ignoring the long-term ramifications. Line supervisors, for example, might let their equipment go without needed tune-ups to reduce maintenance costs.

For jobs that are more service oriented, it is not enough to simply look at production or sales figures. Factors such as cooperation, adaptability, initiative, and concern for human relations are important to the job success of employees too. If these factors are important job standards, they should be added to the evaluation review. Thus, to be realistic, both the results and the methods or processes used to achieve them should be considered.[38]

Management by Objectives

One method that attempts to overcome some of the limitations of results evaluations is **management by objectives (MBO)**. MBO is a philosophy of management that has employees establish objectives (such as production costs, sales per product, quality standards, and profits) by consulting with their superiors. Employees are then evaluated based on these objectives.[39] An MBO system (see Figure 8.7) consists of a cycle that begins with setting the organization's common goals and

FIGURE 8.7

PERFORMANCE APPRAISAL UNDER AN MBO PROGRAM

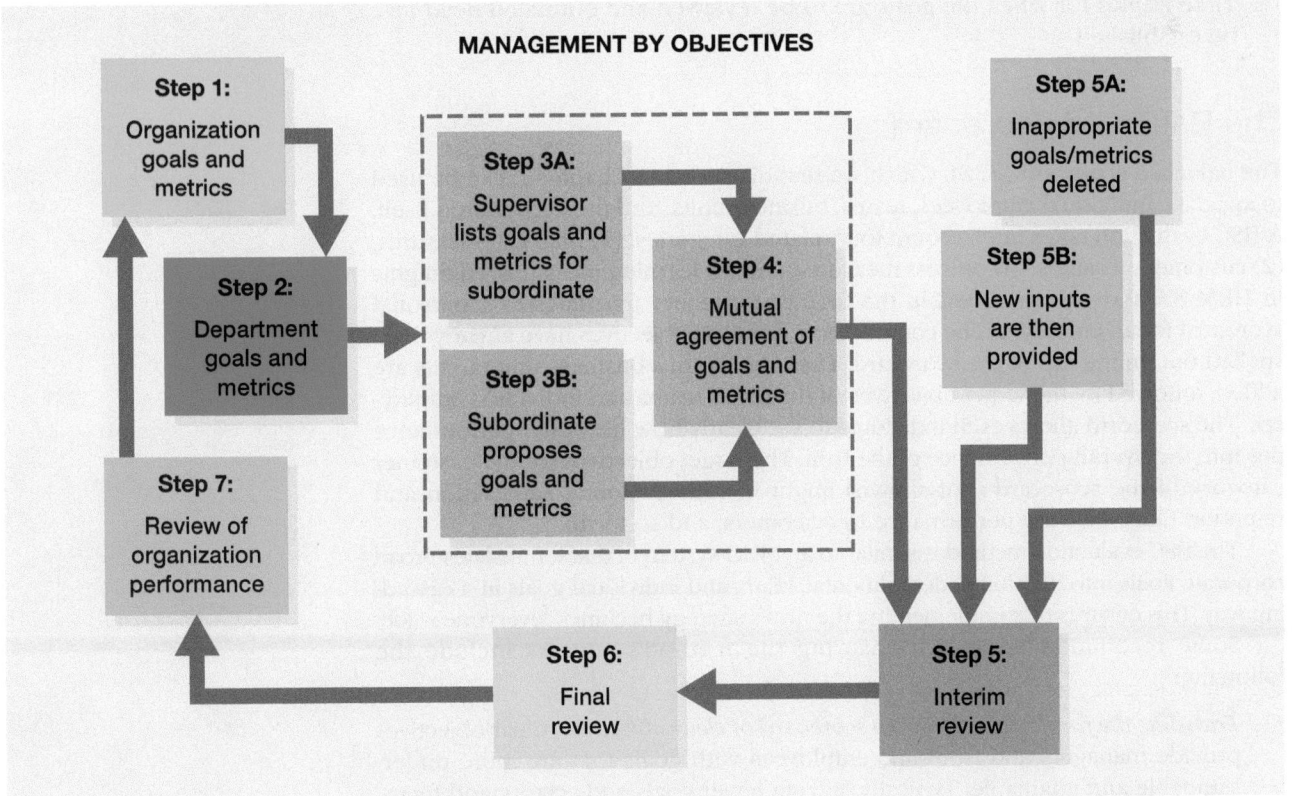

MANAGEMENT BY OBJECTIVES

Step 1: Organization goals and metrics

Step 2: Department goals and metrics

Step 3A: Supervisor lists goals and metrics for subordinate

Step 3B: Subordinate proposes goals and metrics

Step 4: Mutual agreement of goals and metrics

Step 5A: Inappropriate goals/metrics deleted

Step 5B: New inputs are then provided

Step 5: Interim review

Step 6: Final review

Step 7: Review of organization performance

objectives and ultimately returns to that step. The system acts as a goal-setting process whereby objectives are established for the organization (Step 1), departments (Step 2), and individual managers and employees (Step 3).

As Figure 8.7 shows, employees help establish specific goals, but those goals are based on a broad statement of an employee's responsibilities prepared by the person's supervisor. The employee-established goals are then discussed with the supervisor and jointly reviewed and modified until both parties are satisfied with them (Step 4). The goal statements are accompanied by a detailed account of the actions the employee proposes to take to reach the goals and how they will be measured (the metrics).

During periodic reviews, the progress the employee makes toward the goals is then assessed (Step 5). The goals and metrics may be changed at this time as new or additional information is received. After a period of time (usually six months or one year), the employee makes a self-evaluation of what he or she has accomplished, substantiating the self-evaluation with documentation when possible. The final review is an examination of the employee's self-evaluation by the supervisor and the employee together (Step 6). The final step (Step 7) is reviewing the connection between the employee's performance and the organization's. Notice how the steps in an MBO program are similar to the steps in Figure 8.1 at the beginning of the chapter but are more specific.

Goal setting via an MBO or other program can measurably improve how well employees perform because it helps them clearly focus on what they need to do to meet their objectives. It also aids in learning because employees can regularly evaluate their performance against the objectives they've set for themselves.[40] The following guidelines can help an MBO program succeed:

1. The objectives should be quantifiable and measurable and accompanied by a description of how they will be accomplished.
2. The results that are expected must be under the employee's control. Managers must be willing to empower employees to accomplish their goals on their own, giving them discretion over the methods they use (but holding them accountable for the outcomes).
3. The firm's goals and objectives must be consistent, or aligned, with the goals of employees at all levels, including a firm's top managers.
4. Time frames for when the goals are to be reviewed and evaluated need to be established.

The Balanced Scorecard

The balanced scorecard (BSC), which we first discussed in Chapter 2, can be used to appraise individual employees, teams, business units, and the corporation itself. A BSC evaluation takes into account four related categories: (1) financial measures, (2) customer measures, (3) process measures, and (4) learning measures. Highlights in HRM 8.5 shows how a BSC in the financial category translates to a personal scorecard for an employee. The corporation's financial objectives have already been spelled out on the top of the scorecard. Then the various business unit targets are added, followed by the target objectives of the firm's teams and individual employees. The scorecard allows each individual to see clearly how his or her performance ties into the overall performance of the firm. The target objectives for the customer category of the scorecard (not shown) might include customer satisfaction and retention rates, delivery performance to customers, and so forth.

The BSC evaluation method is similar to an MBO system in that it translates broad corporate goals into divisional, departmental, team, and individual goals in a cascading way. This ensures that implementing the firm's strategy becomes "everyone's" job.

Some recommendations for ensuring the method's success include the following:

- *Translate the firm's strategy into a scorecard of clear objectives*. Clear objectives provide managers and front-line employees with goals that are more understandable and attainable. Typically, having fewer goals adds clarity and focus.

Highlights in HRM 8.5

Personal Scorecard

CORPORATE OBJECTIVES

- Double our corporate value in seven years.
- Increase our earnings by an average of 20% per year.
- Achieve an internal rate of return 2% above the cost of capital.
- Increase both production and reserves by 20% in the next decade.

☑ Corporate
❑ Business Unit
❑ Team/Individual

Corporate Targets and Business-Unit Targets									Team/Individual Objectives		
2015	2016	2017	2018		2011	2012	2013	2014	1.		
Financial (millions of dollars)											
100	120	160	180	Earnings							
35	55	85	100	Net profits							
15	35	65	75	Net cash flow					2.		
Operating (millions of dollars)											
35	35	40	50	Production and development costs							
30	30	35	30	Overhead and operating costs							
100	105	108	110	Total annual production (million units)					3.		
Team/Individual Measures					Targets						
1.											
2.									4.		
3.											
4.											

- *Attach measures to each objective.* Each objective should be measurable and the measure included on the scorecard.

- *Provide performance feedback based on measures.* Are employees meeting their targets? Why or why not? Unless managers provide employees with solid feedback, the system is likely to be ineffective.

- *Empower employees to make performance improvements.* One of the benefits of a results-based system such as the BSC is that it gives employees the latitude to continuously improve their work methods.

- *Reassess the strategy.* Information from the process should be used to reassess the firm's strategy and make continuous adjustments. Those who have had the best success with the BSC say the system helps improve communication and learning rather than fixing in place a mechanical set of controls.[41]

WHICH PERFORMANCE EVALUATION METHOD SHOULD YOU USE?

Figure 8.8 lists some of the strengths and weaknesses of trait, behaviour, and results approaches to appraising employees. Although researchers and HR managers generally believe that the more sophisticated and time-consuming methods offer more useful information, this may not always be the case. Ronald Gross, an industrial psychologist and HR consultant, states: "I can't judge a performance appraisal system just by looking at the paperwork. The back of an envelope can

FIGURE 8.8

A SUMMARY OF VARIOUS EVALUATION METHODS

	Advantages	Disadvantages
Trait methods	1. Are inexpensive to develop	1. Have high potential for rating errors
	2. Use meaningful dimensions	2. Are not useful for employee counselling
	3. Are easy to use	3. Are not useful for allocating rewards
		4. Are not useful for promotion decisions
Behavioural methods	1. Use specific performance dimensions	1. Can be time consuming to develop/use
	2. Are acceptable to employees and superiors	2. Can be costly to develop
	3. Are useful for providing feedback	3. Have some potential for rating error
	4. Are fair for reward and promotion decisions	
Results methods	1. Have less subjectivity bias	1. Are time consuming to develop/use
	2. Are acceptable to employees and superiors	2. May encourage a short-term perspective
	3. Link individual performance to organizational performance	3. May use contaminated criteria
	4. Encourage mutual goal setting	4. May use deficient criteria
	5. Are good for reward and promotion decisions	

work just fine. I've seen many systems fail miserably because they're too complex, too time-consuming, and too burdensome. I've never seen a system fail because it was too simple."[42] One way to assess whether an organization's evaluation system is effective is by doing an annual, or at least periodic, audit of the process using a survey instrument that both managers and employees complete on a periodic basis. This should give HR a better sense of whether the evaluation process is improving.

Of course, having a first-rate evaluation method does no good if the manager simply "shoves the information in a drawer." Even a rudimentary system, when used properly, can initiate a discussion between managers and employees that genuinely leads to better performance on the part of individual workers.

PERFORMANCE EVALUATION MEETINGS AND FEEDBACK SESSIONS

After you have evaluated how well your employees are doing using one or more evaluation methods, how should you begin to present the information to them in an evaluation meeting or feedback session? The format for the meeting or session will be determined in large part by its purpose, type of performance management system used, and organization of a firm's evaluation form. The meetings and sessions should be scheduled far enough in advance to allow the subordinate and manager to prepare for the discussion. Usually, 10 days to 2 weeks is a sufficient amount of lead time.

Sometimes discussing an employee's past performance and future development goals can make for a meeting or feedback session that is too long. It can also be difficult for a supervisor to perform the role of both evaluator and counsellor in the same review period. Dividing the meeting into two sessions, one for the performance review and the other for the employee's growth plans, can be helpful. Dividing the sessions can also improve the communication and cooperation between the parties, thereby reducing any stress and defensiveness that might arise.

OUTCOME 4

Imagine that you are a manager (or a friend) trying to get someone to talk about a performance problem. What techniques would you use to facilitate the discussion?

There are three basic types of formats for providing feedback during a performance evaluation meeting or feedback session: tell-and-sell, tell-and-listen, and problem solving.

- **Tell-and-sell**. The skills required in the tell-and-sell format include the ability to persuade an employee to change his or her behaviour in a certain way. This may require the development of new behaviours on the part of the employee and skillful use of motivational incentives on the part of the appraiser/supervisor. But because there is less communication on the part of the employee, this format is less than ideal. However, it may be used if other formats haven't worked, the employee is resistant to change, or the employee is reluctant to participate in the discussion.

- **Tell-and-listen**. In the tell-and-listen format, the appraiser or supervisor communicates the strong and weak points of an employee's job performance during the first part of the session. During the second part of the session, the employee's feelings about the evaluation are thoroughly explored. The tell-and-listen method gives both managers and employees the opportunity to release any frustrating feelings they might have.

- **Problem solving**. This format is the most proactive. Listening, accepting, and responding to feelings are essential elements of it. However, the format goes beyond an interest in the employee's feelings. It seeks to obtain the employee's buy-in for a mutually agreed-upon way to overcome obstacles and improve the person's performance.

Interestingly, Canadian researchers are suggesting that a fourth method, the feed forward interview, may be the most effective way to ensure changes in behaviour. The feed forward method is described in Highlights in HRM 8.6.

Highlights in HRM 8.6

The Feed Forward Performance Evaluation Interview

Critics of performance evaluation interviews claim that the interviews do not result in positive performance change; that employees become demotivated, not motivated; and most interviews are subject to "recency" effects, which do not capture annual performance. But the majority of HR professionals and some managers are reluctant to abolish performance evaluation because of the need for employees to receive feedback. The quest for a mechanism to provide feedback that results in motivated employees willing to change behaviour may have moved a step forward.

Canadian researchers at York University and the University of Toronto have developed an interview protocol that focuses on the positive aspects of employee experiences instead of on "what is wrong." The theory, based on positive psychology, is that the interview should focus on strengths, successes, and values. By focusing on the positive, managers and employees can identify the conditions under which success occurs.

It works like this. Managers are trained, for 2.5 hours, to ask employees questions, paraphrased here, such as "Please tell me about an incident where you felt especially good about achieving a goal" and "What were the circumstances that enabled you to be effective?" and "What can you do in this coming year to create the conditions that will enable you to be successful?" The results show that this interview process increased performance four months later (compared to the standard performance appraisal, where the emphasis was on feedback regarding past performance). The manager was no longer a judge or critic but an enabler of appreciative inquiry.

Sources: Budworth, M. H., Latham, G.P., and Manroop, L. "Looking Forward to Performance Improvement: A Field Test of the Feedforward Interview for Performance Management," *Human Resources Management* 54, 1 (January–February 2015): 45–54; Humber, T. "Fixing the Broken Performance Review," *Canadian HR Reporter* 28, 5 (March 23, 2015): 6.

Managers shouldn't assume that one format is best for every review session. Rather, they can use one or more of the formats depending on the purpose of the session, the topic being discussed, and the receptiveness of the employee.

CONDUCTING THE PERFORMANCE EVALUATION MEETING OR FEEDBACK SESSION

There are probably no hard-and-fast rules for how to conduct an evaluation, but the guidelines that follow can increase an employee's willingness to discuss his or her performance and improve it, accept feedback from his or her supervisors, and increase the person's overall satisfaction with the feedback process.

Ask for a Self-Evaluation

As we noted earlier in the chapter, it is useful to have employees evaluate their own performance prior to the meeting. Research shows that employees are more satisfied and view evaluation systems as more fair when they have input into the process. A self-evaluation can be used to discuss areas in which the manager and the employee have reached different conclusions—not so much to resolve the "truth" as to work toward the resolution of problems. A self-evaluation also ensures that the employee knows against what criteria he or she is being evaluated, eliminating any potential surprises.

Invite Participation

Most experts advise supervisors to encourage their employees to speak freely and listen closely to what they have to say. These experts emphasize that the communication should be a two-way street. To the extent that an employee is an active participant in that discussion, the more likely it is that the root causes and obstacles to his or her performance will be uncovered and that constructive ideas for improvement will be developed. In addition, research suggests that an employee's participation is strongly related to the person's satisfaction with the feedback delivered, the extent to which the person believes it is fair and useful, and the desire to improve his or her performance. As a rule of thumb, supervisors should spend only about 30 to 35 percent of the time talking. They should spend the rest of the time listening to the information their employees volunteer and their responses to questions.

The purpose of a performance appraisal interview is to initiate a dialogue that will help an employee improve his or her performance, making the employee an active participant in the discussion. Such participation is strongly related to an employee's satisfaction with appraisal feedback.

Alina Solovyova-Vincent/Getty Images

Express Appreciation

Because praise is a powerful motivator and employees are seeking positive feedback, it is frequently beneficial to start the session by expressing appreciation for what the employee has done well. Surprisingly, not all supervisors think to do this. They should. A performance review is the perfect time to tell people they are valued, top performers in particular, so they feel encouraged and motivated to continue to come to work day after day and remain with the firm.

Starting the meeting by talking about what the employee is doing well will also make the person less defensive and more likely to talk about aspects of the job that are not going so well. Don't, however, deliberately "sandwich" positive statements followed by negative ones, which are then followed by positive statements. If you do, the individual will be less likely to take the praise seriously and view it instead as a way to soften the bad news. Furthermore, if employees are given feedback on their performance on a regular basis, there will be no need to sandwich bad news between good news.

Be Supportive and Demonstrate That You Care

One of the better techniques for engaging an employee in the problem-solving process is for the manager to ask: "What can I do to help?" Employees frequently attribute performance problems to either real or perceived obstacles (such as bureaucratic procedures or inadequate resources). By being open and supportive, the manager conveys to the employee that he or she will try to eliminate roadblocks and will work with the employee to achieve a higher standard of performance. Good managers also demonstrate during evaluations and on the job that not only do they support their employees' work efforts and ways to improve them, they also care about them personally and want to help them get what they want out of life. No one wants to be just a "cog in the machine."

Minimize Criticism

Even the most stoic employees can absorb only so much criticism before they start to get defensive. If an employee has many areas in need of improvement, managers should focus on the issues that are most problematic or most important to the job. In other words, criticism should be given in small doses.

Some tips for using criticism constructively include the following:

- *Consider whether it is really necessary.* Sometimes a manager's frustration with a performance problem is little more than "letting off steam." Be sure that the criticism focuses on a recurrent problem or a consistent pattern of behaviour over which the employee has control.

- *Consider the person's ability to handle it.* Everyone handles criticism differently. Some people are able to handle it well. Others react very negatively to even the slightest criticism.

- *Be specific and do not exaggerate.* Sometimes we overstate problems in order to be convincing or to demonstrate our concern. Try to keep criticism simple, factual, and to the point. Avoid using terms such as *always, completely,* and *never.*

- *Watch your timing.* Properly timed criticism can often mean the difference between success and failure. Even good criticism given late in the day, for example, can touch a raw nerve if the employee is tired. Take a break or save it for another day.

- *Make improvement your goal.* Frankly, it is hard to change a person's behaviour with a single conversation, so "laying it on the line" is probably not a good idea. Instead of getting into a "blame game" in which both manager and employee enter into a potentially endless discussion of why a situation has occurred, focus on the problem and devise a solution to it.[43]

Because one of the major purposes of the evaluation meeting or feedback session is to improve an employee's future performance, his or her manager should focus the person's attention on the future rather than the past:

- Emphasize strengths on which the employee can build rather than weaknesses to overcome.

- Drop unproductive tasks.

- Limit improvement plans to a few important items that can be accomplished within a reasonable period of time and spell out how they will be achieved. The plans might also include a list of resources, contact information for people who can help the employee achieve the goals, and timetables for following up to ensure that they are met.

- Highlight how both the employee and the firm will excel if the goals are achieved. Some supervisors will be tempted to establish difficult goals with their employees, thinking that these will "motivate" them to achieve more. The ethical issues surrounding unreasonable goals are discussed in Ethics in HRM.

Ethics in HRM

Stretch Goals

Employees are being asked to set performance goals, labelled "stretch goals," that ask them to do such things as double their sales or increase response time to customers threefold. Research has shown that the establishment of goals results in higher productivity. So if goals are good, are supergoals better?

"Not necessarily," says Steve Kerr, General Electric's chief learning officer. In his opinion, most managers do not know how to manage stretch targets. Companies set ambitious goals for their employees but fail to provide them with the resources they need to achieve them. They are saying, in effect, "We aren't going to give you any more people or money, so your solution is to work smarter and be creative." The only resource left to employees is their personal time, so North Americans are working harder than employees in any other developed country. They are working evenings and weekends, with fewer vacations. "That's immoral," says Kerr. "Companies have a moral obligation to provide the tools to meet tough goals." The other risk is that stretch goals may lead to risk-taking behaviour on the part of employees. For instance, U.S. banks set numerical goals for mortgages that resulted in selling mortgages to high-risk customers, who subsequently defaulted, causing a massive meltdown in the home real estate market.

How should stretch goals be managed? The goal must be seen as achievable and not provoke a reaction of "You've got to be kidding." People must also realize that creative energy can be increased. For example, in one innovation training program, teams are given an orange and told that each person must handle the orange, but the orange must end up in the hands of the person who started with it. All teams start by throwing the orange to team members; this takes nine seconds. They try to reduce the time to seven seconds by throwing faster or in tighter circles. When told that it is possible to do this task in one second, they get creative: they stack their hands, and the first person drops the orange through the stacked but open hands and catches it at the bottom.

If the stretch goals are not achieved, then punishment should not be used. Be careful with high achievers who are already stretching or these winners will feel like losers if they cannot meet impossible goals. Provide the tools; asking people to double their quota without ensuring backup is demoralizing. Finally, share the wealth. If the achievement results in additional funds flowing to the organization, split the incremental savings or gains.

Some employees, masters at the politics of organizations, play games with stretch goals. They negotiate hard for modest, achievable goals while arguing that these are stretch targets. Others, with high needs for achievement, accept the stretch targets. At bonus time, the modest goal setters have met or surpassed their goals and receive merit increases. Having failed to achieve impossible targets, the less Machiavellian employees receive nothing.

Sources: Adapted from S. Sherman, "Stretch Goals: The Dark Side of Asking for Miracles," *Fortune* (November 13, 1995): 231; W. Immen, "The Goal: To Set Goals That Really Can Be Met," *The Globe and Mail* (March 20, 2009): B12.

Follow Up Day to Day

Often both managers and employees are frequently happy to finish formal performance reviews and file away the evaluation form. As we have emphasized, a better approach is to have informal talks periodically, perhaps quarterly, to follow up on the issues that were discussed. This puts managers in more of a coaching role versus that of a judge. If you are a sales manager, should you wait to appraise your employees once or twice a year? Probably not. Most likely you would want to monitor their sales on a weekly and monthly basis. Has a particular salesperson met his or her customer contact numbers this week? Why or why not? Is the salesperson closing deals with the people he or she does contact? If at the six-month mark the salesperson isn't making his or her goals, how can you help the person if you haven't provided ongoing feedback? The lack of sales will be hard to make up at this point.

It's not just salespeople who need continual feedback. All types of employees can benefit from ongoing performance conversations with their managers. Managers need to constantly engage in a dialogue with their subordinates. Once the manager and employees have a series of discussions, there is an ebb and flow of ideas, some with the potential to serve as catalysts for improvement within the company.[44] The ultimate purpose is to better both parties. Of course, there is an app to help supervisors provide feedback more often. Using an app called 15five, each week managers at several companies in Western Canada asked employees a few questions that took 15 minutes to answer. Managers then spent five minutes with each employee responding to feedback, discussing issues, and reinforcing successes.

Providing employees with feedback on a continual basis also helps them know where they stand when they receive their formal evaluations. As a result, the anxiety they experience during formal evaluations is often alleviated, and a more meaningful conversation with them and their supervisors can take place. If employees are surprised by their reviews, it is probably safe to say that their supervisors have not been providing them with much ongoing feedback.

IMPROVING PERFORMANCE

What if one of your employees is performing poorly? What can you do to help the person perform better? This requires some diagnosis of the situation. But although performance management systems can often tell us who is not performing well, they typically cannot reveal why.

Identifying the Sources of Ineffective Performance

A person's performance is a function of several factors, but perhaps it can be boiled down to three primary concerns: ability, motivation, and environment. Each individual has a unique pattern of strengths and weaknesses that play a part. But talented employees with low motivation are not likely to succeed. In addition, other factors in the work environment—or even in the external environment, which includes personal, family, and community concerns—can affect a person's performance either positively or negatively. Figure 8.9 provides a better picture of how these three factors (ability, motivation, and environment) can influence people's performance.

It is recommended that a diagnosis of poor employee performance focus on these three interactive elements. As Figure 8.10 shows, if an employee's performance is not up to standards, the cause could be a skill problem (knowledge, abilities, technical competencies), an effort problem (motivation to get the job done), or some problem in the external conditions of work (poor economic conditions, worker shortages due to downsizing, difficult sales territories). Any one of these problem areas could cause performance to suffer.

FIGURE 8.9

FACTORS THAT AFFECT AN EMPLOYEE'S PERFORMANCE

ABILITY	MOTIVATION	ENVIRONMENT
• Technical skills • Interpersonal skills • Problem-solving skills • Analytical skills • Communication skills • Physical limitations	• Career ambition • Goals and expectations • Job satisfaction and frustrations • Fairness perceptions • Relations with coworkers	• Equipment/materials • Job design • Economic conditions • Unions • Rules and policies • Managerial support • Laws and regulations

Too often, however, managers assume that poor performance is due first to a lack of ability, second to poor motivation, and third to external conditions an employee faces. Ironically, research also suggests that we tend to make just the opposite attributions about our own performance. We first attribute poor performance to external constraints such as bad luck or factors out of our control. If the problem is internal, then we typically attribute it to temporary factors such as motivation or energy ("I had a bad day") and only as a last resort admit that it might be due to our abilities or lack of them. This difference in opinion between the two parties can result in a negative feedback cycle if it's not handled properly. Managers who assume that employees are not motivated or not capable may begin to treat them differently (perhaps supervising them too closely or watching for

FIGURE 8.10

PERFORMANCE DIAGNOSIS

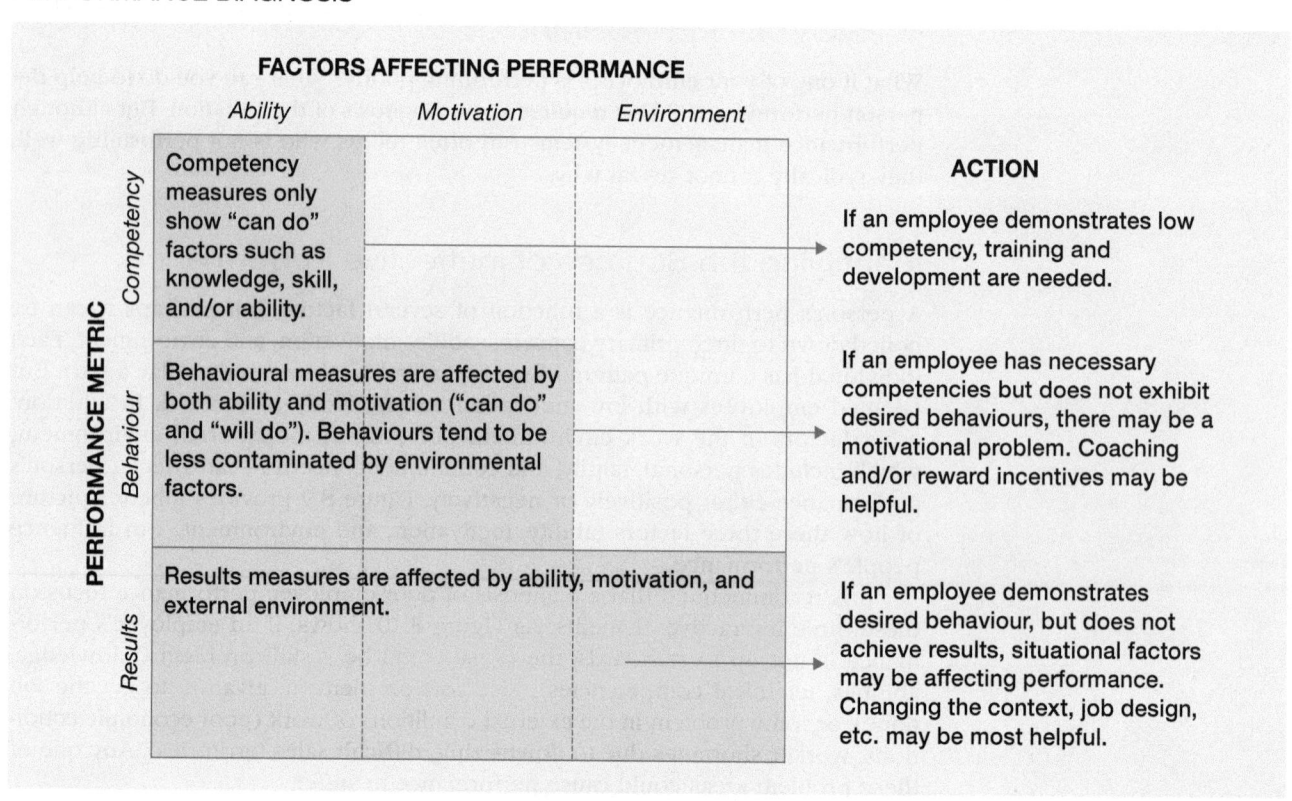

FACTORS AFFECTING PERFORMANCE

	Ability	Motivation	Environment	ACTION
Competency	Competency measures only show "can do" factors such as knowledge, skill, and/or ability.			If an employee demonstrates low competency, training and development are needed.
Behaviour	Behavioural measures are affected by both ability and motivation ("can do" and "will do"). Behaviours tend to be less contaminated by environmental factors.			If an employee has necessary competencies but does not exhibit desired behaviours, there may be a motivational problem. Coaching and/or reward incentives may be helpful.
Results	Results measures are affected by ability, motivation, and external environment.			If an employee demonstrates desired behaviour, but does not achieve results, situational factors may be affecting performance. Changing the context, job design, etc. may be most helpful.

PERFORMANCE METRIC

their next mistake). This can decrease an employee's motivation and cause him or her to withdraw. Seeing this might confirm the manager's initial belief that the employee does not "measure up." As you can probably tell, this "set-up-to-fail" syndrome can be self-fulfilling and self-reinforcing.[45]

Performance Diagnosis

So what can be done to diagnose the *real* reasons for poor performance? More specifically, how can managers identify the root causes and get to work on a solution that improves performance? By comparing different performance measures, managers can begin to get an idea of the underlying causes of performance problems.

For example, as Figure 8.10 shows, results measures cannot distinguish between ability, motivation, and situational determinants of performance. So if someone is not achieving desired results, it could be due to ability, motivation, or external constraints. On the other hand, behavioural measures are less affected by external constraints. So if someone is demonstrating all the desired behaviours but is not achieving the desired results, logic suggests that it might be due to factors beyond his or her control.

Other kinds of diagnoses are possible by comparing different measures of performance. Only by correctly diagnosing the causes of performance problems can managers—and employees—hope to improve them.

Managing Ineffective Performance

Once the sources of performance problems are known, a course of action can be planned. In addition to informal feedback, a formal evaluation and shorter feedback sessions can provide a forum for implementing these actions. This might involve providing training in areas that would increase the knowledge and skills the employee needs to perform effectively. A transfer to another job or department might give an employee a chance to become a more effective member of the organization. In other instances, different ways to motivate the individual might have to be found. Sometimes underperformers do not understand exactly what is expected of them. However, once their responsibilities are clarified, they are in a position to take the corrective action needed to improve their performance.

Focus on Changing the Behaviour, Not the Person

A bad performance on the part of an employee is likely to make his or her supervisor's job harder. As hard as it might be to do, the supervisor has to try to separate the employee from the behaviour—it is not the employee who is bad but his or her actions exhibited on the job. One way to communicate this to employees is not to make suggestions about personal traits they should change but instead to suggest more acceptable ways of performing. For example, instead of focusing on a person's "unreliability," a manager might focus on the fact that the employee "has been late to work seven times this month." It is difficult for employees to change who they are; it is usually much easier for them to change how they act.

If the ineffective performance persists, it may be necessary to transfer the employee, take disciplinary action, or discharge the person from the organization. Not only is the ineffective behaviour likely affecting the manager and the organization as a whole, but it is also probably affecting the person's coworkers. Whatever action is taken, however, should be done legally, fairly, and with an understanding of the feelings of the individual involved. A new manager is likely to need training in this area because it is one of the most difficult aspects of being a manager.

Small Business Application

Does a Small Business Need to Formally Evaluate Its Employees?

So now you have your own business. That means you can dispense with those pesky, time-consuming performance reviews everyone dreads, right? You never liked them as an employee. In fact, maybe they helped solidify your desire to work for yourself. Why would you like them any more as a manager, entrepreneur, or small business owner?

Do not be so fast to dump formal performance evaluations. Without them, you might end up "flying blind" when it comes to some important performance metrics. Evaluating your employees also lets them know they are not just human cogs in the production process—that you care about them, their involvement in the firm, and their personal goals. This can help a small business retain its top employees rather than losing them to big companies, where they are often treated more impersonally. The feedback can be verbal if the reviews are for development purposes only. However, if the evaluations are used in conjunction with raises and promotions, they should be written.

In this chapter, we have covered many appraisal methods under the broad categories of trait, behavioural, and results models. Depending on the context, any of these may be suitable for a small business. However, in a small business, where one's role is unique, a results-based model is likely going to be the most suitable model. For clarity, a results-based model considers the employee's objective outcomes against preestablished objectives. Let's use the example of a carpenter named John working for a small contracting company. Although there are periods when there is enough carpentry work for him to be occupied for the full day, the company regularly also turns to John for assistance on client calls, as well as other miscellaneous work, such as painting. So how does one evaluate John's performance? In essence, John's core responsibility is carpentry, so John will be evaluated based on the effectiveness of his carpentry in terms of quantity, quality, and the manner in which it was delivered. This is a results-based assessment. The other components of John's role fall into the category of "other duties as required." Recognizing that these, even though they are unstructured, form a regular part of John's role, John's manager will likely speak to John regarding his performance in these areas, drawing on the behavioural methods we have reviewed, likely the critical incident method.

Small companies looking for assistance in training in or development of effective performance appraisal may consider working with outside training companies or HR consultants to effectively establish performance appraisal processes. Small businesses with few employees or that are just launching their performance management systems can utilize off-the-shelf systems consisting of either printed forms or software. Popular software brands include Success Factors' Performance Management system, Evaluation Smart, and Halogen's eEvaluation product, the latter two of which are Web based. Generally, a manager can customize evaluation forms in software packages by selecting elements from a list of attributes and behaviours that describe on-the-job success for a position.

Keep in mind that performance reviews are not about the forms, however. They are a two-way discussion designed to benefit both parties. In addition to your employees learning about how they can improve their performance, the evaluations can help you learn how to improve yours as well.

Sources: Amy Linn, "Boost Performance with Performance Reviews," *Small Business Review*, http://smallbusinessreview.com; David Javitch, "How to Survive Employee Appraisals," Entrepreneur.com, http://www.entrepreneur.com.

Summary

OUTCOME 1 Performance management is the process of creating a work environment in which people can perform to the best of their abilities to meet a company's goals. Performance evaluations and feedback sessions, which are used for administrative and development purposes, are the result of a process in which a manager meets with and evaluates an employee's performance relative to the requirements of his or her job and uses the information to show the person where improvements are needed and why. The evaluations are just part of the performance management process, however. Aligning the goals of employees with that of the firm, providing employees with continual on-the-job feedback, and rewarding them are critical as well.

Although some firms believe performance evaluations are ineffective and no longer use them, most organizations continue to do so. The ultimate success or failure of a performance evaluation program depends on the philosophy underlying it, its connection with the firm's business goals, and the attitudes and skills of those responsible for its administration.

OUTCOME 2 Information about how well employees are performing can be derived from a variety of sources, including the employee himself, his or her supervisor, peers, customers, suppliers, and subordinates. Using multiple sources is frequently a good idea because different individuals see different facets of an employee's performance.

Performance management systems must comply with the law and, like selection tests, be job related, valid and reliable, and free from criterion deficiency and contamination. Employees must understand their performance standards in advance, and appraisers must be able to observe job performance, be trained, and have an appeals procedure established. Some companies hold calibration meetings to compare the behaviour of employees and ensure that their managers are accurately evaluating their performance.

OUTCOME 3 Several methods can be used to gauge the performance of employees. These include trait approaches (such as graphic rating scales, mixed-standard scales, forced-choice forms, and essays), behavioural methods (such as critical incident ratings, checklists, BARS, and BOS), and results methods (MBO). The choice of method depends on the purpose of the evaluation. Trait methods are simple to develop and complete, but they have problems in terms of their subjectivity and are not useful for feedback. Behavioural methods provide more specific information for giving feedback but can be time consuming and costly to develop. Results methods are more objective and can link individual performance to the organization as a whole, but they may encourage a short-term perspective (such as annual goals) and may not include subtle yet important aspects of performance.

OUTCOME 4 Although there are various approaches to evaluation meetings, research suggests that employee participation and goal setting lead to higher satisfaction and improved performance. Discussing problems with employees, showing support for them, minimizing criticism, and rewarding them when they perform well are critical. During the meeting, performance deficiencies can be discussed and plans for improvement can be made.

Key Terms

360-degree evaluation, 295
behaviour observation scale (BOS), 306
behaviourally anchored rating scale (BARS), 306
calibration, 291
contrast error, 301
critical incident, 305
customer evaluation, 295
error of central tendency, 299

essay method, 305
forced-choice method, 304
forced distribution, 299
graphic rating scale method, 303
leniency or strictness error, 299
management by objectives (MBO), 308
manager and/or supervisor evaluation, 293
mixed-standard scale method, 304

peer evaluation, 294
performance evaluation, 286
performance management, 286
self-evaluation, 293
similar-to-me error, 301
subordinate evaluation, 294
team evaluation, 295
temporal (recency) error, 301

Discussion Questions

1. Eighty percent of Canadian organizations have performance appraisal systems. List some reasons why 20 percent would not choose to implement one.

2. Develop a list of the characteristics of effective service for fast-food servers at places such as Tim Hortons. Over your next five visits, rate the servers against the criteria that you have developed. Did your criteria meet the performance standards of relevance and reliability, or were they subject to criterion deficiency or contamination?

3. Develop a 10-item checklist to be used to rate student behaviour (e.g., *Always submits assignments on time*). Rate your own behaviour against this list. Then ask friends and family members to rate your behaviour. Are there differences? If so, how would you explain them?

4. Take two of the items from question 3 and develop a BARS for each of these items. Then rate yourself and ask others to rate you using the BARS. Did the ratings change? If so, why?

5. Think of a friend or a family member whose behaviour you wish to change (e.g., your friend is usually late for events that you have organized). Using the problem-solving interview and the suggestions for conducting an effective appraisal interview, provide appraisal feedback to your friend.

HRM Experience

Performance Diagnosis

Managing the performance of employees is a vital—yet delicate—responsibility. One of the toughest aspects of performance management is assessing why someone is not performing well. Although it may be easy to spot who is not performing well, it is not always easy to diagnose the underlying causes of poor performance (such as motivation, ability, and external constraints). But without a correct diagnosis, it is nearly impossible to fix the problem. Managers also need to coach employees to improve their performance.

Assignment

The following are descriptions of three different employees. Describe what the potential causes of poor performance for each of the following employees might be and solutions that could enhance the person's performance.

1. *Carl Spackler* is the assistant greenskeeper at Bushwood Country Club. Over the past few months, members have been complaining that gophers are destroying the course and digging holes in the greens. Although Carl has been working evenings and weekends to address the situation, the problem persists. Unfortunately, his boss is interested only in results, and because the gophers are still there, he contends that Carl is not doing his job. He has accused Carl of "slacking off" and threatened his job.

2. *Clark Griswold* works in research and development for a chemical company that makes non-nutritive food additives. His most recent assignment has been the development of a non-nutritive aerosol cooking spray, but the project is way behind schedule and seems to be going nowhere. CEO Frank Shirley is decidedly upset and has threatened that if things do not improve, he will suspend bonuses again this year, as he did last year. Clark feels dejected because without the bonus he will not be able to make a down payment on the family's swimming pool.

3. *Tommy Callahan Jr.* recently graduated from college after seven years and returned home. His father, Big Tom Callahan, the owner of Callahan Motors, offers Tommy a job in the auto parts factory that makes brake pads. The factory is in severe danger of going under unless sales of the company's new brake pads increase dramatically. Tommy must go on the road with Richard (Big Tom's right-hand man) in a last-ditch effort to save the company. But Tommy proves to be unfocused, inexperienced, and lacking in confidence. Sales call after sales call he meets with rejection, even when the prospect looks promising. Customers express some concern about a warranty on the brake pads, but Richard believes that Tommy's inexperience and awkward approach are the big problems.

MindTap®

Case Study 1

"PROJECT OXYGEN" RESUSCITATES GOOGLE'S POOR-PERFORMING BOSSES

When it comes to gathering data and analyzing them to build new and better products, few companies do it as well as Google. Recently, Google decided to use its info-tech expertise to answer an important question: Since people make the difference between good and great companies, could a data-driven, analytical approach be used to improve Google's HRM function? Such an approach worked for Billy Beane, so surely it could work for Google, couldn't it? Recall from Chapter 2 that Beane, the manager of the Oakland A's, dramatically improved players and the team using data and statistics. (Actor Brad Pitt dramatized Beane's efforts in the movie *Moneyball*.)

One thing Google wanted to know was if it could "build" better bosses. Why? Because despite the many job perks Google's workers get, the company's employee turnover rate was surprisingly high. It's been said that the number 1 reason people leave their jobs is because of their bosses. Could this be true at Google? And if so, could the behaviours of good bosses be pinpointed and used to improve the performance of not-so-good bosses? The researchers at Google wanted to find out. They also wanted to answer these questions using data from their own organization to find out precisely what works for Google rather than other organizations.

To answers these questions, a team of 25-plus Google researchers and scientists began studying the company's supervisors using their performance reviews, surveys from their employees, interviews, and observations of their behaviours. Over 10,000 observations were collected on 100 variables to determine how well the supervisors were performing. Initially, not all supervisors were thrilled to be evaluated by their subordinates and "put under the microscope." Consequently, the effort took some "selling" to Google's top management. The fact that the researchers could point to dramatic differences in the overall ratings employees gave different managers and that some teams performed much better than others helped fuel the fire to get Project Oxygen off the ground. (Presumably, a good boss gives you room to breathe, whereas a bad boss can suck the life right out of you—hence the project's name.)

Once concluded, Project Oxygen yielded a plethora of information, some of which mirrored conventional wisdom and some of which did not: teams with higher-rated managers performed better, the employees in them were happier, and they stayed with the company longer. Their managers had more impact on how the employees felt about their jobs than any other factor. However, it turned out that the best bosses weren't the ones with the greatest technical expertise, as Google had anticipated. Instead, they were those who are even-tempered, help their teams think through problems without micromanaging them, and care about them as people. Google then used the information it gathered to implement training and coaching programs to quickly improve the quality of the bulk of its worst-performing managers.

Specifically, Google identified eight behaviours you should engage in if you want to be a good boss—at least at Google:

1. Be a good coach
2. Empower your team and don't micromanage
3. Express interest in team members' success and personal well-being
4. Be productive and results oriented
5. Be a good communicator and listen to your team
6. Help your employees with career development
7. Have a clear vision and strategy for the team
8. Have key technical skills so you can help advise the team

Questions

1. Why isn't having the greatest amount of technical expertise the key to being a good supervisor at Google?
2. Does Google's research on the performance of its managers surprise you? Why or why not?

Sources: Adam Bryant, "Google's Quest to Build a Better Boss," *The New York Times* (March 12, 2011), http://www.nytimes.com; Meghan Casserly, "Google's Failed Quest to Find Managers Are Evil, and Why You Should Care," *Forbes* (July 17, 2013), http://www.forbes.com; Judith Aquino, "Eight Traits of Stellar Managers as Defined by Googlers," *Business Insider* (March 15, 2011), http://www.businessinsider.com.

Case Study 2

WOW PRODUCTIONS

Wow Productions is a Canadian company specializing in the production of films, documentaries, dramas and animation programs for television. The quality of its productions has earned the company an excellent reputation on the market. Over the last three years, the organization has grown substantially, doubling its workforce. With over 800 employees working in four studios across the country, it has become a major industry player. Furthermore, since it was founded in 1990, Wow Productions has won a number of international awards. A cloud has however appeared on the horizon: in the last 18 months reactions to its productions have been cool and profits have fallen.

The company's president believes that what sets Wow Productions apart in its market segment is its strong talent. Since its inception, it has been able to depend on reliable directors. At their strategic meeting each year, the company reminds the directors of their responsibility to maintain tight control over the management of their studio's productivity and performance.

During a team meeting, some Studio 2 employees learned that, unlike them, Studio 3 employees weren't evaluated each year by their director. The company's president heard about these discussions and wants to understand exactly what's happening. She therefore asks the HR manager to analyze the situation.

The HR manager first meets each of the four studio directors individually before summing up the situation as follows:

Studio 1	Studio 2	Studio 3	Studio 4
The director: • sets performance goals for poor performers only; • meets these employees as often as necessary during the year. In some cases, they are let go or dismissed.	The director: • sets performance goals for all the employees; • holds one-on-one meetings with all the employees twice a year (in mid-year and at year-end).	The director: • does not set any employee performance goals; • holds several one-on-one meetings as needed during the year.	The director: • meets with top performers once a year to congratulate them and recognize their efforts and good performance.

The names and characters in this case study are fictitious, and any resemblance to actual persons living or dead is purely coincidental.

Questions

You are the HR manager and you decide to prepare a report for the president, setting out an overview of the situation and proposing recommendations.

1. Identify four probable causes for the lack of uniformity in the application of performance management practices.
2. What are your top three recommendations to ensure effective management of performance within the organization? Justify your answers.

Notes and References

1. "Infographic: 2013 Employee Performance Appraisal Practices," HR.BLR.com, July 9, 2013, http://hr.blr.com.

2. Susan Scherreik, "Your Performance Review: Make It Perform," *Business Week*, no. 3762 (December 17, 2001): 139; Dick Grote, "Performance Evaluations: Is It Time for a Makeover?" *HR Focus* 77, no. 11 (November 2000): 6–7; "Employers Need to Do a Better Job of Performance Management," *Managing Training & Development* (April 2003): 8; Christopher D. Lee, "Feedback, Not Appraisal," *HR Magazine* 51, no. 11 (November 2006): 111–114; R. L. Cardy and B. Leonard, Performance Management: Concepts, Skills, and Exercises (M. E. Sharpe, Inc., 2011).

3. Dana Jarvis, "Why Should We Continue Performance Appraisals If We Can't Give Raises," *Workforce Management* (September 2010), http://www.workforce.com.

4. Janet Wiscombe, "Can Pay for Performance Really Work?" *Workforce* 80, no. 8 (August 2001): 28–34; Charlotte Garvey, "Meaningful Tokens of Appreciation: Cash Awards Aren't the Only Way to Motivate Your Workforce," *HR Magazine* 49, no. 8 (August 2004): 101–106; Lisa D. Sprenkle, "Forced Ranking: A Good Thing for Business?" *Workforce.com*, http://homepages.uwp.edu/crooker/790-iep-pm/Articles/meth-fd-workforce.pdf.

5. Donna Doldwasser, "Me a Trainer?" *Training* 38, no. 4 (April 2001): 60–66; Rebecca Ganzel, "Mike Carter," *Training* 38, no. 7 (July 2001): 28–30; Carla Joinson, "Making Sure Employees Measure Up," *HR Magazine* 46, no. 3 (March 2001): 36–41; Morton D. Rosenbaum, "Gratitude Adjustment: When a Pat on the Back Isn't Enough," *Meetings & Conventions* 39, no. 7 (June 2004): 20; James W. Smither, Manuel London, and Richard R. Reilly, "Does Performance Improve Following Multisource Feedback?" *Personnel Psychology* 58, no. 1 (Spring 2005): 33–67.

6. Matthew Boyle, "Performance Reviews: Perilous Curves Ahead," *Fortune* 143, no. 11 (May 28, 2001): 187–188; Susanne Scott and Walter Einstein, "Strategic Performance Appraisal in Team-Based Organizations: One Size Does Not Fit All," *Academy of Management Executive* 15, no. 2 (May 2001): 107–116; "Study Questions Performance Appraisal," *Australasian Business Intelligence* (May 1, 2003); Drew Robb, "Building a Better Workforce: Performance Management Software Can Help You Identify and Develop High-Performing Workers," *HR Magazine* 49, no. 10 (October 2004): 86–93.

7. Jonathan A. Segal, "86 Your Appraisal Process?" *HR Magazine* 45, no. 10 (October 2000): 199–206; Barry Witcher and Rosie Butterworth, "Honshin Kanri: How Xerox Manages," *Long-Range Planning* 32, no. 3 (June 1999): 323–332.

8. Ladan Nikravan, "A Needed Change: Make Reviews Proactive, Not Reactive," *Forbes* (September 29, 2013), http://forbes.com.

9. Josh Bersin, "Time to Scrap Performance Evaluations," *Forbes* (May 6, 2013), http://forbes.com.

10. David Javitch, "How to Survive Employee Appraisals," *Entrepreneur.com*, http://www.entrepreneur.com, retrieved April 23, 2011.

11. Doug Cederblom, "From Performance Appraisal to Performance Management: One Agency's Experience," *Public Personnel Management* 31, no. 2 (Summer 2002): 131–140; "Anonymous 360-Feedback Drives Vauxhall Strategy," *Personnel Today* (August 19, 2003): 16; Cindy Romaine, "Staying Relevant: Competencies and Employee Reviews," *Information Outlook* 8, no. 7 (April 2004): 21–25; Jerry K. Palmer and James M. Loveland, "The Influence of Group Discussion on Performance Judgments: Rating Accuracy, Contrast Effects, and Halo," *Journal of Psychology* 142, no. 2 (March 2008): 117–130; "When Promotions Are on the Line, Follow Your Criteria and Beware Supervisor Bias," *HR Specialist: Ohio Employment Law* 3, no. 12 (December 2009): 2.

12. Jason D. Shaw and Nina Gupta, "Job Complexity, Performance, and Well-Being: When Does Supplies-Values Fit Matter?" *Personnel Psychology* 57, no. 4 (Winter 2004): 847–880.

13. Joel Lefkowitz, "The Role of Interpersonal Affective Regard in Supervisory Performance Ratings: A Literature Review and Proposed Causal Model," *Journal of Occupational and Organizational Psychology* 73, no. 1 (March 2000): 67–85; Scott Highhouse, "Assessing the Candidate as a Whole: A Historical and Critical Analysis of Individual Psychological Assessment for Personnel Decision Making," *Personnel Psychology* 55, no. 2 (Summer 2002): 363–397.

14. Joanne Sammer, "Calibrating Consistency," *HR Magazine* 53, no. 1 (January 2008): 73–75.

15. Kathryn Bartol, Cathy Durham, and June Poon, "Influence of Performance Evaluation Rating Segmentation on Motivation and Fairness Perceptions," *Journal of Applied Psychology* 86, no. 6 (December 2001): 1106–1119; Anne P. Hubbell, "Motivating Factors: Perceptions of Justice and Their Relationship with Managerial and Organizational Trust," *Communication Studies* 56, no. 1 (March 2005): 47; Rebecca M. Chory-Assad, "Room for Improvement," *Training* 40, no. 11 (December 2003): 18–20; Deanna M. Merritt, "Appraising the Performance Appraisal," *Supervision* 68, no 4 (April 2007): 3–5.

16. Timothy Aeppel, "Goodyear Ends Ratings System Ahead of Lawsuit," *The Wall Street Journal* (September 12, 2002): B8; "How to Stay 'Legal' with Performance Evaluation and Testing," *Managing Training & Development*, no. 4 (February 2004): 9.

17. Gillian Flynn, "Getting Performance Reviews Right," *Workforce* 80, no. 5 (May 2001): 76–78; David C. Martin, Kathryn M. Bartol, and Patrick E. Kehoe, "The Legal Ramifications of Performance Appraisal: The Growing Significance," *Public Personnel Management*

29, no. 3 (Fall 2000): 381; Deanna M. Merritt, "Appraising the Performance Appraisal," *Supervision* 68, no. 4 (April 2007): 3–5; Kevin R. Murphy, "Perspectives on the Relationship between Job Performance and Ratings of Job Performance," *Industrial & Organizational Psychology* (June 2008): 197–205; Cindy Miller, "Performance Appraisals in a Legal Context," *HR Info*, (July 8, 2008), http://cindymiller.wordpress.com/.

18. Joan Brett and Leanne Atwater, "360-Degree Feedback: Accuracy, Reactions, and Perceptions of Usefulness," *Journal of Applied Psychology* 86, no. 5 (October 2001): 930–942; Bruce Pfau, Ira Kay, Kenneth Nowak, and Jai Ghorpade, "Does 360-Degree Feedback Negatively Affect Company Performance?" *HR Magazine* 47, no. 6 (June 2002): 54–59; Maury Peiperl, "Getting 360-Degree Feedback Right," *Harvard Business Review* 79, no. 1 (January 2001): 142–147; Robert Gandossy and Tina Kao, "Talent Wars: Out of Mind, Out of Practice," *Human Resource Planning* 27, no. 4 (December 2004): 15–20.

19. Corey E. Miller and Carl L. Thornton, "How Accurate Are Your Performance Appraisals?" *Public Personnel Management* (Summer 2006): 153–162; Edward J. Inderrieden, Robert E. Allen, and Timothy J. Keaveny, "Managerial Discretion in the Use of Self-Ratings in an Appraisal System: The Antecedents and Consequences," *Journal of Managerial Issues* 16, no. 4 (Winter 2004): 460–484.

20. Jeffrey Seglin, "Reviewing Your Boss," *Fortune* 143, no. 12 (June 11, 2001): 248; Ann Harrington, "Workers of the World, Rate Your Boss!" *Fortune* 142, no. 6 (September 18, 2000): 340–342; Robert Thompson, "Management Lite: Less Control, More Innovation," *HR Magazine* 44, no. 8 (August 1999): 10.

21. Brett and Atwater, "360-Degree Feedback," 930–942; Paula Silva and Henry L. Tosi, "Determinants of the Anonymity of the CEO Evaluation Process," *Journal of Managerial Issues* 16, no. 1 (Spring 2004): 87–103.

22. John Drexler, Jr., Terry Beehr, and Thomas Stetz, "Peer Appraisals: Differentiation of Individual Performance on Group Tasks," *Human Resource Management* 40, no. 4 (Winter 2001): 333–345.

23. Scott and Einstein, "Strategic Performance Appraisal in Team-Based Organizations," 107–116; Debbie Kibbe and Jill Casner-Lotto, "Ralston Foods: From Greenfield to Maturity in a Team-Based Plant," *Journal of Organizational Excellence* 21, no. 3 (Summer 2002): 57–67; Simon Taggar and Mitchell Neubert, "The Impact of Poor Performers on Team Outcomes: An Empirical Examination of Attribution Theory," *Personnel Psychology* 57, no. 4 (Winter 2004): 935–969.

24. Michael Cohn, "Best Buy Beefs Up Customer Value at the Call Center," *Internet World* 8, no. 6 (June 2002): 42–43; Joe Kohn, "Isuzu Has IDEA for Boosting Sales," *Automotive News* 76, no. 5973 (March 4, 2002): 41; D. L. Radcliff, "A New Paradigm of Feedback," *Executive Excellence* 19, no. 4 (April 2002): 20; Neeraj Bharadwaj and Anne Roggeveen, "The Impact of Offshored and Outsourced Call Service Centers on Customer Appraisals," *Marketing Letters* 19, no. 1 (January 2008): 13–23.

25. Pfau, Kay, Nowak, and Ghorpade, "Does 360-Degree Feedback Negatively Affect Company Performance?" 54–59; Peiperl, "Getting 360-Degree Feedback Right," 142–147; Jack Kondrasuk and Matt Graybill, "From Paper to Computer," *The Human Resource Professional* 13, no. 6 (November–December 2000): 18–19.

26. Gary Meyer, "Performance Reviews Made Easy, Paperless," *HR Magazine* 45, no. 10 (October 2000): 181–184; Douglas P. Shuit, "Huddling with the Coach—Part 2," *Workforce Management* 84, no. 2 (February 1, 2005): 5; "Ceridian and Softscape Announce an Agreement to Deliver Employee Performance and Development Solutions," *Payroll Manager's Report* (May 2004): 13; K. Sanwong, "The Development of a 360-Degree Performance Appraisal System: A University Case Study," *International Journal of Management* 25, no. 1 (March 2008): 16–22.

27. Gary E. Roberts, "Perspectives on Enduring and Emerging Issues in Performance Appraisal," *Public Personnel Management* 27, no. 3 (Fall 1998): 301–320; William Hubbartt, "Bring Performance Appraisal Training to Life," *HR Magazine* 40, no. 5 (May 1995): 166, 168; Filip Lievens, "Assessor Training Strategies and Their Effects on Accuracy, Interrater Reliability, and Discriminant Validity," *Journal of Applied Psychology* 86, no. 2 (April 2001): 255–264; Dick Grote, "Performance Appraisals: Solving Tough Challenges," *HR Magazine* 45, no. 7 (July 2000): 145–150; Leslie A. Weatherly, "Performance Management: Getting It Right from the Start," *HR Magazine* 49, no. 3 (March 2004): S1–S12.

28. Gary P. Latham and Kenneth N. Wexley, *Increasing Productivity through Performance Appraisal*, 2nd ed. (Reading, MA: Addison-Wesley, 1994), 137.

29. Lefkowitz, "The Role of Interpersonal Affective Regard in Supervisory Performance Ratings," 67–85; Edwin Arnold and Marcia Pulich, "Personality Conflicts and Objectivity in Appraising Performance," *The Health Care Manager* 22, no. 3 (July–September 2003): 227; Krista Uggersly and Lorne M. Suksy, "Using Frame-of-Reference Training to Understand the Implications of Rater Idiosyncrasy for Rating Accuracy," *Journal of Applied Psychology*, 93, no. 3 (May 2008): 711–719.

30. Christopher Bartlett and Andrew McLean, "GE's Talent Machine," *Harvard Business School* (2006), Case # 9-304-049.

31. Gail Johnson, "Forced Ranking: The Good, the Bad, and the Alternative," *Training* 41, no. 5 (May 2004): 24–31; Christine A. Amalfe and Eileen Quinn Steiner, "Forced Ranking Systems: Yesterday's Legal Target?" *New Jersey Law Journal* (March 28, 2005); Jessica Marquez, "Is GE's Ranking System Broken?" *Workforce Management* 86, no. 12 (June 25, 2007): 1–3.

32. Adam B. Butler and Amie Skattebo, "What Is Acceptable for Women May Not Be for Men: The Effect of Family Conflicts with Work on Job-Performance Ratings," *Journal of Occupational and Organizational Psychology* 77, no. 4 (December 2004): 553–564; Cheri Ostroff, Leanne E. Atwater, and Barbara J. Feinberg, "Understanding Self-Other Agreement: A Look at Rater

and Ratee Characteristics, Context, and Outcomes," *Personnel Psychology* 57, no. 1 (Summer 2004): 333–337; Mike Schraeder and Jim Simpson, "How Similarity and Liking Affect Performance Appraisals," *Journal for Quality & Participation* 29, no. 1 (Spring 2006): 34–40.

33. Lisa Keeping and Paul Levy, "Performance Appraisal Reaction: Measurement, Modeling, and Method Bias," *Journal of Applied Psychology* 85, no. 5 (October 2000): 708–723.

34. Adam Bryant, "Google's Quest to Build a Better Boss," *The New York Times* (March 12, 2011), http://www.nytimes.com.

35. Kristina E. Chirico, M. Ronald Buckley, Anthony R. Wheeler, Jeffrey D. Facteau, H. John Bernardin, and Danielle S. Beu, "A Note on the Need for True Scores in Frame-of-Reference (FOR) Training Research," *Journal of Managerial Issues* 16, no. 3 (Fall 2004): 382–398; Christopher D. Lee, "Feedback, Not Appraisal," *HR Magazine* 51, no. 11 (November 2006): 111–114.

36. Stephen C. Behrenbrinker, "Conducting Productive Performance Evaluations in the Assessor's Office," *Assessment Journal* 2, no. 5 (September–October 1995): 48–54; Aharon Tziner, Christine Joanis, and Kevin Murphy, "A Comparison of Three Methods of Performance Appraisal with Regard to Goal Properties, Goal Perception, and Ratee Satisfaction," *Group & Organization Management* 25, no. 2 (June 2000): 175–190.

37. Latham and Wexley, *Increasing Productivity*; Tziner, Joanis, and Murphy, "A Comparison of Three Methods of Performance Appraisal," 175–190; Simon Taggar and Travor Brown, "Problem-Solving Team Behaviors: Development and Validation of BOS and a Hierarchical Factor Structure," *Small Group Research* 32, no. 6 (December 2001): 698–726; Paul Falcone, "Big-Picture Performance Appraisal," *HR Focus* 84, no. 9 (September 2007): 1–15.

38. Daniel Bachrach, Elliot Bendoly, and Philip Podsakoff, "Attributions of the 'Causes' of Group Performance as an Alternative Explanation of the Relationship between Organizational Citizenship Behavior and Organizational Performance," *Journal of Applied Psychology* 86, no. 6 (December 2001): 1285–1293; Susan Leandri, "Measures That Matter: How to Fine-Tune Your Performance Measures," *Journal for Quality and Participation* 24, no. 1 (Spring 2001): 39–41.

39. Peter F. Drucker, *The Practice of Management* (New York: Harper & Brothers, 1954), reissued by Harper-Collins in 1993; Janice S. Miller, "High Tech and High Performance: Managing Appraisal in the Information Age," *Journal of Labor Research* 24, no. 3 (Summer 2003): 409–425.

40. E. Locke and G. Latham, *A Theory of Goal Setting and Task Performance* (Englewood Cliffs, NJ: Prentice Hall, 1990). See also John J. Donovan and David J. Radosevich, "The Moderating Role of Goal Commitment on the Goal Difficulty-Performance Relationship: A Meta-Analytic Review and Critical Reanalysis," *Journal of Applied Psychology* 83, no. 2 (April 1998): 308–315; Cindy Romaine, "Staying Relevant: Competencies and Employee Reviews," *Information Outlook* 8, no. 4 (April 2004): 21–25; Gail Johnson, "Room for Improvement," *Training* 40, no. 11 (December 2003): 18–20.

41. Jack Steele, "Transforming the Balanced Scorecard into Your Strategy Execution System," *Manage* 53, no. 1 (September–October 2001): 22–23. See also Robert Kaplan and David Norton, "Strategic Learning and the Balanced Scorecard," *Strategy & Leadership* 24, no. 5 (September–October 1996): 18–24; Robert Kaplan and David Norton, "Using the Balanced Scorecard as a Strategic Management System," *Harvard Business Review* (January–February 1996): 75–85; Joe Mullich, "Get in Line: People Talk about Aligning Corporate, Departmental and Employee Goals, But Not Many Actually Do It," *Workforce Management* 82, no. 13 (December 2003): 43; "Good Appraisal Is Simple, Happens Often, Experts Say," *The Orlando Sentinel* (via *Knight-Ridder/Tribune News Service*) (December 3, 2003); Li-cheng Chang, "The NHS Performance Assessment Framework as a Balanced Scorecard Approach," *International Journal of Public Sector Management* 20, no. 2 (2007): 101–117.

42. Deloris McGee Wanguri, "A Review, an Integration, and a Critique of Cross-Disciplinary Research on Performance Appraisals, Evaluations, and Feedback," *Journal of Business Communications* 32, no. 3 (July 1995): 267–293; Tziner, Joanis, and Murphy, "A Comparison of Three Methods of Performance Appraisal," 175–190; "Good Appraisal Is Simple, Happens Often, Experts Say"; Joanna Haworth, "Measuring Performance," *Nursing Management—UK* 15, no. 3 (June 2008): 22–28.

43. Kwok Leung, Steven Su, and Michael Morris, "When Is Criticism Not Constructive? The Roles of Fairness Perceptions and Dispositional Attributions in Employee Acceptance of Critical Supervisory Feedback," *Human Relations* 54, no. 9 (September 2001): 1155–1187; Ted Pollock, "Make Your Criticism Pay Off," *Electric Light & Power* 81, no. 1 (January 2003): 31; "Five Ways to Tackle Poor Performers," *Law Office Management & Administration Report* 6, no. 12 (December 2006): 9.

44. "Focus on Success," *Aftermarket Business* 115, no. 2 (February 2005): 1.

45. Helen Wilkie, "The Tricky Art of Criticism," *HR Magazine* 49, no. 12 (December 2004): 77–83.

CHAPTER

SUCCESSION MANAGEMENT

CHAPTER LEARNING OUTCOMES

AFTER READING THIS CHAPTER, YOU SHOULD BE ABLE TO:

- Understand why succession management is important.
- Trace the evolution of succession management from its roots in replacement planning, comparing the two models with respect to focus, time, and talent pools.
- List the steps in the succession management process.
- Compare and contrast the job-based and competency-based approaches to aligning future needs with strategic objectives.
- Discuss the four approaches to the identification of managerial talent.
- Describe several ways to identify high-potential employees.
- Evaluate the advantages and disadvantages of the five management development methods: promotions, job rotations, special assignments, formal training, and mentoring and coaching.
- Recognize the difficulties in measuring the success of a management succession plan.
- Outline the employee's role in the succession management process.
- Describe the role of HR in succession management

Edwards Lifesciences is a manufacturer of medical products with more than $1 billion in sales and 5700 employees. Its CEO dedicates 20 percent of his time to talent management issues. This highly profitable company attributes its succession management success to its identification of 75 critical positions (which it refuses to reveal for competitive reasons). Each of these 75 positions has at least two employees identified as replacement candidates. The company spends millions of dollars annually to develop qualified candidates for these positions, including e-learning initiatives and weeklong leadership programs for upper management and promising talent. Almost 70 percent of jobs are filled by internal candidates. Every board meeting and every management meeting includes an item on succession management. For its program to track and retain candidates for critical positions, Edwards Lifesciences was awarded the 2007 Optimas Award for Competitive Advantage.[1]

// IMPORTANCE OF SUCCESSION MANAGEMENT

> **Succession management**
> The systematic process of determining critical roles with the organization, identifying and evaluating possible successors, and developing them for these roles

Executives of any organization must develop the next generation of leaders, just as sports teams need to develop the next generation of players. **Succession management** refers to the systematic process of determining critical roles within the organization, identifying and evaluating possible successors, and developing them for these roles.[2] (Succession management might be viewed as part of the talent management process of an organization that focuses on the flow of employees, starting from selection to career management to exit, through the organization.) The importance of succession management is discussed in HR Planning Notebook 7.1.

Succession management used to focus mainly on the CEO. However, there must be a pipeline of talent for the most critical roles:

1. The CEO
2. The senior management team (executives)
3. Critical roles based on long-term value to the organization (such as scientists or customer relationship specialists)[3]

Organizations must view succession management as a critical activity aligned with the organization's business strategy. Due to factors such as the impending retirement of millions of baby boomers, the large increase (53 percent) in the turnover of CEOs and the need to transfer corporate knowledge, there is increasing pressure on organizations to develop succession plans. Companies without a succession plan experience a drop of about one-third in business after the transition to new management. The effective implementation of succession management has been linked to these outcomes: the retention of key talent; increase in shareholder value; reduced senior executive turnover after succession. Moreover, organizations that have developed a reputation for developing key talent have a significant value proposition to attract new employees and retain key ones.

Sources: Stadler, K. 2011. "Talent Reviews: The Key to Effective Succession Management," *Business Strategy Series*, 12. 5, 264–271, www.pwec .com/ca/en/private-company/lets-talk/succeding-through-succession.

Succession management consists of a process of identifying employees who have the potential to assume key positions in the organization and preparing them for these positions. The identification of talent is always paired with ongoing programs to develop that talent. Succession management ensures continuity in leadership and, like any rookie program, develops the next generation of players. The goals of succession management programs are to identify and prepare future leaders and to ensure business continuity.[4] The first priority of any succession management program is to have a plan to replace its leaders. Organizations with positive reputations for leadership brands tend to outperform their peers.[5]

As Peter Drucker says, the ultimate test of good management is succession management, ensuring that there is a replacement for the CEO.[6] Organizations must prepare for expected and unexpected turnover, for key players die, retire, or quit. Unfortunately, only about half of organizations answered "yes" when asked the question "If your president or CEO resigned today, do you know who would take charge of the company?"[7] At McDonald's, the excellent succession management program enabled the company to designate a replacement within six hours of the CEO's sudden death, compared to a more typical delay of six months. The research shows that delays in naming a successor result in decreasing operating performance, and that these negative effects can last up to two years.[8] Fiery young entrepreneurs who build hugely successful businesses often see them fail in the hands of their untrained children. Many Canadian dynasties (e.g., Eaton's, Simpsons) have failed because their heirs were incapable of managing the business.

Succession management is needed even when retirements and company sellouts are predictable. The baby boomers who currently hold most of the leadership positions are retiring. Twenty percent of top management positions and 25 percent of middle management positions will become vacant in the near future, and retirements of baby boomers (the first of whom turned 65 in 2011) will accelerate this trend.[9] And 75 percent of executives are worried about their ability to develop leaders.[10] Yet this worrying does not result in action plans, as only 25 percent of companies report having a formal succession plan in place.[11] About one-half of the HR managers don't consider grooming potential leaders a high priority.[12]

At a minimum, firms need to plan for replacements, and personnel planning was the first step in the march toward sophisticated models of succession management. Some reasons for succession management are listed in HR Planning Notebook 7.2. The next section traces this evolution.

HR PLANNING NOTEBOOK 7.2

WHY ORGANIZATIONS HAVE SUCCESSION MANAGEMENT PROGRAMS

1. Improve internal candidate pools.
2. Assure business continuity.
3. Reduce skill gaps.
4. Retain employees.
5. Help individuals realize their career plans within the organization.
6. Develop leaders more quickly.
7. Encourage the advancement of diverse groups.
8. Improve employees' ability to respond to changing environmental demands.

Sources: K. Lamoureux, "Developing Leaders," *Leadership Excellence*, Vol. 25, No. 7 (July 2008): 11, 12; A. Paradise, "Many Barriers Inhibit Success of Succession Planning," T1D, Vol. 64, No. 6 (2010): 60.

EVOLUTION OF SUCCESSION MANAGEMENT

Replacement planning can be defined as the process of identifying short-term and long-term emergency backups to fill critical positions. If the CEO dies, who will be prepared to take over that position? Is there a replacement for the vice-president of marketing if she suddenly quits to take another job? The events of September 11, 2001, tragically presented a worst-case scenario. Bond trading firm Cantor Fitzgerald lost 700 of its 1,000 World Trade Center staff, including most of its executives.

Formal and methodical replacement planning has existed for over 30 years. This section examines how replacement planning has evolved into succession management by:

- Broadening the focus
- Expanding the time horizon
- Creating a talent pool of replacements
- Improving the evaluation system

BROADER FOCUS

The focus of replacement planning was the job, and having a replacement ready to fill that job if the incumbent died or quit. This concept referred mainly to the succession and replacement charts for the high-level or key positions in the organization, as discussed in Chapter 6. Each key position was represented by a box on the chart, with the name and possible retirement or departure date of the incumbent in the box. Below the box were the names of two or three potential successors, with codes next to their names. These would be, for example, codes such as "PN" for "promotable now" or "RD" for "ready with development."

In short, replacement planning consisted of a periodically updated table of employees who might be nominated if a need arose. This type of planning focused on the high-potential candidates (replacement track stars), all ready to step into vacant positions, and in doing so set off a chain effect throughout the organization. This model assumed that people have single careers within one organization. Thus, replacements were replicas of the current jobholders.

This planning depended on a stable future, in which the knowledge, skills, attitudes, and other attributes (KSAOs) of future managers looked pretty much like those of the current managers. Jobs of the next five to ten years were assumed to be identical to the existing jobs. Organizational structures (i.e., how the organization was set up along divisional lines, product lines, or functional lines) were unchanging, and few new competitors were seen on the horizon. Obviously, this type of scenario just doesn't exist for most companies.

In replacement planning, the starting point was the job, whereas in succession management, the starting point is the strategy of the organization. Employees are selected on the basis of long-term goals, and the developmental plans for employees are aligned with strategic plans, not position replacements.

A case might best illustrate how succession management aligns with strategy. Traditionally, the goal of a large utility like Ontario Hydro was to provide safe, reliable energy. Its core competencies were reliability of distribution, measurement of

consumption, and the maintenance of its power plants. However, deregulation and a more competitive environment forced Ontario Hydro to compete on price and services. Sales and marketing were the new competencies needed. The strategy changed from providing energy to marketing energy. Thus, in the long run, Ontario Hydro must identify or develop managers who have not only sales and marketing abilities but also the ability to change a production culture to one of marketing.[13]

TIME HORIZON

The traditional planning approach was concerned with immediate and short-term replacements. Who is our backup for the vice-president we are planning to promote in six to twelve months? A strategic focus of under one year is a "business as usual" perception, which, if repeated, will not be true over a ten-year period. This short time perspective does not allow for the intake or career management of those with different skills in growth areas.

Succession management looks at a longer term (after ensuring that immediate replacements are in place) and focuses on a future of two years or more. Obviously, this is harder to do, and so, rather than identify one replacement, succession managers identify talent pools.

TALENT POOLS

Traditional models of HR planning looked at succession as the passing of the baton to the next capable runner. Managers would identify their top performers and groom them for success. Sometimes two or three successors would be identified, and they would be in a race to the finish line of executive promotion. This practice may have worked when organizations consisted of dozens of levels, each manager having many assistant managers. Currently, organizations have found that their designated backup personnel fill only 30 percent of the open positions for which they were slotted.[14] Flatter organizations with fewer "apprentices" can no longer rely on this approach. The key is not to develop a specific successor to fill any position (done by about one-third of organizations) but to develop several multiple successors (about two-thirds of organizations do this) for every position.[15] The place to start is with positions that are difficult to fill because of talent shortages.

As employees cannot trust organizations to provide lifetime job security, so too organizations cannot rely on single individuals or a small group of employees for their succession plans. Organizations are trying to identify and develop as many employees as possible to ensure employee departures and changing needs will not leave them harmed. But what is the right number of employees to develop? One rule of thumb that David Ulrich and Norm Smallwood use in their consulting and research is that about 10 to 15 percent of the work force is high-potential talent.[16]

At MDS, a medical supply company, many of the high-potential employees are not aware of being tracked, because "we do not want to create a culture in which some people feel they are special and others feel their potential is not being recognized."[17]

By not telling employees this, companies risk having employees leave the organization for one that offers better opportunities, and they also risk having to groom someone who may not want the job. (However, most employees realize their special status through the frequency of their promotions, assignments, and training.)

Employers must avoid promises such as "You will become CEO in five years"; such promises are an implicit contract that may be judged to be binding.

Does identifying many successors solve these problems? Surely competition among successors will ensure that the best candidate wins by trying harder and demanding better training. Furthermore, if one successor does not develop to the potential that was anticipated or quits the organization, then others are willing and ready. But this approach has problems too. One is that candidates might sabotage each other by not sharing important information or by raiding key employees to improve their own track records. As well, many might engage in managing impressions and performing for short-term results in order to be evaluated more highly. This strategy does not encourage team playing, which is a force in organizational culture.

There is no easy solution to these problems. The key is to communicate to these star employees that they are valued and that they have leadership potential, without ever promising anything. Another approach is to tell high-potential employees about their status, and then explain that they will be given a series of developmental challenges, and their potential will be continually assessed.

Any organization needs a pool of talent and must develop many employees with flexible job skills and competencies. A "pool" is a good description of the next generation of talented leadership because the term implies fluidity and responsiveness to the impact of forces. The talent pool is considered a corporate resource and is not the property of individual organizational units. This evolution from personnel planning to succession management has led to a model of generating pools of leadership talent within an organizational context of global competition, environmental turbulence, de-layered organizations, and new technologies. Talent segmentation, the identification of employees who are critical to the success of the organization, is expected to become as important as customer segmentation.[18]

Furthermore, a succession management approach should depend not only on internal candidates, but should also track external candidates. Rather than rely on inbred internal managers, the new generation of succession managers tracks high performers in the external market, thus ensuring that new skills and ideas flow into the organization. Large companies such as IBM and AT&T have recruited over half their executives from outside the organization to obtain the skills that these mega-companies were unable to predict they would need or to develop internally. HR Planning Notebook 7.3 compares the advantages and disadvantages of internal and external candidates. The list of advantages of internal candidates is more robust than for those of external candidates, and the reality is that about two-thirds of internal candidates do succeed.[19] Moreover, it appears that when a company is doing well, internal candidates are favoured to sustain high performance, because they possess valuable firm-specific knowledge.[20] But overall, it appears that companies that are performing well do better by hiring from within, and those companies that are struggling show better returns by hiring outsiders.[21] Interestingly, it appears that if the former CEO stays in the company (usually as chair of the board), this retention has a pronounced effect in preventing the new CEO from making significant changes.[22]

RATING SYSTEM

Traditional planning relied on the identification of the replacement people by a single rater. Previously, only the boss of the high-potential employee supplied information about that employee, and the information on which succession plans were based could be both out of date and unreliable. The gathering and recording of these judgments may

Advantages of Internal Candidates

- Organizations have more and better information about internal candidates.
- Organizations that offer career development and opportunities to internal candidates increase commitment and retention among their employees.
- Internally developed leaders preserve corporate culture.
- Internal candidates can hit the road running, because they know the organization, its people, and its processes. Other employees know the internal candidate, and there is less internal disruption waiting to see who the new executive is and what changes he or she will make. Internally chosen executives do not replace those who report to them as often as external candidates do; externally chosen candidates often get rid of the "old guard."

- Recruitment and selection costs are lower. For example, the replacement cost of a CEO is estimated to be $750 000, including the use of a search firm and lost opportunities getting the external candidate up to speed. Additionally, internal candidates do not have to be compensated at the higher levels demanded by external candidates (who face the risk of starting in a new organization).

Advantages of External Candidates

- The external candidate may have better skills to lead the organization through a major transformation or change in strategy.
- The external candidate brings new knowledge and skills to the organization and prevents the organization from becoming inbred and stale.

have been seen as a personnel function, which incorporated little understanding of the real needs of the organization. Thus, managers may not have bought into the process.

In a succession management approach, several raters give current evaluations on an employee's performance. The increasing use of 360° feedback mechanisms sheds light on various aspects of any candidate's style and performance. HR Planning Notebook 7.4 compares replacement planning and succession management.

A manager rates the potential of an employee.

© iStock/Thinkstock

COMPARISON OF REPLACEMENT PLANNING WITH SUCCESSION MANAGEMENT

FACTORS	PLANNING	MANAGEMENT
Environment	Stable	Dynamic
Focus	Jobs	Strategy
Time frame	6–12 months	2+ years
Selection criteria	Job experience	Competencies
Appraiser	Immediate manager	360° feedback
Selection pool	Internal	Internal and external
Successors	Slated individuals	Talent pools
Development	Limited	Flexible, multiple

SUCCESSION MANAGEMENT PROCESS

The succession management process links replacement planning and management development. Until recently, in some organizations, succession planners worked with one database, management trainers with another. Now, both databases are integrated, with succession managers working in strategic planning committees, performance management groups, and organizational learning and training functions.

The succession management process is simple to understand but difficult to implement. The process involves five steps, each of which we will now consider in some detail.

1. ALIGN SUCCESSION MANAGEMENT PLANS WITH STRATEGY

Management development must be linked to business plans and strategies. If the business plan focuses on global markets, then managers have to be trained to manage global businesses. How does this translate into everyday skills? To build global talent, an organization could start by asking these questions: What are the specialized skills and perspectives necessary to compete globally? How many managers possess these skills? What percentage of employees could represent the firm to the world? How many could have an extended dinner with key international customers?[23]

The strategic connection is important, so organizations must start with the business plan. Using this, coupled with environmental scanning, managers try to predict where the organization will be in three, five, or ten years.

2. IDENTIFY THE SKILLS AND COMPETENCIES NEEDED TO MEET STRATEGIC OBJECTIVES

From the strategic plan, managers can then develop a list of the employee skills and competencies needed. There are at least two approaches to identifying the characteristics of successful managers: the job-based approach and the competency-based approach.

JOB-BASED APPROACH The first impulse is to start with the job. We know that employees have jobs with duties and responsibilities. The job-based approach suggests that employees who have significant experience as managers, and who have acquired job skills such as motivating, delegating, marketing, or managing finances, will make successful managers.

Others suggest that this job-based approach to successors is inadequate because jobs change rapidly. Furthermore, the increase in knowledge work has led many organizations to search for a different approach to employee development, particularly for those employees at the managerial level. Therefore, many organizations are turning to a competency-based approach, in which the capabilities of individuals are the primary focus.[24]

COMPETENCY-BASED APPROACH Competencies are groups of related behaviours that are needed for successful performance.[25] A competency can comprise skills, abilities, knowledge, and personal characteristics (ability to motivate others, for example[26]). Competencies are measurable attributes that differentiate successful employees from those who are not. These competencies are a collection of observable behaviours and can be "hard" or "soft." Hard competencies might be the ability to build new technologies. Soft competencies might be the ability to retain top talent.[27] Given an uncertain future in which skill needs change rapidly, succession management should focus on the development of competencies.

Consulting firms are the perfect example of companies in which the skills and capabilities of individuals drive the business, and business opportunities drive the development of new capabilities. Thus a list of skills (rather than jobs or positions) forms the basis for succession management. Rather than moving *up* a career ladder, individuals move *through* a certification process, developing increasingly complex capabilities along the way. There may be several skill acquisition paths, rather than one sure path to the top.

A good place to start preparing a list of competencies is to look at what experts have said about the competencies of successful managers. Many lists are available that outline the kinds of generic skills and competencies managers should possess. HR Planning Notebook 7.5 presents a list of these characteristics.

The skills that managers need to possess are endless, and each "expert" develops a preferred list. These lists could be used as a starting point and then be customized to identify and develop managers in any organization. By emphasizing competencies rather than job skills, individuals will be more flexible in adapting to changing organizational needs. ("Skills" and "competencies" are terms that are often used interchangeably. However, skills are narrower and refer more specifically to skills for one job; competencies are broader and can be applied to many jobs at many levels. For example, proficiency in PowerPoint and installing Windows are skills;

the abilities to think creatively and work in teams are competencies.) Catano and his colleagues provide a full discussion of competencies; they distinguish between several types:

- *Core competencies:* Characteristics, such as thinking skills, that every member of the organization is expected to possess
- *Role or specific competencies:* Characteristics, such as business knowledge, shared by different positions within an organization
- *Unique or distinctive competencies:* Characteristics, such as expertise in media relations, that apply only to specific positions within an organization[28]

HR PLANNING NOTEBOOK 7.5

MANAGERIAL COMPETENCIES

- *General mobility skills and knowledge:* These competencies facilitate reemployment and include effectiveness in group process, communication skills, and flexibility and adaptation.
- *General managerial core competencies:* These competencies were identified by studying successful managers and include "being able to build a cohesive team" and "being able to persuade employees to accept much needed organizational changes."

- *Detailed, job-specific competencies:* Job-specific competencies vary by function, but in HR would include "the ability to implement a change program" and to "identify the best selection tool to identify high-potential candidates." These abilities would vary by level, with a junior manager mastering the ability to identify performance gaps in a subordinate and a senior manager being able to initiate change programs to improve performance.

Source: Adapted from E.H. Burach, W. Hochwarter, and N.J. Mathys, "The New Management Development Paradigm," *Human Resource Planning,* Vol. 20, No. 1 (2000), pp. 14–21.

3. IDENTIFY HIGH-POTENTIAL EMPLOYEES

After we know what competencies are needed, we can turn to the identification of employees who might ultimately acquire these sets. Regularly scheduled discussions about succession force the leaders of the organization to think about the future of the business and the kinds of employee skills needed to facilitate the chosen strategy. By concerning themselves with the future directions of the organization, executives focus on the managers who will guide that future. The performance appraisal process becomes meaningful and not just another personnel form to complete. Executives come to "own" the succession and development plans, because they are integral to the success of the organization.

In HR, we often state that the best predictor of future performance is past performance. Executives must be able to move beyond descriptions of high-potential employees that use descriptions such as "She is very bright and very strategic" and "He has the support of his team" to listing specific achievements.[29]

Organizations use several approaches to identify managerial talent, including the following:[30*]

1. *Temporary replacements:* At the most primitive level, most individual managers will have identified a designated backup and potential successor. This is done in case the manager is away from the office for extended periods (e.g., vacations, training). A manager who fails to pick a successor may never be promoted, as no replacements would be ready to succeed him or her.

2. *Replacement charts:* At the next level, some organizations prepare replacement charts with predicted departure dates of the incumbents, along with a shortlist of possible successors. This is usually done around performance appraisal time, using the performance evaluation data. Typically, a handful of senior executives targets a diverse list of employees for growth and creates annual development plans. These executives stay in touch with each individual assigned to them and become responsible for the development of the leadership competencies of those individuals. The list identifies those candidates who are ready now, those who will be ready in three to five years, and the long shots. These approaches tend to replicate current strengths (and weaknesses) and are not necessarily future oriented, nor are they strategically aligned with the needs of the business. This stair-step approach is too rigid during times when organizational structures are changing rapidly and employee loyalty is weak.

3. *Strategic replacement:* A more advanced succession management program exists in an organization that is less inclined simply to replicate existing incumbents, but instead identifies the leadership competencies it needs, on the basis of organizational plans. The organization then tries to support and train these managers from within. The identification of high-potential people moves beyond the evaluations conducted by one or two managers. The Public Service Commission of Canada, for example, uses a formal assessment centre to identify those public servants who will become the future executives in the federal public service. Wary of evaluations done by only one individual with one perspective on employee performance, many organizations are moving to a 360° evaluation. For many employees, such an evaluation is the first time they have received feedback on how others perceive them. Some employees have likened the experience to holding up a mirror, others to a breath of fresh air.[31] Employees who had undergone 360° feedback reported that they felt their peers often knew better than their managers how to improve their performance.

The above three systems favour the selection of internal candidates. As a result, these systems have a motivating impact on employee performance. However, they are limited in their ability to introduce new ways of thinking and working, and may not suit the strategic direction of the organization. In the next approach, the managers more actively scan the environment to identify and retain top talent.

4. *Talent management culture:* Many organizations, whose CEOs lie awake at night worrying about their ability to find and keep top talent, have adopted a talent management culture.[32] The winners in the war for talent have developed a talent mindset—that is, they believe that talent matters and it must be developed not only at the top level but also at all levels. Managers are committed to define and model an employee value proposition that answers the question, "Why would a talented person want to work here?" The employee "brand" is

---

* Joinson, C. 1998. "Developing a Strong Bench," *HRM Magazine* (January): 92–96.

managed as much as the company brand. The organization wants its reputation (i.e., its brand) to be one where current and future employees believe that it is a great place to work based on attributes that candidates' desire. See HR Planning Today 7.1 for a discussion of brand positioning to attract and retain employees. Organizations with employer brands outperformed others in three critical areas: revenue, net income and share price.[33] Managers actively scan the environment (e.g., for the actions of their competitors or the actions of the world's best industry leaders in other areas with overlapping functions, such as finance or logistics) looking for external talent. They have developed both internal and external lists of high-potential candidates.[34]

Those with a talent management culture use conferences to identify top talent.

© Jacobs Stock Photography/Getty

Recruitment is opportunistic—that is, when a top candidate is found, that person is hired regardless of whether there is a vacancy. For example, MDS is so interested in securing talent that it will hire even when no position is open, and make that person an "executive-in-residence" and give him or her a special project to manage until a vacancy arises.[35] As David Guptil, vice-president of HR for Lafarge Canada, a large supplier of construction materials, states:

> *What keeps me awake at night is my very thin bench strength. … We are resisting that temptation to scale back on strategic recruiting. And when I say strategic recruiting, what I mean is that you don't wait for a vacancy and the predicted retirees. I and our senior managers are always on the lookout for talent that may be available. If I find a very talented person … my freedom is to go out and hire that person whether we have a vacancy or not.[36]*

The process of continually searching for talent is correlated with success. A McKinsey study found that nearly one-third of HR directors at top-performing companies constantly search for talented executives, contrasted with less than 10 percent at average-performing companies.[37] These talent management companies analyze turnover statistics and always include in their reports the reasons for the voluntary turnover. Managers, not HR, have the responsibility for identifying and cultivating talent.

Finally, some companies operate with all four approaches, using replacement planning for highly predictable jobs such as accounting, and talent management to deal with rapid changes in strategic needs.

Assessing employees to identify high-potential candidates must be done both fairly and accurately: fairly so that employees buy into the process and feel that the search for talent is an equitable procedure, and accurately so that the selection process is both reliable and valid. Organizations typically use the direct supervisor's informal judgments and formal evaluations such as performance appraisals and assessment centres. (More information can be found in the performance evaluation chapter of any introductory HRM text.) Caterpillar's annual talent assessment includes the employee's manager, the business unit manager, and the executive office. The discussion centres on the employee's next three moves and the kinds of career experiences needed for these moves.[38] HR Planning Notebook 7.6 contains a brief description of common assessment methods. Usually about 10 percent of employees are identified as high potential. Syncrude Canada Ltd., an oil producer, with headquarters in Fort McMurray, Alberta, has identified about 8 percent of its 3600 employees as high potential.[39]

However, the use of annual reviews of talent can result in a mechanical approach leading to the goal of completing the forms provided by HR, rather than quality dialogues about leaders. Some managers simply update forms to meet a deadline. A better process would be to commit to quarterly reviews and the allocation of one full day to choose the top candidates by ranking them against all other candidates. Even these discussions can become politicized when:

- Executives rate their own candidates too positively
- People are hesitant to criticize the choices of others
- Members distrust the motivation of others' recommendations ("passing the trash")
- Running conflicts between executives result in cheap shots about candidates
- Information about the best players is withheld as executives want to own this talent

- *Performance appraisals:* Managers identify high-potential employees through performance appraisal systems. Raters, who may include the supervisor, colleagues, customers, and subordinates of an employee, evaluate the employee against some pre-developed standards. The goal is to identify and communicate the employee's performance strengths and weaknesses. The information is then used for developmental purposes so that gaps in performance can be closed. High-potential employees are tracked in this way using a standardized organizational assessment tool. Managers are forced to identify high-potential employees through performance appraisal systems and may be rewarded for developing employees.

- *Assessment centres:* Assessment centres involve a process by which candidates are evaluated as they participate in a series of exercises that closely resemble the situations faced on the job. Simulations include negotiating a merger, handling the press, managing interdepartmental conflicts, or making a decision without all the facts.

Trained and experienced managers observe the candidates' behaviour during this process and provide an evaluation of their competence and potential. The newest form of assessment centre is the acceleration centre, in which the first stop is a website where candidates learn about the fictitious company they will manage for a day. All testing, correspondence, and decisions are completed online, enabling the assessors to compare candidates more objectively.

- *Human Resources Management Systems (HRMS):* Large amounts of information about employees' KSAOs can be stored in databanks and used to identify employees with needed skills. Employees' files can document their experiences, skills, abilities, and performance evaluations. Employees' interests and career objectives may also be recorded. Basic matching to identify high-potential candidates is simplified with an effective HRMS. A useful feature of an HRMS is its ability to construct scenarios. Planners can create "what if?" models to determine the effect of employee movements.

To minimize the politics involved in identifying talent, management should develop a set of principles such as "Talent is managed in the larger interests of the company. Managers are simply stewards of this talent, and companywide interests prevail."[40]

4. PROVIDE DEVELOPMENTAL OPPORTUNITIES AND EXPERIENCES

Before we discuss the methods used to develop managers, we should first consider two issues:

- Are leaders born or made?
- Should organizations produce their own managerial talent or buy it on the open market?

Born or made? Many great leaders have had no formal management training. Shouldn't we just select leaders with the inherent qualities of leaders and not try to teach leadership skills?

Peter Drucker, considered by many to be the founder of management as a discipline, is credited with saying, "*Most managers are made, not born. There has to be systematic work on the supply, the development, and the skills of tomorrow's management. It cannot be left to chance.*"[41]

Buy or make? Organizations invest many dollars and other resources to develop managers, but perhaps experienced, trained managers could simply be hired from other organizations.

Some organizations do prefer to pick up their needed executive talent by buying it on the open market. For example, Elliot Whale, president and CEO of Dylex Ltd., had been president of Toys "R" Us (Canada) and director of player personnel for the Toronto Blue Jays baseball club before he moved to Dylex. Selecting outsiders allows companies to bring in fresh perspectives, people who can lead the organization through a transformation. By bringing in an outsider, the board of directors sends a strong message to employees and shareholders that the old way of doing things is going to change.[42] Other organizations feel strongly that they want to indoctrinate and train their own leaders, who then have a deep commitment to the organizational vision.

There are no easy answers to these questions. Organizations may find outstanding leaders by chance, or they may commit to the development process. Some may choose to hire from the outside to obtain fresh approaches; others will commit significant time and money to train their own managers. However, most large organizations have a policy of promotion from within. There are many advantages to this: the organization has accurate records of employees' past performance, and employees understand and are committed to organizational objectives, know the ropes, and know how to get things done. Another reason to recruit internally is that CEOs recruited from the outside delivered annual returns 3.7 percent lower than insiders.[43] Most large organizations have formal management development programs to ensure a ready supply of "promotables." Let us look at some of the methods such organizations use.

MANAGEMENT DEVELOPMENT METHODS In the succession management process, the focus in management development is on the development of competencies, not just on job preparation. Because the goal is to develop many skills that may be needed in an uncertain future (in contrast to simply replicating the skills of the present incumbents), management is much more open to various approaches to develop the talent pool. More traditional approaches might have relied on a senior leadership course and one developmental assignment, perhaps mimicking exactly what the current CEO did. The key point is that the approach has changed from one of providing training to fill jobs to one of providing experiences to realize leadership potential. The most common development methods are promotions, job rotations, special assignments and action learning, formal training and development, and mentoring and coaching.

PROMOTIONS A promotion refers to an employee's upward advancement in the hierarchy of an organization and usually involves increased responsibilities and compensation. Traditional models of management development saw managers moving up a pyramid, managing larger and larger units until they reached their appointments at the top. Each organization had its favourite route to the top, some through sales, others through operations. These paths became worn over time, and few succeeded by using other paths, such as an HR track. One organization used a system of temporary rotations, resulting in a win–win combination. Senior executives nearing retirement were given the option of a week's vacation in every month, which they welcomed, and were replaced by high-potential employees who could try new leadership skills in a safe setting. In flat organizations, where promotions are rare, a preferred developmental method is job rotations—developing managers horizontally rather than vertically.

> **Promotion**
> An employee's upward advancement in the hierarchy of an organization

JOB ROTATIONS **Job rotations** are lateral transfers of employees between jobs in an organization. Rotations involve a change in job assignments but not necessarily more responsibility or money. For example, one way of orienting a new employee quickly is to place him or her in a new department every few weeks, providing an overview of the organization. The CEO of Maritime Life Insurance believes that rotation is the best indicator of whether an employee is ready for a top position. To avoid costly placement decisions, staff with potential are placed in a variety of roles across the organization. Succeeding at rotation is a prerequisite for a top-level position.[44]

Rotations have several motivational benefits for employees, including the reduction of boredom and fatigue. Trying out new jobs also benefits employees who have reached a career plateau. The development of additional skills may increase an employee's job and career prospects. Almost all the research suggests that job rotation makes employees more satisfied, motivated, involved, and committed.[45]

From the organization's standpoint, rotations are useful for orientation and career development. Rotations allow an employee to increase his or her experience. A common use of job rotation is to take a functional specialist, such as an accountant, and rotate this specialist through both HR and operations in preparation for management positions. An information technology specialist, before a rotation in sales, might try to sell his idea to management by saying, "We have to invest in a multiprotocol router," and might be met with complete incomprehension. After a rotation through the sales department, the same specialist might sell the same program by explaining, "We're building an infrastructure so that salespeople can access product or inventory information from anywhere." The technician has learned a business skill.[46] Jet Form, an Ottawa-based business with about 650 employees, uses cross-functional mobility as a key part of its strategic planning.[47] The results are encouraging, and employees are regularly rotated between functions to increase their knowledge and skills.

Besides the additional knowledge of the functional areas, such as sales, and management areas, such as business knowledge, the rotated employee is making contacts and establishing a network that might prove useful in the future. Learning new ways of doing things, with different co-workers and bosses, also might make employees more adaptable in their managerial jobs. The research shows that rotation improves an employee's knowledge of the organization (e.g., of business, strategy, and contacts) and improves his or her ability to cope with uncertainty. Furthermore, employees who have tried out several jobs gain a better insight into their own strengths and weaknesses. However, job rotation produces generalists and should be supplemented by training for any specific skills needed.

Of course, the downside of employee rotations includes the increased time needed to learn the new jobs, the cost of errors while learning, and the loss of efficiency that otherwise is gained through repetition and specialization.[48] In other words, workload may increase for the employee while productivity decreases, and other employees absorb additional work and stress in efforts to socialize, orient, and train the newcomer.

At the managerial level, employers should be concerned about producing a short-term orientation in the organization's leadership ranks. Employees in six-month jobs may put their efforts into creating fast results, which might hurt the unit in the long term. For example, employees with a short-run focus may neglect plant safety in a rush to exceed production quotas. Furthermore, the rotation of managers places new expectations on performance, creates new goals, and results in reassignment of work, producing stress on the unit managed by rotation.[49]

One approach is to give an employee a number of assignments within the company or a related sector. Ultimately, managers may be better formed by developing skills horizontally, throughout an organization, rather than by developing specialized skills vertically, up a career ladder.

SPECIAL ASSIGNMENTS AND ACTION LEARNING On-the-job learning is still a favoured path to the development of managerial skills. Most organizations test high-potential employees by giving them an assignment in addition to their regular duties. For example, the manager of corporate banking might be placed on a task force that is considering the acquisition of another bank. A manager who needs international experience might be sent to work in China with a vendor to the company. In another case, a team of managers might be given a special assignment, such as developing an equity plan for the organization or developing an e-commerce plan for the company. These types of special projects enable candidates for future executive positions to network and test their skills in new environments. Mistakes must be tolerated, as candidates may quickly assume that these special assignments are synonymous with failure, fostering a culture of fear in which no employee dare be innovative or take bold measures, and, finally, derailment from the fast track. Recognizing the value of experience, even negative ones, is important. For example, there is a story about the executive called into his boss's office expecting to be fired because of a business decision that cost the company a million dollars. The CEO instead gives him another special assignment, reasoning, "Why should we fire you? We just invested $1 million in your development." Interviewers for executive positions routinely ask candidates about a difficult challenge or unsuccessful project. If the candidates indicate no failures, the executive search firm concludes that the candidate is not open about these experiences, or he or she may not have the skills to handle an unsuccessful project in the next assignment. The best assignments are those that entail a high degree of risk and accountability, such as launching a new business or turning around a struggling project. If these are coupled with decision-making authority and the opportunity to manage a large group of people, this is the recipe for producing effective executives.

FORMAL TRAINING AND DEVELOPMENT Management training and education is big business. Hundreds of thousands of dollars may be spent preparing one executive to become the CEO of the organization. This cost appears relatively minor when it is estimated that the total career investment in an individual employee is 160 times the initial starting salary.[50] In this book, we use the term *management development*, but others label a similar process *executive education* or *leadership training* or a combination of any of these words.

The majority of companies use traditional and passive instructional techniques and rate them least effective, but they are fast and easy to use. Most use lectures, seminars, and discussion groups more often than behaviour modelling and experiential learning.[51] Senior managers need the soft skills of delegation and motivation, rather than hard technical skills such as website development or benefits management. Thus we would recommend that role-playing, case studies, behaviour modelling, and action learning, which are effective techniques, be used as training methods for management development. Through case studies and action learning, the courses offer managers a chance to practise and receive feedback. Unlike professional athletes or musicians, managers seldom get a chance to practise their skills and try out new ideas and methods.

MENTORING AND COACHING Many very successful managers explain that their successes resulted directly from having been mentored: A senior executive took an interest in them and their careers at a critical time in their lives. **Mentors** are executives who coach, advise, and encourage junior employees. The mentor takes an active interest in the career advancement and the psychosocial development of the protégé. Career development aspects include examining approaches to assignments and learning how tasks should be handled, which conferences or networks have high career value, and which senior managers to emulate. Psychosocial considerations include building the self-confidence of the protégé, as well as offering counselling and friendship to make him or her aware of the political open doors and open pits of the organization. Studies show that protégés do indeed derive these psychosocial benefits (increased confidence, self-esteem, reduced feelings of isolation etc.) as well as career benefits (increased compensation, promotions, career development opportunities, etc.).[52] One company offers coaching to help high-potential candidates understand the executive derailers—those personality traits that might cause an otherwise effective executive to fail (such as arrogance, micromanagement, risk aversion, volatility, and low tolerance for ambiguity).[53]

Mentoring used to happen informally, but organizations have recognized the value of having a senior manager take a career interest in a junior employee and so have started formal mentoring programs. One survey showed that 70 percent of highly productive organizations have mentoring programs, and employees in these programs report greater career satisfaction and experience faster career growth.[54] These programs link executives who have the motivation and time to nurture managerial talent with employees who are motivated to advance quickly. Two-thirds of the top-performing companies provide high-potential employees with frequent access to the CEO, and opportunities to interact on projects with senior managers.[55] Mentors are almost always more senior people who volunteer within an organization, while coaches tend to be paid counsellors from outside the organization. Internal mentors are best for strengthening and assuring continuity of organizational culture.[56] The advantages of external coaches are described in HR Planning Notebook 7.7. Closely related to mentoring is sponsorship. In one study of the careers of CFOs, many described the importance of a sponsor, a manager who provided a critical opportunity on the career journey.[57]

While it is necessary for discussion purposes to separate management development methods, all companies will use a combination of methods. Some focus on formal programs, such as a three-week leadership course followed by an assignment in a foreign country. Other companies, such as 3M, allow their employees to choose assignments and to work on ad hoc committees to manage new projects, as well as giving them free time to tinker and play with ideas. Cisco, a leader in hardware and software technology, uses the 3E Model: 70 percent of development occurs through Experience (assignments, rotations, special projects), 20 percent through Exposure (feedback, mentoring, and shadowing), and 10 percent through Education (readings, e-learning, and courses).[58] The choice of a method depends on the employee's learning style and the goals to be achieved. Learning about foreign cultures is best done by spending time in a foreign office or with representatives from overseas, not from a book; nor is shadowing an IT employee the best way to learn about IT.

Table 7.1 outlines the most common leader development activities, and how HR managers rate their effectiveness.

Some companies follow these processes but press the fast-forward button for candidates to intentionally accelerate their development. These candidates are part of an acceleration pool and

- Obtain assignments that offer the most intense learning and high visibility
- Spend less time in assignments
- Are given stretch assignments
- Receive more training
- Are given developmental activities designed especially for them
- Are assigned a mentor
- Are not guaranteed promotion[59]

Companies that do this well are called "academy companies"–a kind of executive finishing school–known for breeding the best leaders. In Canada, these incubators are PepsiCo, IBM, General Electric, Procter & Gamble, Petro-Canada, and Manulife Financial.[60] Headhunters go to these companies to poach new leadership blood. These top companies for leaders offer many benefits, as outlined in HR Planning Notebook 7.8. Does this mean that companies risk losing leaders if they invest in them? Not necessarily, according to research by Canadian professors Jack Ito and Celeste Brotheridge, who concluded that supervisory support for career development strengthens employee's intentions to stay.[61] Generally, providing opportunities to grow and develop new skills is seen as a good retention tool.

ACADEMY COMPANIES

Academy companies offer these experiences to become top companies for leaders:

- Working abroad/international experiences
- 360° feedback to assess and critique leadership attributes, skills, and traits
- Assessment centre solely for leadership development of high potentials
- Mentor with admired senior leader
- Rotational job assignments

- Spending 10 percent to 24 percent of top leadership's time on talent management issues
- Organization has special/different career development process to retain high potentials
- Organization prepares specific development plans for high potentials
- Organization makes lateral moves attractive to high potentials

Source: Donlon, J.P. "Best Companies for Leaders," *Chief Executive*, December 2007, 230, 58–62.

TABLE 7.1

USE AND EFFECTIVENESS OF LEADER DEVELOPMENT ACTIVITIES

USE	% VERY EFFECTIVE	% MODERATE OR EXTENSIVE USE
Special projects within one's own job responsibilities	77	69
Special projects outside one's own job responsibilities	46	55
Expatriate assignments	26	54
Coaching with internal coaches or mentors	48	45
Formal workshops	85	42
Coaching with external coaches or mentors	28	42
Articles/books	65	27
Tests, assessments, or other measures of skills	52	26
Computer-based learning	38	16

Notes: Leaders rated effectiveness; HR professionals rated usage; table made from bar graph.

Source: Bernthal, P. & Wellins, R. 2006 "Trends in Leader Development and Succession," *Human Resource Planning*, Vol. 20, Issue 2, page 35.

Another reason for using different methods is that the development of a senior executive may take 25 years. It is unusual to see a vice-president of a large company who is younger than 40 years old. So some companies, such as Walmart, start early, grooming the store managers under a mentoring system to take on more and more responsibility.

5. MONITOR SUCCESSION MANAGEMENT

Some succession plans are placed on an executive's top shelf, ready to be dusted off to prepare for the annual discussion. They do not form part of a strategic plan, nor are they used to guide employee development. To measure the effectiveness of succession management, succession planners used to count the number of predicted "high-potential replacements" with the actual number of those placed in the position. However, if the needs of the business change dramatically, this may be a poor way of measuring. Others suggest measures such as:

- Increased engagement scores
- Increased positive perceptions of development opportunities
- High-potential employees' perceptions of the succession management process
- Higher participation in developmental activities
- Greater numbers involved in the mentoring process[62]

Nevertheless, there are internal ways to judge whether a succession management program is successful, including HR metrics, which may be viewed as lag measures such as:

- Increased average number of candidates for key positions
- Reduced average number of positions having no identified successors
- Increased percentage of managers with replacement plans
- Increased percentage of key positions filled according to plans
- Increased ratio of internal hires to external hires in key positions
- Increased retention rates of key talent
- Increased percentage of positive job evaluations after promotion
- More positive assessment of the quality of preparedness for new roles
- Increased number of bosses as talent developers[63]

The above measures need benchmarks, perhaps simply improvements over the previous year for the organization. Benchmarks will emerge for these measures. For example, one benchmarking organization suggests that effective organizations have 1.6 candidates for each key role.[64] However, one study found that the single most important driver of an effective plan was that the executive team modelled the behaviour, believed in it, and held managers accountable (in performance reviews and bonuses) for developing employees. Top-performing companies allocate 20 percent of executive bonuses to leadership development and assess them on the ability to retain this talent.[65]

One expert asked, "If this process worked perfectly and everything happened the way it was supposed to happen, what would the results look like?"[66] The answer? Employees would receive regular feedback based on the assessment process and would participate in development plans. The best result would be an organization with skilled employees prepared to contribute to the goals of the organization under changing conditions. Organizations measure their success not only by the percentage of positions filled by designated high-potential employees but also by attitude surveys of these employees, as well as exit interviews if these high potentials leave the organization. The word "success" in succession is illuminating in that studies are starting to show that corporations with strong succession management programs are higher performers measured by revenue growth, profitability, and market share.[67]

Another international study surveyed thousands of leaders, employees, and HR staff from 117 organizations in 14 countries and identified the following characteristics as critical to perceptions of succession management effectiveness:

- A timeframe for achieving planned action
- Flexible adjustments to changes in strategic plans
- The sharing of information about the nomination process performance and rankings with identified candidates
- Visible support from top management
- The involvement of line management in the identification and development of candidates.[68]

So far, we have examined succession management from the organizational perspective. We will now consider the employee's perspective.

An employee has a responsibility to update her skills as part of her own career planning.

EMPLOYEE ROLE IN SUCCESSION MANAGEMENT A top-down, organization-directed approach to succession management assumes that employees are ready and willing to be prepared for the next generation of leadership. A top-down approach treats employees as pieces in a chess game. But employees are not pawns; their voices need to be heard.

The first consideration is that an employee's relationship with any organization is not permanent. The employee can quit, or the employer can terminate him or her. Today's new employment contract does not guarantee jobs to anyone, even to those performing competently. The former contract was built on an implied promise of a long-term, mutually satisfying relationship. However, market forces create turbulence that sometimes causes companies to restructure or fail. These changes have resulted in a change in the psychological contract that an employee has with the employer. The traditional employment contract with the organization was built on an implicit understanding that the employee would work hard, would develop additional skills provided mainly by the employer, and, in return, would be promoted on a regular basis. At a minimum, the employer would reward the loyalty and efforts of employees with job security. This contract is dead. Today's career model may be perceived as a transactional one in which benefits and contributions are exchanged for a short period.[69] The new contract, transactional in nature, lists the responsibilities and rights of each party in the employer–employee relationship, and employees want this contract stated explicitly in writing. If loyalty to any organization still exists, it is to the professional organization, to a network of peers, and to certifiable credibility that confers collegiality and respect. HR Planning Notebook 7.9 contains a comparison of the two concepts of career management.

This transactional view of employer–employee relationships suggests that as organizations develop employees, they must take into consideration employee aspirations and goals. Employees will participate in management development programs more eagerly if their goals match the succession plans of the company. Employees will enthusiastically engage in self-development if they are aware of the strategic goals of a company, thus enhancing their own job security or marketability. If, for example, employees of *The Globe and Mail* knew

COMPARING TRADITIONAL AND EMERGING CAREER MANAGEMENT CONCEPTS

CHARACTERISTICS	TRADITIONAL	EMERGING
Employment contract	Implicit	Explicit
Duration	Long term	Useful term
Career responsibility	Employer	Self-directed
Career identity	Organization	Profession/occupation
Benefits	Focus on security	Focus on experience
Loyalty	To the organization	Profession, friends, family
Mindset	Inward, political	Outward, entrepreneurial
Development	Formal training	Work experiences
Career progression	Vertical	Horizontal
Employment stability	Job security	Employability
Role of manager	Control/coordination	Coach
Career goal	Corporate success	Meaningful contributions

Sources: Adapted from D. Hall and J.E. Moss, "The New Protean Career Contract: Helping Organizations and Employees Adapt," *Organization Dynamics*, Winter 1988, pp. 22–37; E.F. Craig and D.T. Hall, "The New Organizational Career: Too Important to Be Left to HR?" *Reinventing HRM: Challenges and New Directions*, R.J. Burke and C.L. Cooper, eds. (New York: Routledge, 2005).

that the company was changing from a newspaper publishing business to an international information marketing business, employees would likely undertake, on their own time and at their own expense, to study languages or marketing. Managerial preferences cannot be the sole determinant in employee development. Career counselling and discussions at performance appraisal time will help ensure that the employee's voice is heard. While organizations cannot promise lifetime employment, competition for leadership talent is so intense that high-potential employees must be given a reason to stay with an organization.

An added benefit of listening to employees is the opportunity to customize the development plan. Employees are very aware of their strengths and weaknesses and their preferred learning styles. One employee might suggest that she could learn decision making by being given a leadership role; another might prefer a seminar on decision making. Some organizations, such as Ford Financial, which has 20 000 employees around the world, provide information to employees that enable them to make their own career plans. Ford Financial has a sophisticated skill and competency-based learning program with direct links to the company's three core businesses and job requirements. Employees can determine the skills and competencies needed for any job within the organization, then undertake a self-development plan to master any of the 15 knowledge domains, 80 functional areas, and 800 separate skills.[70]

By creating a process that invites employee participation, succession managers are more likely to gain employee commitment to and ownership of the plans. We turn now to a discussion of the role of HR in this process.

MANAGING TALENT: THE HR ROLE Most researchers and consultants will argue that the CEO should own the succession management function, and that HR should simply provide some tools for doing so. But HR are professionals and know more about succession management best practices (and pitfalls) than CEOs do. HR should own the talent management process in order to mitigate three types of risk to an organization:

1. *Vacancy risk:* Organizations that are unable to fill key vacant positions quickly with effective leaders may suffer business losses and/or an inability to move forward on strategic goals.

2. *Readiness risk:* HR must develop employees so that when opportunities arise, there are qualified and motivated personnel in place.

3. *Transition risk:* In addition to preparing employees for key roles, HR must develop programs to retain key employees, and to monitor competitors and others to be able to quickly identify external candidates.[71]

In order to manage these risks, HR promotes a culture of talent management, develops successors for all key positions, identifies gaps between current competencies and those needed in the future, and encourages development at all levels.

// SUMMARY

In this chapter, we defined succession management and contrasted it with personnel planning. The five-step model of effective succession management includes these steps: (1) align succession management plans with strategy; (2) identify the skills and competencies needed to meet strategic objectives; (3) identify high-potential employees; (4) provide developmental opportunities and experiences through promotions, job rotations, special assignments and action learning, formal training and development, and mentoring and coaching; and (5) monitor succession management. The employee's role in the process must be considered. The HR function has to assume responsibility for the succession management process.

KEY TERMS

job rotations p. 176
mentors p. 178
promotion p. 175
replacement planning p. 164
succession management p. 162

WEB LINKS

HR Council.ca provides a toolkit for succession planning
http://hrcouncil.ca/hr-toolkit/planning-succession.cfm

The Government of New Brunswick publishes a succession planning overview.
http://www2.gnb.ca/content/gnb/en/departments/human_resources/career_devel-opment/content/succession_planning/overview.html

DISCUSSION QUESTIONS

1. Ganong Bros., a manufacturer of candy and chocolates, is based in St. Stephen, New Brunswick. In 2008, for the first time in its 135-year history, an outsider succeeded a member of the Ganong family as president of the company. (Two children who work in the business were deemed "not ready.") This decision is a result of two years of succession planning by the Ganong board, which is dominated by outsiders. What are the advantages and limitations of choosing an outsider to head the company?

2. About half of all Canadian companies offer paid leave to volunteer, ranging from one day to two weeks annually. According to Mario Paron, KPMG's chief HR officer, "Employees return with a fresh perspective—new skills learned in a non-traditional environment and learning and sensitivity in dealing with people from different backgrounds, that is invaluable when they return to work."[72] Do you think that volunteering is a good management developmental tool? Why or why not?

3. This chapter has focused mainly on managers, implying that they are the key talent that needs to be managed. However, there are people who believe that the organization's most critical employees are not those who make the highest salary, but those who have the most impact on the customer: for example, the couriers at FedEx and the street sweepers at Walt Disney World. Describe why these people should be considered key talent, and what succession management plans could be used for them.

EXERCISES

Consider the following three scenarios:

1. Lee Ki Chung managed all the operating systems for 8 Star Manufacturing Company. Always reliable and never absent, Lee was indispensable. One day, Lee phoned to say that he had been diagnosed with cancer, had to enter treatment immediately, and did not know when he would return to the office.

2. The president of Overseas Banking Corporation, the second-largest bank in the country, had chosen as his successor the vice-president of finance. However, as the president's retirement date approached, he began to worry that this star employee could no longer handle the stress and long hours of banking. The VP was absent for extended periods as he tried to deal with his son, who was a drug addict, which in turn caused problems in his marriage.

3. Hi Tech Corp is a company created by the next generation of Bill Gates clones. They had succeeded in attracting the best and brightest to help them build a billion-dollar company to develop the ultimate software applications. On Tuesday, October 10, the entire design team announced they were quitting to start a rival company and recapture that entrepreneurial culture of the early years.

Could succession management have mitigated the impact on the organization of any of these situations? How could succession management mitigate the seriousness of the consequences?

The North American automotive industry has been facing significant challenges in recent years as the "Big Three" restructure their operations to respond to increased foreign competition, difficult economic conditions, and shifting demand as consumers migrate toward more fuel-efficient vehicles. In light of these dynamic business conditions, Ford of Canada relies heavily on organization and personnel planning processes and tools to ensure that the organization structure, internal selection practices, and succession management systems are aligned to support the future needs of the firm and the needs of its employees. With a strategic focus on maintaining a "People Development Framework," succession planning is a key element of the organization and personnel planning function.

The HR team reviews four major areas of focus in order to make better decisions about the organization's future direction for personnel requirements. In addition to assessing the impact of external factors such as world events, the changing marketplace, and workforce demographics, team members regularly review the operational plans in place so that functional HR objectives and action plans are properly developed and aligned to meet the long-term goals of the business. Ongoing reviews of the organization structures are conducted to ensure that the delivery of the organization's business priorities is achieved in an efficient, flexible, and affordable manner by assessing factors such as the size of the organization, the percentage of resources deployed at each level and function, and the attraction and retention potential of the leadership level and salary grade system. Lastly and most importantly, the "people equation" is evaluated on an ongoing basis to ensure that the organization has the right people in the right positions at the right time to help the organization achieve success.

Personnel development committees (PDCs) play a central role within Ford of Canada to identify and match employee capabilities to key positions to ensure appropriate bench strength is in place. Committees exist for three broad levels of the organization including senior executive, business unit management, and line management, and PDC composition includes managers from all functional business areas to ensure cross-functional opportunities can be efficiently explored and utilized for employee development. In conjunction with department managers, PDC members are charged with the responsibility of identifying employees who demonstrate outstanding leadership abilities, strong and continual learning, and superior job performance, and then matching employees to key positions.

PDCs assess candidate bench strength for particular key positions or job families using a visual aid called a "T" chart. Employees immediately qualified are plotted on the horizontal section of the "T" while employees with future potential who require further development are identified in rank order in the vertical region of the tool. Using a graphic aid such as a "T" chart allows review committees and managers to see and compare bench depth across key positions; it further assists in the communication process as succession planning information moves vertically to other PDCs as vacancies are being filled or when bench strength is being assessed.

An integral component of the People Development Framework is the engagement and participation of the individual employee in his or her own professional development and career management. With consultation from their immediate supervisors, employees are engaged in the process through the completion of a Leadership Development Employee Profile (LDEP) and an Individual Development Plan (IDP) on an annual basis. The LDEP acts as an internal résumé to capture individual employee information for PDC or hiring manager review that includes current position details, previous Ford position history, the employee's viewpoint on Ford, and non-Ford key accomplishments, as well as preferred developmental assignments.

The IDP reinforces the need for each employee to invest in his or her own professional development and provides an opportunity for career planning activities to further develop strengths and areas of improvement in alignment with career goals and business needs. Plans are developed between an employee and supervisor that identify developmental actions that improve current assignment performance and also position the individual for his or her desired future assignments. While partnership with the supervisor is necessary for establishing the content and implementation timing of an IDP, it is inherently critical that employees take personal ownership of the formation and maintenance of their own career plans for this tool to be successful.

As Ford of Canada business units strive to "do more with less" in a manner that delivers an efficient, profitable, and competitive position, an assessment of key position requirements and employee leadership and technical competencies is critical to ensure that employee developmental needs and placements support the delivery of the desired business outcomes. The process tools and governance structure under the People Development Framework serves to reinforce the inherent linkage and shared responsibility between employee, manager, and PDCs in the success of the organization and of individual employees.

Source: Case prepared by Ron Derhodge, Human Resources Manager, Parts Distribution Centre, Ford Motor Company of Canada, Limited.

QUESTION

Analyze the effectiveness of Ford's succession management program. Include in your report the strengths and weaknesses of the model and suggestions for increasing its effectiveness.

EXECUTIVE SUCCESSION MANAGEMENT PROGRAM AT EMEND MANAGEMENT CONSULTING

When company executives and boards need advisory services on succession, they sometimes seek external support, from consulting firms such as EMEND. Ellie Maggio, CEO and Managing Director of EMEND, describes the necessary transformed interest of Boards and executives in succession planning:

Over the past decade, succession plans have really become important due to CEO departures leaving organizations scrambling. Moreover, heightened board governance and regulatory compliance have raised the bar on this important function. If succession plans are not implemented, shareholders may view their investment at risk.

At EMEND, when working with boards, a six-step process is used in developing executive succession management programs:

1. PLAN

- Determine or clarify CEO and board expectations of the succession management process
- Ensure top-level responsibility/accountability
- Ensure plan is business oriented, pragmatic, and endorsed at the highest levels

2. ASSESS

- Review executive contracts for content related to succession plans and how they may relate to development plans, performance plans, compensation plans, termination, retirement, organization departure, and transition
- Review existing replacement plans, performance reviews, talent/high potential/development plans

3. STRATEGIZE

- Engage executives in the development of the new/refined program
- Ensure clear linkages to other programs related to risk management, talent management, performance management, and compensation programs
- Ensure the succession management method and process is reflective of stakeholder requirements

4. DEVELOP

- Create talent review criteria/competency models for executive and critical jobs
- Develop talent review tool(s) linked to the leadership development program, performance management process, and executive compensation
- Develop talent review process steps and timeline for implementation

5. IMPLEMENT

- Conduct talent reviews (e.g., 180°/360° assessments)
- Analyze talent reviews and link findings to criteria/competency models
- Facilitate the process by using an electronic "talent skills inventory"
- Communicate succession plans and ensure internal and external transparency
- Educate/train decision makers

6. TRACK AND MEASURE

- Develop metrics to measure success of the new program. Metrics may include but are not limited to:
  - Quality/readiness of potential leaders
  - Number of vacancies
  - Success rate of new executives
  - Executive assessment of new plan
  - Identification of potential leaders
  - Response and completion rate of plans
  - Ratings from employee satisfaction surveys
- Track success and make enhancements as required

Source: Correspondence with Ellie Maggio, CEO and Managing Director, EMEND Management, June 2011.

QUESTIONS

1. What steps might you include or remove from this process?
2. What additional techniques might be used to assess talent?
3. How would this process apply to non-executive succession planning?

// REFERENCES

1. Ruiz, G. "Edwards Lifesciences: Optimas Award Winner for Competitive Advantage," http://www.workforce.com, retrieved October 13, 2008.

2. Stadler, K. 2011. "Talent Reviews: The Key to Effective Succession Management." *Business Strategy Series*, 12.5, 264–271.

3. Conlon, R. and R.V. Smith. 2010. "The Role of the Board and the CEO in Ensuring Business Continuity." *Financial Executive*, Vol. 26, No. 9: 52–55.

4. Paradise, A. 2010. "Many Barriers Inhibit Success of Succession Planning." *T+D*, Vol. 64, No. 6: 60–61.

5. McLaughlin, V. and C. Mott. 2010. "Leadership Brand Equity: HR's Role in Driving Economic Value." *Strategic HR Review*, Vol. 9, No. 4: 13–19.

6. Drucker, P. 1998. "Management's New Paradigms." *Forbes*, October 5: 152–177.

7. "Succession Management in C-Suite Is Lagging: A Korn Ferry Study Finds That the Majority of Companies Do Not Have a C Suite Succession Plan in Place." *T+D*, Vol. 64, No. 1 (2010): 23.

8. Behn, B.K., D.D. Dawley, R. Riley, and Y. Yang. 2006. "Deaths of CEOs: Are Delays in Naming Successors and Insider/Outsider Succession Associated with Subsequent Firm Performance?" *Journal of Managerial Issues*, Vol. 18, No. 1: 32–45.

9. St. Onge, S. 2007. "Planning Ahead." *CA Magazine*, Vol. 140, No. 1 (January/February): 51–52.

10. Anonymous. 2008. "Top Trends for 2008: Leadership Talent and Metrics Will Be Key." *HR Focus*, Vol. 85, No. 1: 8.

11. Henneman, T. 2012. "Most Companies Err on Preparing Heir Apparents." *Workforce Management*, 91.1, pp. 8–9.

12. Immen, W. 2011. "Getting a Jump on the Fast Track." *The Globe and Mail*, June 25, 2011, p. B18.

13. Leibman, M., R. Bruer, and B.R. Maki. 1996. "Succession Management: The Next Generation of Succession Planning." *Human Resources Planning*, Vol. 19, No. 3: 16–29.

14. Byham, W.C. 2002. "A New Look at Succession Management." *Ivey Business Journal*, Vol. 66, No. 5 (May/June): 10–12.

15. Corporate Leadership Council, 2003. *Hallmarks of Leadership Success: Strategies for Improving Leadership Quality and Executive Readiness*. New York: Corporate Executive Board.

16. Ulrich, D. and N. Smallwood. 2012. "What Is Talent?" *Executive Forum*, Winter, 2012, pp. 55–61.

17. Immen, W. 2005. "Rising Stars Get a Chance to Shine." *The Globe and Mail*, November 16, pp. C1, C3.

18. Boudreau, J.W., and P.M. Ramstead 2005. "Talentship, Talent Segmentation, and Sustainability: A New HR Decision-Science Paradigm for a New Strategy Definition." *Human Resource Management*, Vol. 44, No. 2 (Summer): 129–136.

19. Bernthal, P., and R. Wellins. 2006. "Trends in Leader Development and Succession." *Human Resource Planning*, Vol. 29, No. 2 (2006): 31–40.

20. Hoskisson, R.E., M.A. Hitt, and R.D. Ireland. 2004. *Competing for Advantage*. Mason, OH: Thomson South-Western.

21. Conlon, R. and R.V. Smith. 2010. "The Role of the Board and the CEO in Ensuring Business Continuity." *Financial Executive*, Vol. 26, No. 9: 52–54.

22. Quigely, T.J. and D.C. Hambrick. 2011 "When the Former CEO Stays on as a Board Chair: Effects on Successor Discretion, Strategic Change and Performance." *Strategic Management Journal* 33, pp. 834–859.

23. Eichlinger, B., and D. Ulrich. 1996. "Are You Future Agile?" *Human Resource Planning*, Vol. 11, No. 2: 30–41.

24. Lawler, E.E. III. 1994. "From Job-Based to Competency-Based Organizations." *Journal of Organizational Behaviour*, Vol. 15: 3–15.

25. Catano, V.M., S.F. Cronshaw, W.H. Wiesner, R.D. Hackett, and L.L. Methot. 2010. *Recruitment and Selection in Canada*. 4th ed. Toronto: ITP Nelson.

26. Kashi, K and F. Vaclav. 2013. "Managers' Core Competencies." *European Conference on Management, Leadership and Governance*, November 2013, pp. 384–393.

27. Ulrich, D. et al. 2008. *HR Competencies Mastery at the Intersection of People and Business*, Provo, RBL Institute, 2008.

28. Catano et al., 2010.

29. Kessler, G.C. 2002. "Why the Leadership Bench Never Gets Deeper: Ten Insights About Executive Talent Development." *Human Resources Planning*, Vol. 25, No. 1: 32–45.

30. Joinson, C. 1998. "Developing a Strong Bench," *HRM Magazine* (January): 92–96.

31. Lenz, S.S., and S. Wacker. 1997. "Career Development in an Uncertain World." Paper presented at the Human Resource Planning Society Symposium, Ithaca, New York.

32. Gore, N. 2000. "Managing Talent Replaces Static Charts in a New Era of Succession Planning." *Canadian HR Reporter*, Vol. 13, No. 15 (September 11): 12.

33. McLaughlin, B., and C. Mott. 2010. "Leadership Brand Equity: HR Leaders' Role in Driving Economic Value." *Strategic HR Review*, Vol. 9, No. 4, pp. 13–19.

34. Joinson, 1998.

35. Immen, 2005.

36. Guptil, D. 2003. "HR Leaders Talk." *Canadian HR Reporter*, February 10: 16.

37. Yancey, G.B. 2001. "Succession Planning Creates Quality Leadership." *Credit Union Executive Journal*, Vol. 41, No. 6 (November/December): 24–27.

38. Fulmer, R., S. Stumpf, and J. Bleak. 2009. "The Strategic Development of High Potential Leaders." *Strategy and Leadership*, Vol. 37, No. 3 (2009): 17–22.

39. Newell, E. 2001. "CEOs Talk." *Canadian HR Reporter*, Vol. 14, No. 17 (October 8).

40. Kessler, 2002: 34.

41. Walter, G. 1996. "Corporate Practices in Management Development." *Conference Board*, Report No. 1158-96-RR. New York: Conference Board Inc., 89.

42. Church, E. 1998. "New-Style CEOs Follow Zig-Zag Path." *The Globe and Mail*, February 20, p. B23.

43. Gagne, C. 2004. "Get Good Help." *Canadian Business*, Vol. 77, No. 14/15: 71–72.

44. Black, B. 2002. "CEOs Talk." *Canadian HR Reporter*, October 7: 17.

45. Campion, M.A., L. Cheraskin, and M.J. Stevens. 1994. "Career-Related Antecedents and Outcomes of Job Rotation." *Academy of Management Journal*, Vol. 37, No. 6 (December): 1518–1525.

46. Horwitt, L. 1997. "It's Your Career: Manage It." *Network World*. March 17: 39–43.

47. Francis, K. 2001. "CEO's Talk." *Canadian HR Reporter*, Vol. 14, No. 11 (June 4): 17.

48. Horwitt, 1997.

49. Chereskin, L., and M.A. Campion. 1996. "Study Clarifies Job Rotation Benefits." *Personnel Journal*, November: 31–38.

50. Dahl, H.L. 1997. "Human Resource Cost and Benefit Analysis: New Power for Human Resource Approaches." *Human Resource Planning*, Vol. 11, No. 2: 69–78.

51. For a fuller discussion of these methods, see Saks, Alan M., and Robert R. Haccoun. 2010. *Performance Management Through Training and Development*, 5th ed. Toronto: Nelson.

52. Haynes, R.K., and R. Ghosh. 2008. "Mentoring and Succession Management: An Evaluative Approach to the Strategic Collaboration Model." *Review of Business*, Vol. 28, No. 2 (Winter 2008): 3–7.

53. Byham, 2002.

54. Butyn, S. 2003. "Mentoring Your Way to Improved Retention." *Canadian HR Reporter*, January 27: 13.

55. Hewitt Associates. 2005. "How the Top 20 Companies Grow Great Leaders." *Research Highlights*. Toronto: Hewitt Associates.

56. Haynes and Ghosh, 2008: 3.

57. Kambit, A. 2010. "Developing the Next Generation of Leaders." *The Journal of Business Strategy*, 31.2: 43–45.

58. Chatman, J. O'Reilly, C., and V. Chang. 2005. "Cisco Systems: Developing a Human Capital Strategy." *California Management Review*, Vol. 47, No. 2 (Winter 2005): 137–167.

59. Busine, M., and B. Watt. 2005. "Succession Management: Trends and Practices." *Asia Pacific Journal of Human Resources*, Vol. 43, No. 2: 225–237.

60. Pitts, G. 2005. "Need a Leader: Just Look for a GE Graduate." *The Globe and Mail*, July 11, p. B11.

61. Ito, J., and C.M. Brotheridge. 2005. "Does Supporting Employees' Career Adaptability Lead to Commitment, Turnover or Both?" *Human Resource Management*, Vol. 44, No. 1 (Spring): 5–19.

62. Bernthal and Wellins, 2006.

63. Corporate Leadership Council, 2003; Fulmer, R.M. 2005. "Keys to Best Practice Succession Management." *Human Resources*, October 14, 2005: 17–18.

64. Anonymous. 2010. "2010 Benchmarks: Key Measures to Monitor." *HR Focus*, Vol. 87, No. 1: 1, 13–15.

65. Hewitt Associates Inc., 2005.

66. Borwick, C. 1993. "Eight Ways to Assess Succession Plans." *HRM Magazine*, Vol. 38, No. 4: 109–114.

67. Willins, R., and W. Byham. 2001. "The Leadership Gap." *Training*, Vol. 38, No. 5 (March): 98–106.

68. Bernthal, A., and R.S. Wellins. 2003. *The Leadership Forecast: A Benchmarking Study*. Pittsburgh, PA: Developmental Dimensions International.

69. Hall, D., and J.E. Moss. 1988. "The New Protean Career Contract: Helping Organizations and Employees Adapt." *Organization Dynamics*, Winter: 22–37.

70. Greengard, S. 2001. "Make Smarter Business Decisions: Know What Employees Can Do." *Workforce*, Vol. 80, No. 11 (November): 42–46.

71. Lockwood, N. "Talent Management: Driver for Organization Success." *HR Magazine*, Vol. 51, No. 6 (June 2006): 1–12.

72. Lane, P. "Time Off to Save the World." *National Post*, July 26, 2008.

CHAPTER

CHANGE MANAGEMENT

CHAPTER LEARNING OUTCOMES

AFTER READING THIS CHAPTER, YOU SHOULD BE ABLE TO:

- Understand the importance of organizational change.
- Discuss the role of change as part of organizational planning.
- Discuss the steps of a generic change project.
- Define and discuss the process of planned change.
- Understand how emergent change occurs.
- Understand the principles of a learning organization.
- Discuss how the principles of a learning organization are important to both planned and emergent change.

NEL

When Marissa Mayer took over as CEO at Yahoo! in mid-2012, she instituted a change in organizational culture aimed at increasing Yahoo!'s focus on the customer. Part of the strategic vision at Yahoo! is to produce products that end users want to use every day on any or all their devices. In addition to communicating the vision, Mayer has used several HR practices to move the culture toward it. For example, Yahoo! issued smartphones to all employees, partly so that they could develop a better understanding of how and why people might experience Yahoo! on mobile devices. She also changed the company policy around telecommuting by stopping the practice of allowing employees to work from home during business hours. Mayer's justification for this controversial move was that Yahoo!'s human capital needs are better served by collocating employees within the workplace so that creativity and innovation could emerge from increased levels of employee interaction. While the research on telecommuting points to many benefits from this flexible work practice, Mayer defended the change on the basis that it was not the ideal choice for Yahoo! at the time. This shift was reinforced by a new policy to offer free food to all employees at the office. Mayer also introduced a new formal system for employees to voice problems and complaints about Yahoo!

These changes are intended to bring about a renewed culture of collaborative innovation and customer focus at Yahoo! A few months after the policy change to telecommuting, Mayer attributed the development of a new weather app to the collaborative efforts of the weather group and the Flickr group within Yahoo! as support for the effectiveness of the policy decisions. Planned change is often initiated from the top of the organization, and its success is contingent upon a great deal of communication

Marissa Mayer was hired to implement changes at Yahoo.

partnered with policy or practice changes to move employees towards new behaviours that are consistent with the change direction.[1]

Sources: www.inc.com: "Yahoo CEO: Why I Was Right About Telecommuting"; www.forbes.com: "5 Ways Mayer's Trying To Kick-Start The Yahoo! Culture"; www.allthingsd.com: "Because Marissa Said So – Yahoos Bristle At Mayer's QPR Ranking System and Silent Layoffs": www.en.wikipedia.org: "Marissa Mayer."

// WHY IS ORGANIZATIONAL CHANGE IMPORTANT?

Organizational change lies at the heart of the planning process. Organizations are dynamic entities, constantly growing or contracting, and responding to internal and external changes, some of which are within the control of the firm and others beyond its control. The planning process anticipates organizational resource requirements in response to organizational change using a variety of methods to forecast demand and supply, and by connecting resource requirements with strategic and operating imperatives. In order to

effectively plan for and anticipate resource requirements, organizational planners must have a strong understanding of organizational change. Chapter 1 introduced the roots of organizational planning and change in firm strategy. In that chapter we learned that strategy is a plan for establishing and maintaining a competitive advantage in the market, and that the firm's strategy provides the ideological context within which organizational change takes place. Later chapters cover specific change initiatives such as downsizing and restructuring, outsourcing, and mergers and acquisitions. In this chapter we span the gap between change at the level of conceptualizing strategy and change at the level of specific initiatives by examining the change process itself.

THE INCREASING PACE OF CHANGE

Innovations like the World Wide Web connect people and ideas across the boundaries of time and space to enable change in ways that we are only beginning to grasp. Crowd-funding, open-source software development, collaborative knowledge repositories such as wikis and shared folders, mass customization, and other communication-enabled advancements are changing the way businesses operate, and now connect innovators with each other, their competitors, and customers to bring about dramatically faster product developments. These changes are occurring amid unprecedented levels of economic, political, and environmental uncertainty. In response to these levels of change and uncertainty, organizations are moving toward systems that enable faster response and adaptation to change. Flatter organizational structures, more fluid job roles, greater employee autonomy, and team-based learning and decision making are all efforts that can facilitate organizational knowledge acquisition and action based on that learning.

Given the quickening pace of change and higher levels of uncertainty in today's business environment, firms that are able to manage change effectively are in a position to outperform their slower, less change-capable competitors. The ability to manage change is such an important organizational competency that some scholars believe that it is the only form of sustainable competitive advantage.[2] Where other forms of competitive advantage are susceptible to erosion through imitation, competition, or changing consumer needs, firms that are able to adapt to their environment faster maintain the ability to stay ahead of their competition. Accordingly, the most important aspects of the job of a general manager include creating and directing strategy, and managing change.[3]

// SOCIETAL, INDUSTRIAL, AND ORGANIZATIONAL LEVELS OF CHANGE

Organizational change occurs in response to societal, industrial, and firm-level developments. At the societal level, economic and environmental issues can be strong drivers of change. For example, after the 2008 recession, big-box stores such as Best Buy, Walmart, Target, and Home Depot found that revenues were dropping in their large-format stores. Several of the big-box stores have even begun to close their large stores, while others have found that the big-box format is either restricting growth by not allowing the format to serve smaller communities, or that the number of useful locations for these large shopping outlets is becoming saturated. Furthermore, as people turn increasingly to online shopping, the big-box format is becoming less relevant to shoppers. Big-box retailers are now developing smaller versions of their stores in an attempt to adapt to these societal changes.

At the industrial level, change typically follows an S-curve pattern in which sales of a new product or service begin slowly as demand builds, followed by rapid growth as the market for the product or service becomes mature, which leads to a tapering as consumer demands develop and change. The market for tablet computing devices showed a slow start as the computer industry struggled to put together all the attributes of size, weight, ergonomics, and technological capabilities that make a successful tablet device. Apple found a winning design in iPad, and the market took off, leading to successful designs from competitors as well. As sales of the original iPad began to peak and competition increased from other firms and devices such as smartphones with larger screens, Apple brought out a smaller version at a different price point and with slightly different features, and also began actively pursuing new markets for the tablet through partnerships like its alliance with IBM to bring iPad to the corporate market.

Firm-level developments occur largely as a result of demands from stakeholders. Shareholders, a particularly powerful group of stakeholders, might demand higher return on equity, new leadership might prefer a different strategic direction, or internal resource constraints might lead to strategic change. Large firms like GE, with multiple business units in different industries, might develop interesting opportunities in multiple industries, but resource constraints such as managerial capabilities or financial resources might lead to difficult decisions resulting in changes to the decisions around the projects that are approved and the projects that are downsized or shelved. Thus, decision making based on internal, firm-level choices can be a strong source of organizational change.

Given the multiple levels from which the need for organizational change can arrive, it is no surprise that firms experience an ongoing state of change. However, organizations do not always change when they should, and even when they do change, they often experience failure. Research suggests that up to 70 percent of organizational change efforts fail.[4] We will examine several models of organizational change that attempt to model, understand, and mitigate these reasons for failure.

// MODELS OF ORGANIZATIONAL CHANGE

There are many models of organizational change. In this section we will examine the view of organizations as open systems, and how this view impacts our understanding of organizational change through three basic models that form the basis of most models of change. The first is a generic model of change that demonstrates the attributes that are common to the many models of organizational change. The other two models include a model of planned change, followed by a model of emergent change.

ORGANIZATIONS AS OPEN SYSTEMS

The term *system* refers to a set or arrangement of interrelated parts that interact to form a whole.[5] Organizations are systems that comprise multiple subsystems. A corporate functional group, such as the marketing department or the HR department can be considered a subsystem within the organization, as can the retail division of the firm. These subsystems interact in complex ways. An open-system perspective views the organization not from the point of view of an individual subsystem or even groups of subsystems, but from the perspective of the organization as a whole, and its interaction with its environment. Organizations are **open systems** because they interact with their external environment, and because the internal subsystems interact with one another.[6]

Open system
A system that receives inputs from its external environment

Organizations impact and are impacted by their external environment and by the other subsystems working within them. The unpredictable and interconnected nature of these open system dependencies are primary reasons that organizational change can be so difficult, and so prone to failure.

THE IMPORTANCE OF FEEDBACK

Open systems are input-throughput-output systems in that they take or receive inputs from their environment, transform or convert those inputs, and then output the finished products or services back to the environment. The factor that defines the structure of an open system is its purpose; goals are used as indicators of whether the system is functioning according to its purpose. The objective of an open system approach in organizations is to structure and coordinate all the subsystems in a manner that ensures that the firm is collectively pursuing its overall purpose.[7] Therefore, organizations must use feedback to determine whether or not they are achieving their goals, and ultimately their strategic purpose. Two basic forms of feedback are positive and negative feedback. Negative feedback is the kind of information that tells whether the system is achieving its goal. For example, the thermometer in your room operates through negative feedback; the set temperature is its goal, and it will operate the heater until the room temperature rises to the set temperature before shutting off. If an organization determines that it needs to produce 1000 pairs of shoes every month, it will use negative feedback to determine if its daily production is on track.

Positive feedback, on the other hand, is the kind of information that a system uses to determine if its purpose is suited for its environment. Positive feedback helps the organization to determine if it should be producing 1000 pairs of shoes a month, or what styles of shoe it should be producing. Organizational change implementations must take into account the potential effect of changes on other subsystems and on the environment, and all models of organizational change incorporate methods for utilizing negative and positive feedback into the design and decision-making processes around change. However, benefitting from feedback implies learning. Organizations must also have systems in place for learning in order to use feedback, and different methods of learning are required to access negative and positive feedback. Chris Argyris, a thought leader and noted researcher in the area of organizational behaviour referred to these methods of learning as single-loop and double-loop learning.[8]

SINGLE-LOOP LEARNING

Single-loop learning
The attempt to solve a problem using a single strategy, without examining the validity of the problem itself

This type of learning is more related to problem solving in the form of identifying and correcting errors. **Single-loop learning** is the type of learning around negative feedback, and essentially seeks to learn how to achieve a set goal within the current set of governing variables. Single-loop learning permits the organization or the individual to proceed according to the status quo, and can impede change implementations, especially when the change requires new and different goals. Argyris also suggests that individuals can seek to avoid potential embarrassment or threat by remaining within the current set of governing variables.[9] This tendency can lead to organizational defensive routines, which are actions that are intended to prevent individuals from experiencing embarrassment or threat, but that ultimately prevent the identification of the actual underlying causes of the threat. Organizational defensive routines can be used to explain actions such as those of

the managers of the Peanut Plant Corporation of America who in 2008 faked lab results of their peanut paste to indicate that a tainted shipment was free of salmonella. That shipment of peanut paste led to the deaths of 9 people and sickened over 700 others.[10] One manager testified that the plant samples had received multiple positive tests for salmonella contamination over a period of several years. It is possible that defensive routines had led the managers to convince themselves that the positive tests for salmonella in the peanut butter paste were unlikely to lead to any kind of public health hazard. In an effort to avoid the embarrassment of admitting to error, defensive routines can reinforce single-loop learning, and prevent the underlying issues from being examined.

DOUBLE-LOOP LEARNING

Double-loop learning involves questioning the tacit assumptions and attributions that people have around their decision making. In organizational settings, this involves questioning the extent to which the strategy itself, and the systems and structures that implement the strategy support the underlying purpose of the organization. When managers and employees examine the assumptions they have used to arrive at a point of view, they are using double-loop learning that enables them to bypass the assumptions that may be locking them into a particular frame of mind, and preventing them from viewing the problem from a different perspective. **Double-loop learning** is typified by encouraging participation in

> **Double-loop learning**
> A method of learning that involves questioning current assumptions, examining a problem from different perspectives, and questioning the validity of the problem

---

HR PLANNING NOTEBOOK 9.1

OVERCOMING SINGLE-LOOP LEARNING

Single-loop learning can prevent the learner from developing an understanding of underlying or root issues. It is typified by the following values:

1. The desire to remain in unilateral control.

Predetermined goals and existing methods of achieving those goals provide a sense of control. It is generally easier to change the things that fall within our direct control than to change things that are not. For example, when asked to find ways to increase profits, managers often seek to cut costs, which are known and within the control of managers, than to increase revenues, which are less certain. One way to reduce the tendency to want to remain in unilateral control includes allowing more democratic and inclusive methods of decision making by pushing decision-making to groups or giving individuals greater autonomy in decision making.

2. A focus on maximizing winning and minimizing losing.

Success is important, and failure is difficult to accept. Organizations can increase their learning abilities by encouraging experimentation, and allowing members to make mistakes. Individuals and groups can move beyond defensive routines when they accept their mistakes, and learn from mistakes from a more objective frame of mind.

3. Leaving potentially threatening or embarrassing facts out of the decision-making process.

This tendency relates strongly to the previous point about the importance of encouraging experimentation. When errors can be career limiting or when they can negatively impact performance appraisals, it is only rational to want to ignore them. However, by accepting errors or misfires as part of the risk-taking process of creativity and innovation, learning can be enhanced.

Sources: C. Argyris, "Teaching Smart People How to Learn," *Harvard Business Review, 3* (1991): 99–109; C. Argyris, R. Putnam, and D.M. Smith, *Action Science*, San Francisco: Jossey-Bass, 1985.

decision making and open expression of conflicting views, using valid information, and widespread and open testing of evaluations. Had the managers at the Peanut Plant Corporation of America employed double-loop learning, they would not have covered up the lab tests and defended their current course of action; they would have questioned how salmonella got into the paste, and embarked on a program to uncover and eliminate the cause. While this may sound like an obvious solution, it is likely that you can recall one or more examples where you have witnessed the results of single-loop learning and the tendency to pursue goals without questioning the goal itself or the assumptions that led to a course of action.

The success of organizational change is therefore dependent on the methods of feedback that organizations use, the validity of information that is gathered and shared, the alignment of goals to the organization's purpose and to the change implementation, and the extent to which double-loop learning is fostered. Models of change must allow for these factors to be considered, and differences between models often come down to issues relating to the scale of the change or method in which these variables are taken into account.

// THE GENERIC MODEL OF CHANGE

Many models recognize that the process comprises several critical periods of change as shown in Figure 9.1.[11] This figure represents an overview of the change process, and incorporates the need for constant review of the change process as well as the need to monitor and adapt to the internal and external changes that may be affecting or caused by the change process.

RECOGNIZING THE NEED FOR CHANGE AND STARTING THE PROCESS

This is one of the most difficult stages in the change process. Change requires not only that a need to change is identified, but that the need is broadly felt among all participants involved in the change process. Without full buy-in from all stakeholders, change

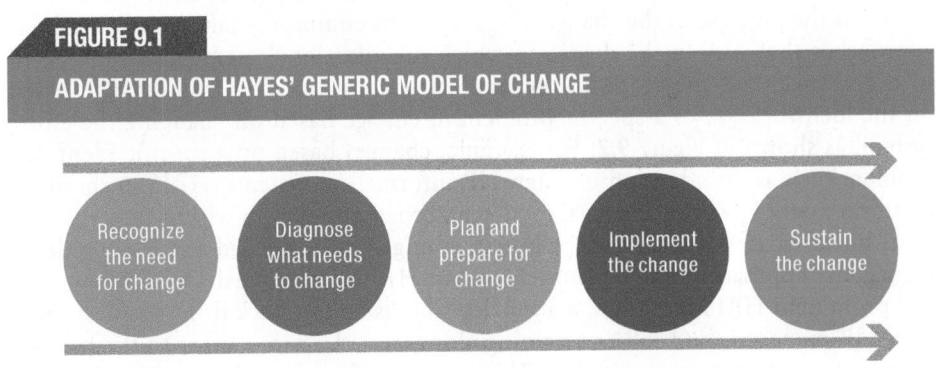

FIGURE 9.1

ADAPTATION OF HAYES' GENERIC MODEL OF CHANGE

Recognize the need for change → Diagnose what needs to change → Plan and prepare for change → Implement the change → Sustain the change

Source: Adapted from Hayes, J. (2010). *The Theory and Practice of Change Management* (3rd ed.). New York: Palgrave MacMillan.

efforts are likely to fail. Once the need for change has been identified, the motivation for that change must be spread throughout the firm. This motivation can come in the form of incentives tied to organizational goals that are aligned to the desired outcomes of the change, or in the form of a high-involvement/high-commitment strategy that aligns employee values with organizational values.[12] Successful change initiatives tend to involve management and employees in the process of discovering the problems and developing the solutions, as this inclusive style tends to promote a shared understanding of the issues.

DIAGNOSING WHAT NEEDS TO BE CHANGED

Organizational change is complex, involving multiple stakeholders, unpredictable outcomes, and unexpected consequences. Models of organizational change tend to deal with the diagnosis of what needs to change by examining the leadership of the change process, the overall purpose of the change, and the degree of planning involved in the change process. Will leadership be a top-down style in which management determines what needs to change and communicates goals down through the organization, or a bottom-up approach in which all levels of employees share in determining what needs to change and teams are charged with developing plans of action? Is the purpose of the change to maximize the economic value of the firm by focusing on shareholder value, in which case a top-down approach may be utilized—or is the purpose to develop the human capability to implement the firm's strategy, where a bottom-up approach may be a better choice? Is the level of planning detailed, with firm goals and a timeline outlined from the beginning, or is the planning loose, with a general direction and plenty of room for experimentation? All these manifestations of change planning can be successful, but they must be implemented in suitable situations. Change models help the strategic planner to understand how to use these methods.

PLANNING AND PREPARING FOR CHANGE

The type of change intervention that will be most successful will depend on the organization culture, leadership, timeline available for the change to be implemented, as well as the purpose of the change. Organizations commonly take implementation approaches that vary in the degree to which organizational members are involved in the change, and the scope of the implementation, ranging from change based on the identification of a specific problem to change based on changing the entire system, as shown in Figure 9.2. For example, changes based on a specific identified problem such as the adoption of a new HR information systems (HRIS) technology platform might have the potential to affect a broad population within the organization; however, this type of change initiative might be addressed using a top-down managerial approach. Senior managers within HR might request an RFP from several prominent HRIS providers, make a decision using feedback from business unit–level HR managers, and roll out training along with the new system to the broader organization upon implementation. This example of a narrow level of involvement for a broad implementation can be contrasted against change implementations that seek to involve a much broader group of stakeholders. The proliferation of high

FIGURE 9.2

COMMON CHANGE IMPLEMENTATION STYLES

		LEVEL OF INVOLVEMENT	
		CONSULTANTS OR TOP-DOWN MANAGEMENT TEAMS	ALL EMPLOYEES
SCOPE OF IMPLEMENTATION	System-wide change	Tight structure. Top-down, planned change initiative	Loosest structure. Emergent change, or combination of emergent and planned approach.
	Change to solve a specific problem	Tightest structure. The problem, proposed solution, and implementation plan come from management. Incremental change intended to bring localized improvement.	Tight or loose structure, depending on organization culture and management approach to the problem.

involvement (often referred to as high performance) work practices in recent years suggests that firms are moving more toward greater levels of employee involvement in organizational decision making and change implementation. An example of a high-involvement work practice is a gainsharing compensation plan, where employees are rewarded for reducing production costs and increasing organizational efficiencies. Such a plan motivates employees to think creatively about developing and implementing new ways to be more efficient.

More tightly structured and larger-scale changes will require many changes to organizational systems and processes, while loosely structured changes will require deep organizational learning around the firm's vision and values. As organizations seek to involve more constituents in the process of developing and implementing change, the structures that guide the change process, including goals, levels of autonomy in decision making, and feedback systems tend to be broader and more loosely controlled. According to John Kotter, good leaders tend to focus on setting direction rather than plan, they align people to a common purpose rather than organize them, and they motivate people to move in a particular direction rather than problem solve around the systems and processes used to push people in a particular direction.[13] This view of leadership suggests that any change process should begin with the establishment of a clear understanding of the firm's overall vision and direction. When anchored around a common understanding of the firm's vision, highly structured change implementations can be constructed such that all the goals, processes, and practices that are intended to move the organization in the direction of the change are internally aligned. A common understanding of the firm's vision is even more important to loosely structured change initiatives, where leadership tends to express very loose goals around which organizational processes and practices emerge. For example, Bob Galvin, CEO of Motorola, in 1983 helped to transform the company by challenging his executives to "renew the organization."[14] Such a challenge would lack impact or even meaning without a strong understanding of the firm's broader purpose.

Employees often have very good ideas about how to improve processes.

IMPLEMENTING THE CHANGE

Implementing change demands particular skills from both the change leaders and those involved in the change. Successful change leaders rely on their ability to make use of the complex social networks that connect people within organizations, and their political skills, which can be defined as the ability to persuade, manipulate, and negotiate to achieve a particular outcome.[15] **Social networks** in organizations are rarely reflected by the formal reporting structures. These networks are instead based on the extent to which people routinely communicate with one another and whom people turn to for information relating to getting their work done. Social networks in organizations can be complex and very difficult to observe, and employees who become influential members of a social network are often those with high levels of firm-specific human capital in that they are instrumental to getting work done or helping others to get work done better or faster. An influential role in a social network can therefore be a very important tool in helping to achieve buy-in from others around the importance of the change initiative and in bringing about shared mental models of the firm's vision and purpose.

Political skills are also important in achieving widespread buy-in for a change initiative. Persuading others is rarely done using a single, convincing argument. Rather, persuasion is a process that involves listening to others, learning about the positions and perspectives of others, and incorporating those views into an argument. Persuasive skills are quite similar to the dimensions of political skills, which include social astuteness, interpersonal influence, networking ability, and apparent sincerity.[16] Leaders involved in a change process must to be able to exercise political and persuasive skills, and to draw from social networks in order to ensure the success of the change implementation.

Social networks
The networks of ties that an individual has with other individuals

THE SCIENCE OF PERSUASION

The ability to persuade others is an important skill not only for managing change but also as a general leadership skill. A good argument requires support and understanding from others, and those who are better able to supplement a strong argument with persuasive skills are more likely to find that support. One model of persuasion suggests that there are four steps to persuading others:

1. Establishing credibility with the audience by demonstrating expertise and gaining trust. People are less likely to follow those whom they do not trust. An important first step is to help others to see how your position is informed through expertise, and that you are a trustworthy source.

2. Framing your position in a way that will appeal to the audience by emphasizing the advantages. The way in which people respond to ideas is partly dependent on the way the information is presented, or framed. This is done in politics, of course, where politicians choose words carefully to elicit an emotional response that frames an issue in a preferred manner. For example, referring to the US *Patient Protection and Affordable Care Act*, (otherwise known as Obamacare) as *socialized medicine* or as *health insurance reform* frames the act in very different ways that illicit potentially different responses. Strong persuasive skills involve framing an argument in a manner that the audience will be able to relate to and find appealing.

3. Providing evidence through the use of supporting data and appealing stories, metaphors, or analogies to help the audience visualize your position. Metaphor is an excellent tool for communicating something new or different by relating it to something with which people are already familiar. For example, children who are not equipped with language to describe sensations like a foot falling asleep will communicate the odd feeling using a metaphor such as "a hundred bees are buzzing on my foot." People skilled in persuasion help others to understand their position by creating shared mental models to describe unique, novel, or abstract ideas.

4. Connecting emotionally by matching the emotional state of the audience. To do this, good persuaders require emotional intelligence. Emotional intelligence involves an ability to be aware of and capitalize on one's own emotions and the emotions of others. Effective persuasion requires an emotional appeal in addition to a rational argument.

Sources: Conger, J.A. (1998). "The Necessary Art of Persuasion," *Harvard Business Review*, 76, 84–95.

SUSTAINING THE CHANGE

Implementing organizational change also requires a firm-wide approach to enable the change process, regardless of its scope. Change initiatives that are of a narrow, more focused approach may make use of a new business process, with a commensurate level of training around the new process, whereas large-scale change initiatives may involve many unknowns that cannot be completely anticipated. Such changes require organizational learning and experimentation in order to plot a successful change path. We will cover two prototypical models of organizational change in the next section that address how organizational change can be implemented.

Once change has been implemented, steps must be taken to ensure that the organization does not slip back into its pre-change mode. While new methods or processes can be put into place, these methods will likely not endure if they do not fit with the

ORGANIZATIONAL CHANGE AT YOU.I

When Rogers and Shaw announced the launch of Shomi in August 2014 as their video streaming service intended to compete with services like Netflix, they revealed that the user interface for Shomi will be produced by You.i, a young Canadian high-technology firm based in Ottawa, Ontario. You.i is a small technology firm of approximately 50 employees that is planning to double in size over the next year. Change in the high-technology industry is constant and fast paced, especially in small firms that are in the process of developing a market niche (i.e., a portion of the market that contributes value to the consumer, and is not currently being served, or is underserved). Jason Flick, co-founder and Chief Executive at You.i explains that the vision behind the firm is "to bring the best user experience to all screens." This vision is focused on the video market space, and is further enlivened by the guiding principles of having well-designed workflow, cross-platform capability (that is, it works on all hardware platforms including smartphones, tablets, and computers of all major brands), and high performance (such as quick video rendering, fast loading and response, etc.). You.i seeks to keep its vision at the forefront of employees' minds by making the vision a focal point during product meetings. You.i conducts several employee retreats every year in which all employees are brought together to discuss and have input on what the vision means at You.i and how it impacts their work. Flick further explained that the company's vision is communicated to both employees and customers through the creation of prototype software. The software is only for demonstration purposes, and shows how You.i envisions the future blending of art and science in the world of video streaming. Its purpose is to not only give potential customers an idea of what You.i can do, but also help to affirm the aspirations of the employees at You.i, and give them the opportunity to bring You.i's current vision to life, to give it substance.

In a recent example of change, You.i was working on a video streaming solution that was intended to extract the highest video performance from smart devices that did not have a built-in graphics chip. However, rapid advancements in the hardware configurations of smart devices led the team at You.i to realize that the market was moving toward a widespread use of graphics chips in these devices. You.i had to make a major change in its organizational activities. Management decided to abandon some of their high-priority projects relating to maximizing video performance without using the graphics chip; but this shift in focus remained true to the overall vision and the guiding principles of You.i. As a result, much of the learning that went into the abandoned projects served as a springboard to guide the resulting projects, ultimately leading to a rethinking of You.i's rendering engine, and a subsequent breakthrough in the speed of its video rendering software. The speed of You.i's rendering software is a critical aspect of one of the guiding principles, and is a strong differentiating feature of You.i's product in the marketplace. In this change incident, You.i quickly realized that the mental models it was using around how to implement its vision of bringing "the best user experience to all screens" were no longer relevant due to changing environmental conditions, and adapted new mental models around how to deliver its vision. When organizations are focused on a clear understanding of a future vision, and carry the ability to adapt and learn, environmental changes can bring opportunities where other firms may see a dead-end.

Vision and the use of mental models helped make You.i a success.

Source: Based on interview with Jason Flick, President and CEO, You.i, and Deborah Naczynski, Head of Education and Outreach, You.i.

firm's culture, or if they are not incorporated into existing mental models of how things work within the organization. For example, despite the potential benefits of merging to both Daimler and Chrysler in terms of expected market development and resource sharing, and despite all the systems put in place to merge these two firms, the inattention to integrating the cultures of these two very different firms ultimately led to one of the most notable merger failures in the auto industry.[17] Sustaining change usually involves a set of measures to provide feedback to the organization that indicate when goals that relate to successful change are being met, and systems that can lead to the development of adaptations when those goals are not being met.

// THE PLANNED MODEL OF CHANGE

It has been argued that Kurt Lewin's three-step model of planned organization change is the model around which most subsequent change models were conceived.[18] Kurt Lewin (1890–1947) was a behavioural psychologist who focused much of his work on situational and group influences on individual behaviour. Lewin developed the three-step model in the early 1940s as part of the Planned Approach to change that comprises four elements in total: field theory, group dynamics, action research, and the three-step model. Together these four elements form an interrelated approach to understanding and developing solutions to change problems. We will briefly touch upon each of these elements while focusing more on the three-step process.

FIELD THEORY

Lewin developed field Theory as an approach to understanding and changing individual or group perceptions and behaviours by seeking to understand the interdependent forces that act on individuals or groups and that motivate them toward certain courses of action and restrain them from others. According to Lewin, the totality of all the psychological forces (that is, their needs, goals, and intentions) that maintain an individual's or group's set of behaviours in a given situation such as home-life or work-life can be described in what Lewin called a *life-space*. The forces acting on a particular life-space are always in flux, always changing, but they form a state of quasi-equilibrium, which is referred to as the status quo. The status quo can be changed by altering the forces that make up the life-space. Behavioural change is therefore a matter of understanding the forces that act on an individual's or group's life-space, and reinforcing those forces that act to move the individual or group toward the desired behaviour, and reducing the strength of the forces that act to prevent the individual or group from moving toward the desired behaviour. The analysis of these forces acting on individuals or groups is also called force-field Analysis.

Force-field analysis
A framework for analyzing a problem that seeks to identify all the relevant factors and stakeholders that are acting to either sustain the current state or to move away from the current state

FORCE-FIELD ANALYSIS

The purpose of force-field analysis is to analyze a condition and to plan corrective actions. As Figure 9.3 shows, the analysis begins therefore with a statement of the current state or condition, and a statement of the desired future state or condition. The analysis then attempts to plot the forces that are supporting or driving toward the future state as

FIGURE 9.3

FORCE-FIELD ANALYSIS

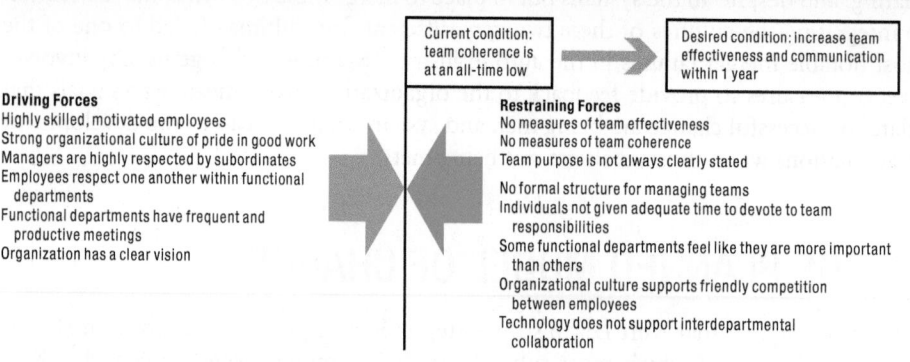

Source: Based on French, W.L., & Bell, C.H. (1999). *Organizational Development: Behavioral Science and Interventions for Organizational Improvement* (6th ed.). Upper Saddle River: Prentice-Hall.

well as the forces that are restraining the future state from being put into action. A force-field analysis is an important first step in a change plan. It helps organizations to identify issues by requiring change planners to first identify a future desired state rather than to focus solely on existing problems. It also helps planners to identify suitable courses of action to initiate a change implementation.

GROUP DYNAMICS

A group can be any aggregation of two or more people. Groups can be assembled for a specific purpose or task, or groups can form spontaneously as a result of people assembling around a common cause (for example, an audience at a concert, or a social network at work, or witnesses at the scene of a car accident). A common element of groups is that they form structures to determine what kinds of behaviours are expected or permitted within the group. While not all groups have formal rules or codes of conduct, they develop norms over time that govern or constrain the behaviours of the individuals who comprise the group. Thus, a group is more than merely the sum of the individuals within it; a group establishes normative behaviours that alter the actions of group members. Solomon Asch and Muzafer Sherif were social psychologists who performed several groundbreaking experiments on group norms in the 1930s and 1940s. Collectively, their work demonstrated that individuals are willing to ignore their own perceptions in order to agree with group norms, and that once group norms have been established, group members will tend to take on those normative behaviours as their own, such that when group members are removed from the group and new members are introduced to the group, the original norms tend to persist. And so group norms are innate aspects of the group itself that have the capacity to influence the identities of the individuals who comprise the group. Furthermore, groups are capable of harnessing collective knowledge in a way that goes beyond the knowledge of any individual in the group. For example, in his book *The Wisdom of Crowds*, James Surowiecki[19] points out how groups can make predictions that tend to be more accurate than expert predictions.

FORCE-FIELD ANALYSIS

Force-field analysis can be used as a problem-solving tool as well as a change management tool. Some of the benefits of a force-field analysis include the development of a strong understanding of the current situation, and a clarification around how it differs from an ideal future state or situation. Force-field analysis can be used to decide whether a change is appropriate and, if so, what actions should be taken to move toward the new direction. French and Bell break the force-field analysis down to the following steps:

1. Describe the current state (i.e., the status quo), and why it must be changed. Ultimately this will lead to a statement of the current condition such as "team coherence is at an all-time low."

2. Describe the desired future state. The future condition should ultimately be described in a sentence or a few sentences, such as "increase team effectiveness and communication within one year."

3. Identify the forces that are supporting or driving toward increasing team coherence as well as the forces that are restraining or preventing increased team coherence. Techniques that access a wide variety of stakeholder viewpoints such as surveys, brainstorming sessions, and nominal group technique might be useful to perform this step.

4. Examine the valence of each of these forces. Which forces are the strongest and which are the weakest? Which of these forces can be controlled or are susceptible to behavioural intervention?

5. Develop strategies to reduce the strength of the restraining forces and strategies to amplify the driving forces.

6. Implement the strategies developed in step 5. As restraining forces are reduced in strength and number and driving forces are amplified and increased in number, behaviours should begin to shift toward the desired state.

7. Develop strategies to stabilize the driving and restraining forces into a new state of quasi-equilibrium. How do we make this the new status quo?

After using a force-field analysis, organizational planners can begin the process of moving toward the future state through a series of trial-and-error attempts to implement the strategies developed in step 5 to reduce restraining forces and amplify the driving forces. After moving to the new state, planners must develop strategies to stabilize the driving and restraining forces into a new state of quasi-equilibrium; to turn the change into the new status quo.

Source: Based on French, W.L., & Bell, C.H. (1999). *Organizational Development: Behavioral Science and Interventions for Organizational Improvement* (6th ed.), Upper Saddle River: Prentice-Hall, 1999.

Lewin believed that organizational change could only be achieved by changing behaviours at the group level. Accordingly, efforts focused on changing individual behaviours alone would be insufficient to bring about effective and sustainable change. In other words, individual behaviour in organizational settings is to some extent a function of the group setting. Change implementations must be viewed from the perspective of the group, which involves focusing on the values, norms, and roles within the group.

ACTION RESEARCH

While an important stage in the change process is understanding that the status quo is not sustainable, the decisions around what needs to change are filled with uncertainty and risk. Lewin believed that change is most likely to succeed when stakeholders are involved in both

making and implementing decisions. This implies a level of interaction between research and practice whereby the practitioners are also the researchers. **Action research** is theory based, but rather than seeking findings that are universal or generalizable across all situations, it is embedded in the specific context of the practitioners, and is intended to help identify and solve practical problems in a methodical, evidence-based manner. Figure 9.4 shows the five stages of the cyclical process of action research. As practitioners move from diagnosis to planning, taking action, evaluating the outcomes of those actions, learning based on the outcomes, and back to diagnosing, this cyclical process is intended to spiral deeper toward greater insight into the problem and its ultimate set of solutions as new learning occurs through each cycle.[20] Action research is used in many fields including management, education, sociology, psychology, anthropology, and politics, to name a few.[21]

One of the main benefits of action research is that each of the successive steps taken to implement change is based on input from stakeholders and uses information from prior steps.[22] When each step of an implementation informs the following steps using action research, it is possible to understand how a change implementation can be methodical, but allow for improvisation and unpredictability in the process. The end result of such a process of inquiry may be quite different from the original problem definition, as insights from each cycle of action research have the potential to lead to previously unanticipated courses of action.

Action research
An iterative trial-and-error process of discovery that involves diagnosing a problem, planning a solution, acting on the solution, evaluating the results of the actions, learning from the outcomes, and asking new questions

THREE-STEP MODEL

This model is the main component of the Planned Model of Change, and is the primary change framework for this chapter. The three steps of unfreezing, moving, and refreezing have become the foundation of many subsequent models of organizational change. Lewin's choice of wording has led to criticisms of this model, as some have argued that the static notions of unfreezing and refreezing do not adequately address the need for models of change to incorporate the constant ebb and flow of change within organizations.[23] However, when the three-step model is embedded in the four interconnected

FIGURE 9.4

THE PROCESS OF ACTION RESEARCH

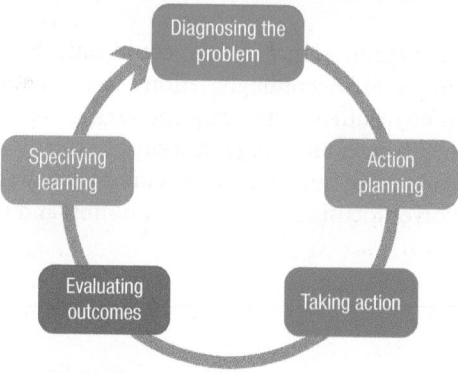

Source: Adapted from Susman, G.I. (1983). *Action Research: A Sociotechnical Systems Perspective* (95–113). Ed. G. Morgan. London: Sage.

elements of the planned model of change, it becomes clear that the model is far from static in its consideration of organizational change. To better understand this, we will examine the three steps of unfreezing, moving, and refreezing in closer detail.

UNFREEZING

As was discussed in the section on field Theory and the force-field analysis, Lewin proposed that organizational conditions exist in a state of quasi-equilibrium that is loosely maintained by opposing forces acting to drive and restrain conditions. Because individual behaviours are partly dependent on group forces such as norms, values, and roles, the equilibrium brought about by the various forces and by the norms, values and roles within the group must be destabilized so that new learning, new norms, and new conditions can take root.

A great deal of research has been done on the tendency to resist change, and the unfreezing stage represents the part of a change process where resistance to change is broken down. The open-system view of organizations presupposes that organizations, like organisms, tend toward homeostasis in that they try to maintain their equilibrium in changing environments, and are naturally "change resistors."[24] In addition to systemic sources of resistance to change, individuals may resist change actively by finding fault in or ridiculing the change plan, or passively by verbally agreeing to a course of action but failing to actually act, by refusing to share information, or by not following through with plans.[25] Destabilizing the status quo requires that resistance to change is overcome. Edgar Schein is a social psychologist who expanded on Lewin's three-step model by suggesting that the process of **unfreezing** requires three conditions to unfreeze current behaviours:[26]

1. *Disconfirmation of the validity of the status quo:* Essentially, this means that stakeholders must be convinced that the current modes of behaviour and way of doing things are no longer successful paths to achieving goals. This is done by

2. *Inducing survival anxiety:* Individuals and groups must develop a sense of survival anxiety, or pressure to change, in order to overcome resistance and to move away from current behaviours and toward new learning and new behaviours. However, new learning and new behaviours carry with them learning anxiety, or the fear of failure. In the context of a force-field analysis, survival anxiety can be considered a driving force, and learning anxiety a restraining force. Therefore, moving away from the status quo would require both increasing the driving force and reducing the restraining force (learning anxiety). Schein suggests that decreasing learning anxiety can be facilitated by

3. *Creating psychological safety:* Psychological safety is the belief that an individual can take certain risks and openly discuss workplace issues without fear of reprisal or threat to mental well-being. Schein recommends that psychological safety can be increased through interventions such as providing a strong organizational vision, consistent systems and structures, training, role models, and support groups, as well as by involving the learner. Thus, unfreezing requires that stakeholders develop the understanding that the current way of doing things is no longer acceptable, that continuing along the current path will lead to meaningful negative consequences, and that taking a risk on a new path or expressing new ways of doing things will not be judged negatively. Without satisfying these three conditions, change efforts are likely to be hampered by resistance.

UNFREEZING AT IBM

For decades IBM was considered a model corporate enterprise. IBM hired the smartest employees and gave them an excellent working environment and job security; customers knew that they could trust IBM's information technology and management solutions. It was a safe bet to buy IBM products and services. But by the mid-1990s, IBM was quickly running out of cash, and heading toward disaster. In the mid-1970s, IBM focused its resources on large mainframe computing, when the market was headed to miniaturized, stand-alone workstations. As the market for mainframe computers quickly dwindled through the 1980s and early 1990s, IBM did not have the resources to develop a competitive advantage in the personal computing market. However, the corporate culture at IBM that had been developing since the early 1960s was very strong. IBM was focused on developing and implementing integrated, large-scale solutions, whereas the information technology market had been cut into segments, where smaller, faster innovators were capturing market share. Having been accustomed to market domination and success, the culture at IBM was highly resistant to change, even in the face of broad media criticism.

Senior management at IBM looked outside the firm for the first time in its history to hire a new CEO. They were looking for a change agent who could transform the company. IBM had become frozen in its current condition after years of market dominance; as its market began to disappear, the company lacked the ability to "unfreeze"' to the point of its near demise. When Louis Gerstner took over as CEO in 1993, he set about unfreezing this behemoth of a company. By the time Mr. Gerstner arrived at IBM, employees had a strong sense that the status quo was no longer viable. Revenues from the mainframe computer market had fallen by more than 50 percent over the course of a couple of years, and the media coverage of IBM's woes had helped push several banks to reconsider their lending situation with IBM. The company that had a reputation for "no layoffs"' had seen the departure of roughly 120 000 employees in just three years.

To instill psychological safety, Mr. Gerstner called upon IBM's original strategy of offering customers a complete, unified solution, but using different activities. He confronted the criticism of many media outlets that IBM had become too big to change this late in the game by suggesting that IBM eliminate its bureaucratic ways, and he dealt with the employees honestly by admitting that the days of no layoffs at IBM were gone; IBM would have to change its size and its core activities. After laying out the overall customer strategy and focus, Gerstner left much of the implementation to managers' understanding of what the market needed. Rather than extensive planning, he wanted quick action, even if it led to occasional mistakes. Finally, Gerstner pointed out that while he was looking for small wins in the short term, this effort was going to take years.

IBM sold its last computer in 2005. Today it is the largest consulting organization in the world that connects hardware, software, and decision making to provide data analysis and information-based solutions to its customers. Many factors came together to bring about the unfreezing of IBM's culture and strategy back in the early 1990s; the board of directors, employees, and U.S. media and society helped unseat the status quo, while Louis Gerstner did much to bring about a sense of psychological safety that allowed the firm to progress into the moving stage of change. Without these factors coming together, IBM would not be the successful firm that it is today.

Sources: Gerstner, L.V. Jr. (2009). *Who Says Elephants Can't Dance?* Harper Collins e-books; "Chronological History of IBM," www-03.ibm.com/ibm/history/history/decade_1990.html; IBM corporate website www-03.ibm.com/employment/news/200908_volume3art2_realibm.html; *Business Week Magazine* www.businessweek.com/chapter/mills.htm.

MOVING

The unfreezing and moving stages of the three-step model parallel the action planning process. The unfreezing stage involves identifying the problems and action planning

around methods of enhancing driving forces and reducing restraining forces, and the moving stage of the three-step model focuses on taking action and evaluating the outcomes of those actions. Lewin mentions that the complexity of the interplay between the forces involved in change renders outcomes impossible to predict. Thus, the **moving** stage is the process of trial-and-error that can cycle back and forth between unfreezing and moving as change agents monitor the strength and effects of the moving process on driving and restraining forces. Successful movement requires experimentation, where mistakes can occur. Organizations that encourage experimentation must also develop a culture in which mistakes are accepted as part of the learning process. Organizational cultures that do not accept mistakes or that punish employees for mistakes will generally lead to defensive routines and single-loop learning.[27] When double-loop learning is employed during this step, change agents not only strive to achieve movement in the direction of the originally proposed change, but also seek to determine whether the original set direction or outcome is still the most important or relevant goal. This iterative process of action and research continues until a set of behaviours, values, and attitudes that are consistent with the overall change effort are achieved.

Moving
As the second stage of a change process, the moving stage involves the trial-and-error process of taking action to move the firm through the intended change

---

HR PLANNING NOTEBOOK 9.4

THE SIMILARITIES BETWEEN ORGANIZATIONAL CHANGE AND ADDICTION TREATMENT

Addiction treatment programs have long recognized that if individuals in need of treatment do not accept the fact that they have a problem, and desire to change, treatment is likely to fail. Popular television series like *Intervention* have acquainted us with the idea of gathering family and friends together with a loved one who is in need of help to confront the individual with the reality of his or her situation. An intervention is an effort to bring about an epiphany and the desire to change deeply entrenched behaviours. Organizational consultant Keith Ferrazzi notes that there are many similarities between addiction treatment programs and organizational change efforts. Where addiction treatment often includes an intervention in order to stimulate readiness to change, Lewin's three-step model of planned change includes an unfreezing stage, where change participants must develop a sense of survival anxiety, in which the status quo is no longer acceptable. Both programs imply that change will not occur without readiness for and deep acceptance of the need for change. Kotter refers to the need for short-term wins in his eight-step model for change; this is reflected in the 12-step program for Alcoholics Anonymous, which embraces short-term objectives like "not taking a drink today." Acknowledging that failures occur and that behavioural change includes setbacks is an important aspect of both organizational change and addiction treatment; short-term wins can assist in the motivation to persevere despite these difficulties. Overcoming addiction is difficult work. It offers some guidance to organizational change efforts by reminding us that significant changes to established patterns of behavior require not only individual introspection and change, but also change to our surrounding environment. Without changing our environment or culture, the cues to enact past behaviours remain strong, which increases the likely of reverting to the pre-change state.

Sources: Ferrazzi, K. (2014). "Managing Change, One Day at a Time," *Harvard Business Review*, 92, 23–25; www.recovery.org; "About the Alcoholics Anonymous (AA) 12-Step Recovery Program"; Ziedonis, D.M., Zammarelli, L., Seward, G., Oliver, K., Guydish, J., Hobart, M., & Meltzer, B. (2007). "Addressing Tobacco Through Organizational Change: A Case Study of an Addiction Treatment Organization." *Journal of Psychoactive Drugs*, 39, 451–459.

REFREEZING

The purpose of this stage is to establish new norms and modes of behaviour that are likely to reinforce the change that has taken place. The term **refreezing** may suggest that the organization is placed in a new form of stasis, but recall that the quasi-equilibrium that Lewin refers to in the unfreezing stage refers to a balance of forces that are supported by a set of norms and behaviours. Unless there are new group norms and routines to support individual behaviours, Lewin suggests that changes to individual behaviour will regress to their pre-changed state. In this phase, organizational structures, processes, and systems such as new compensation and benefits plans, revised selection criteria, training initiatives, job designs, or team or reporting structures are put into place to reinforce new cultural norms. The lack of attention to refreezing may be exemplified by the nature of popular organizational management techniques such as outsourcing or TQM, which rapidly become management fads and then quickly lose some of their popularity as the intended benefits fail to emerge for many firms. The implementation of these techniques themselves may be clearly codified and followed, but the development of organizational structures and practices to root them into the newly changed system may not be given sufficient managerial attention to allow them to flourish within the organization.

> **Refreezing**
> The third and final stage of a change initiative, refreezing involves putting policies, practices, and structures in place to establish new norms around the change

// DEVELOPMENT OF THE PLANNED CHANGE APPROACH

Planned change has endured since Lewin's approach was introduced in the 1940s, and has been further developed in many ways by many researchers and practitioners. One of the more popular approaches is John Kotter's eight-step model of change.[28] You may not be surprised to learn that this approach bears many similarities to Lewin's model, which suggests that the overall process has endured the test of time. Kotter's eight steps, and their relation to Lewin's planned approach are shown in Figure 9.5. The first three stages of this model, which include (1) *establishing a sense of urgency*, (2) *forming a guiding coalition*, and (3) *creating a vision* are clearly activities that mirror Lewin's unfreezing stage.

FIGURE 9.5

RELATIONSHIPS BETWEEN LEWIN'S THREE-STEP MODEL AND KOTTER'S EIGHT-STEP MODEL OF CHANGE

Lewin's 3-step Model

Unfreezing
- Disconfirm the status quo
- Create psychological safety

Moving
- Experiment

Refreezing
- Reinforce new norms & behaviours

Kotter's 8-step Model

i) Establish a sense of urgency
ii) Form a guiding coalition
iii) Create a vision

iv) Communicate the vision
v) Empower others to act on the vision
vi) Create short-term wins
vii) Consolidate improvements and produce more change
viii) Institutionalize new approaches

Source: Kotter, J.P. (2007). "Leading Change: Why Transformation Efforts Fail," *Harvard Business Review*, 85, 96–103.

The next four stages move the change process, and even include the reiterative nature of cycling between unfreezing and moving by (4) *communicating the vision*, (5) *empowering others to act on the vision*, (6) *planning for and creating short-term wins*, and (7) *consolidating improvements and producing still more change*. Finally, (8) *institutionalizing new approaches* clearly reflects the refreezing process. Common to all models of planned change is the assumption that change is a process that can be segmented into discrete and necessary steps that organizations all pass through en route to successful change. Kotter warns that the change process usually takes more time than managers suspect, and that skipping steps in a planned change effort in the hope of saving time or increasing efficiency is unlikely to yield positive results.[29]

// EMERGENT CHANGE

All planned approaches to change assume that change is initiated at the top of the organization based on identifiable and definable issues, has discrete steps, and includes a beginning and end point. This planned, linear approach might be used in a situation such as the implementation of a financial incentive plan that is designed to better align

---

HR PLANNING TODAY   9.3

EMERGENT CHANGE THROUGH VISION AND VALUES AT MENNONITE SAVINGS AND CREDIT UNION

An important element to successful emergent change is a shared understanding of the simple rules that drive the system. Credit unions are member-owned cooperatives in which members can draw low-interest loans from pooled deposits. The Mennonite Savings and Credit Union centred in Kitchener, Ontario, is such a cooperative, where members agree to embrace a faith-based set of convictions. By sharing similar religious beliefs, members develop rich mental models of the guiding principles of the Mennonite Savings and Credit Union, which are integrity, compassion, and responsible stewardship. These institutional values are directly associated with personally held religious values, which imbues the credit union's values with deep meaning and an understanding of the kinds of actions and behaviours that reflect those values. Furthermore, a main purpose of this credit union is to invest in the local community, and to return profits to the members. As such, the institution exists to serve the needs of its members.

When an organization is able to clarify and consistently message its members around its central principles, and when members identify strongly with the purpose of the organization, then member activities are likely to complement the needs of the organization. In a credit union, this means that members are less likely to abuse the credit-granting aspects of the institution, thereby lowering costs of defaults for all members. The kinds of loans that are granted and the types of services that are offered to members are not determined by what competitors are offering, or whether the organization can achieve economies of scale or scope through these activities, but whether the activities serve the needs of the members. When it comes to organizational change, a strongly shared understanding of the central principles and purpose of the organization can lead to thinking, actions, and innovations that are in step with the needs of the organization. Rather than stating a specific need or even a specific goal, these institutions develop necessary capabilities spontaneously and as the need arises.

Source: Mennonite Savings and Credit Union. https://www.mscu.com/AboutUs/MissionAndVision/

employee goals with organizational goals. However, if the change plan recognizes that change must take place, but has difficulty identifying the exact courses of action to take, and has goals that are broadly defined—for example, a goal to "improve customer service," the planned approach can be overly restrictive. Furthermore, as Lewin's notion of quasi-equilibrium based on a balancing of opposing forces suggests, change is often complex, dynamic, and unpredictable. Organizations are complex systems, and relationships in such systems tend to be nonlinear and highly interconnected, which lead to unintended consequences.[30] These characteristics evoke a process that is much more chaotic than the carefully controlled nature of the planned approach to change. Change researchers have recently begun to embrace the chaotic nature of change by applying chaos theory to models of organizational change.

CHAOS THEORY AND EMERGENT CHANGE

The development of organizational management over the past century has been focused on establishing order from chaos through systemization and control. **Chaos theory** recognizes that attempts to do this assume that the future can be both known and to some extent, controlled. However, scientists have learned that even models that perfectly match dynamic systems cannot predict the outcome of that system at a given point in time. For example, you may be familiar with the children's toy that is a pendulum with a magnet at the bottom of the pendulum as well as a magnet on the base of the toy underneath the pendulum. When the pendulum is put into motion, the two magnets interact to make the pendulum move in chaotic patterns. While it is possible to predict things like the average distance the pendulum will be from the base at a given moment, or the average length of time the pendulum will remain in motion, it is impossible to predict the exact position of the pendulum at any given moment during its travels. The properties of the system interact with one another in unpredictable ways to produce outcomes that simply cannot be predicted with accuracy.[31]

> **Chaos theory**
> Complex systems are based on some form of order, but can behave in unpredictable ways. The unpredictability of these systems results from the many interactions of the system variables and the consequences of differences in the initial states of those variables.

This is the essence of chaos theory, and it flies in the face of the popular Newtonian worldview of business as a controllable, predictable machine. We tend to think of chaos as a complete lack of order; however from a scientific perspective, chaos refers to a form of disorder in which behavioural patterns emerge in unpredictable and yet similar ways.[32] While the perfect model of a dynamic system may not be able to perfectly predict the state of that system at a given point in time, the model will produce outcomes that are consistent with the behaviour of that system. This can be understood through the myriad examples of the outcomes of chaos theory in our daily lives; for example, through the way snowflakes are formed by the same process that leads to all having six sides, and yet each is unique.[33] Chaos theory has been used in the study of business to demonstrate how small changes in the function of supply chain models can lead to unpredictable outcomes.[34] In short, chaotic systems produce recognizable patterns, with unpredictable outcomes.[35]

In the context of managing change, chaos theory provides a frame for understanding how a broadly defined goal such as "to improve customer service" can provide the basis on which successful change can be patterned. Dee Hock, former CEO of Visa, coined the term *chaordic organization* (a combination of the words chaos and order) to describe a management style whereby firms focus less on structure and control, and more on a guiding purpose. A clearly understood and shared guiding purpose provides the order necessary for organizations to spontaneously develop their own structure and system.[36]

Tetenbaum[37] points out that chaos is actually governed by underlying rules, and in Hock's chaordic organization those rules are the firm's purpose and the principles that guide employees toward behaviours that are harmonious with that purpose. Examples of chaordic behaviour in nature are the tendencies for birds to flock together or fish to swim in tightly coordinated schools.[38] Flocks of birds dart through the air with a degree of coordination that suggests an extremely high level of communication and integration. How is a signal to turn in a particular direction transmitted instantly through a flock of hundreds of birds? Craig Reynolds, a software engineer developed a computer simulation model of the flocking behaviour of birds using three simple rules: (1) *separation*; avoid crowding other members of the flock, (2) *alignment*; steer towards the average direction of other members of the flock, and (3) *cohesion*; move toward the average position of members of the flock. These three simple rules created a model of flocking behaviour that replicates the flocking of birds so well that it was adopted by Hollywood to create bird and bat flocking animations in the *Batman Returns* movie.[39]

Using the principles of chaordic behaviour to manage change therefore suggests that emergent change is a bottom-up process in that it originates from and is enacted by all members at all levels of the organization, and that it is guided by simple principles that are widely held throughout the organization. For example, Apple's success can in part be attributed to the fact that all the company's products demonstrate a commitment to their guiding principles of ease of use, integration of products, and innovative industrial design. One can imagine that when developing innovations at Apple, hardware engineers, software engineers, and designers all have these guiding principles at the forefront of their thinking, which may explain why Apple's products have been enormously successful, time and time again.

The idea of a chaordic organization also suggests that firms must focus on creating systems and structures that communicate the guiding principles in a consistent and unambiguous manner, on giving employees the skills and autonomy to be adaptive in their environment, to leverage diversity to broaden the creative scope of the firm, to make use of teams so that employees can interact and develop ideas, and to encourage information sharing among employees.[40] Change in the context of a chaordic organization is an emergent phenomenon rather than planned. Change occurs as a form of adaptation and as a result of learning, and so the most important attributes an organization can develop in order to promote emergent change are those of a learning organization.

ORGANIZATIONAL LEARNING

How does an organization improve its products, its services, its manufacturing process, or its customer service? Should strategy always be developed at the top of the organization and implemented down to the business lines? Should change? If not, how can strategy or change come from the bottom of the organization? Top-down strategies for learning, strategy development, or change can involve focus groups, customer surveys, six-sigma or TQM methods, or formal training, among other activities. The strategies for bottom-up learning, strategy development, or change are very different. Imagine an organization in which the employees working in the assembly plant to produce the same product many times over develop such a high degree of competence that they begin to find successful shortcuts, or better ways of assembling the product; or the organization in which the sales staff develop a rich understanding of what the customer is looking for in your products. Employees have direct contact with the products of their labour

Coffee is one of the most traded agricultural commodities in the world. It is also one of the most valuable commodities exported by developing countries. As a commodity-based industry, the market price for coffee is set according to its global availability more than its quality. Because of the speculation in coffee prices and the global reach of the coffee market, coffee farmers can lose money on their crops due to the fluctuations in the global price of coffee. In the commodity market, farmers deliver their crop to a central co-op, where their crop is combined with those of other local farmers, and the farmer is paid according to the going rate for green (unroasted) coffee. These coffees are then purchased by the large coffee buyers such as Kraft, Proctor and Gamble, and Nestlé.

The specialty coffee industry is the portion of the coffee industry that is focused on the highest quality coffee. Quality in coffee is defined in terms of the transparency of the process that led to the production of the coffee, from farm and soil, to how the coffee beans are separated from the coffee cherries, to transportation, roasting, and finally to the brewing process itself. This is an industry that is emerging from the commodity coffee industry, and it has grown from 1 percent of the total coffee market in the 1970s to roughly 50 percent of the market today. A few of the companies leading the evolution of the specialty coffee industry include Intelligentsia Coffee (based out of Chicago), Stumptown Coffee Roasters (in Portland, Oregon), and George Howell Coffee (in Acton, Massachusetts). The values that guide this industry are quality and transparency. These values are associated with the principle that everything done to the coffee cherry once it is plucked from the tree can degrade the quality that is locked into the bean. The process of delivering that bean to the cup must preserve as much of that quality as possible.

Guided by this principle and these values, the leaders in the specialty coffee industry travel to the areas where coffee is produced throughout the world and develop relationships with farmers who are interested in adhering to these values. By doing so, the farmer steps away from the commodity market, and develops a purchase agreement with the specialty coffee retailer at rates well above the commodity market price. This begins the process of transforming not just the way the coffee is farmed, but how the coffee is processed, and how it is transported from the farm in Ethiopia or Peru to the roastery in Portland or Chicago. Every farm and every geographic region has its own unique qualities and problems to overcome, and so the solutions can range from planting more shade trees around the coffee trees to long-term projects to bring water to remote farming communities to facilitate the washing and processing of the green coffees. Relationships in the specialty coffee industry are more intimate, where the retailer knows the farmer, and the farmer learns how his green coffees are brought to and consumed by the rest of the world. Problems are solved locally, and decision making is more democratic and is highly decentralized. The participants in this industry develop more of a system view of the coffee value chain, and every member of that value chain, from farmer to barista (and ultimately the consumer) understands the basic guiding principle and values, and each plays a role in the transformation and development of the specialty coffee industry.

Source: SCAA. "U.S. Specialty Coffee Consumption Report." www.scaa.org/?page=resources&d=statistic-and-reports. Retrieved March 12, 2015.

and can develop a highly nuanced understanding of their jobs and consequently how to improve aspects of the organization that are separated from senior management often by several layers of management. Employees also have a keen understanding of how organizational processes fit together. How many people do you know who have at least one story about an organizational process or practice that makes no sense or that runs contrary to stated organizational objectives? If the firm could harness the knowledge in these employees and further encourage this kind of inquisitive thinking, it could tap into a diverse and almost limitless source of innovation and improvement. Peter Senge[41] discusses the concept of organizational learning in his seminal book *The Fifth Discipline*,

which explains the concept and benefits of organizational learning, and outlines the necessary conditions for organizational learning.

One of the first aspects of **organizational learning** is to move away from viewing the organization from the perspective of a singular focus such as "maximizing shareholder value." Such a single-minded objective tends to engender single-loop learning, and brings with it the difficulties of trying to predict and bring about a particular future state. Instead, Senge suggests that "our primary tasks in complex human systems are to become more reflective on the reasoning that guides our actions and to gradually improve our theories in use."[42] This sounds very much like double-loop learning, as it requires managers and employees to re-examine the practices, processes, and assumptions that guide current activities.

Senge further suggests that rather than becoming focused on specific numeric goals, which have the potential to limit our natural tendency to try to make sense of our overall environment, organizations should seek to promote the learning processes that people would otherwise use to improve.[43] These natural learning processes are supported through the principles of a learning organization. Thus, organizational learning is one of the most important attributes necessary to bring about emergent change. The elements of organizational learning comprise (1) *personal mastery*, (2) *mental models*, (3) *building a shared vision*, (4) *team learning*, and (5) *systems thinking*.

> **Organizational learning**
> An approach to learning that applies double-loop learning and an attempt to understand how the entire system may be affected by change. Organizational learning allows knowledge from any individual in the organization to become incorporated into the firm's culture and processes.

PERSONAL MASTERY

Developing personal mastery is not necessarily about becoming very good at what one does, although people who have a high level of personal mastery do become very good at what they do. **Personal mastery** has more to do with personal development, a commitment to learning, and to achieving what one really wants, one's personal vision.[44] Vision flows from a sense of purpose. Where purpose can be thought of as a vocation, a calling, what one truly cares about in life, vision represents a picture of where one wants to be. Goals provide measurable markers of success toward that vision. Think of what you would like to be doing professionally in five years; how does this vision connect with your sense of purpose? Do you have goals to help you to indicate whether you are on track with your vision? Now imagine that you get that job. What comes next for you? Re-establishing a new vision that is connected to your purpose is the source of energy that people with a strong sense of personal mastery use to propel themselves through life. When organizational change is connected to a clearly articulated organizational vision, and that vision connects with the individual, Senge suggests that personal mastery will lead employees to be more committed to their work, and take more initiative at work.[45] Senge further suggests that organizations can actively promote personal mastery in the workplace through building climates that foster the development of personal visions, that encourage frank and open discussions about the workplace, and that question the status quo.[46]

> **Personal mastery**
> The understanding of one's purpose and the development of a personal vision

MENTAL MODELS

These are the organized knowledge structures that individuals use to help navigate the volume and complexity of information that we perceive from our environment. **Mental models** help us to describe, ascribe cause to, and explain our surroundings.[47] Our mental models help to shape the heuristics, the rules-of-thumb that we use to simplify

> **Mental model**
> An internal representation of the way things work. Mental models influence the causal attributions that we make.

and increase the speed of decision making.[48] At the team level, shared mental models contribute to higher team performance.[49] We are largely unaware of the mental models that we employ, but they are responsible for many of the causal attributions that we make; for example, if we meet someone who claims to like classical music, we may think that person is well educated.

Because mental models are assumptions or generalizations that are ingrained within us, they can limit our openness to learning or to understanding novel situations or information in new ways. In organizations, institutionalized mental models can limit the firm's ability to take advantage of opportunities, or to change, or to understand when change is necessary. Furthermore, organizational defensive routines can insulate the firm from examining its mental models.[50] The importance of mental models to a learning organization is that when we become aware of the mental models that guide and limit our actions, we can hold them up to the light, and are in a better position to evaluate the quality and context of our decision making. When organizational groups become aware of their mental models and open them up to critical examination, organizations can understand when their mental models no longer serve them successfully in a changing environment, and can adapt their mental models to the changing conditions. A planning method that organizations can use to challenge existing mental models is scenario planning (see Chapter 5).[51] Other methods to institutionalize the questioning and testing of mental models include practices that encourage reflective skills in employees, and a culture that allows employees to challenge organizational thinking.

SHARED VISION

Senge defines shared vision as "… the answer to the question 'What do we want to create?"[52] A shared vision helps to connect people to a greater purpose, which facilitates organizational identification, and accepting the organization's goals as one's own goals.[53] Great leaders tend to encourage a shared vision by creating pictures of the future that are embedded in important social values.[54] When Steve Jobs shared his vision for NeXT in the mid-1980s, a computer company that built computers intended for higher education and business markets,[55] his vision was to "revolutionize the educational system of a nation."[56] People want to do work that matters, and when an organization can galvanize employees around a shared vision that reflects an important social purpose, it connects the individual with the other employees and with the organization in a deep and meaningful way.[57] In terms of organizational learning, a shared vision is the bonding element that brings together and focuses the efforts of employees to pursue personal mastery in ways that are relevant to the goals of the firm, and helps employees to understand current shared organizational mental models and develop new shared mental models.[58]

TEAM LEARNING

Have you ever been part of a group that made you feel as though you were performing at a higher level than you could have ever achieved on your own? We experience team learning when working with a particularly good team at work, in a successful group project at school, or with a sports team or a group of musicians. When experiencing **team learning**, our individual ideas and efforts are combined with the team's, and amplified by others within the team to arrive at something we could not have achieved on our own. The most important element of team learning is open dialogue, where team

Team learning
The interaction of individual ideas and efforts toward a team objective that result in outcomes that exceed the capabilities of any individual on the team

members feel free to discuss and share ideas openly and without fear of embarrassment or reproach. Dialogue is important because it is what enables people to see beyond their own perspective and to better understand the boundaries of their own mental models. When we include the views of others into our own thinking, we are broadening our understanding and incorporating *systems thinking* in our decision processes.

SYSTEMS THINKING

A great deal of organizational thinking tends to be linear in nature: we look at systems in terms of input-to-output, and we analyze decisions in terms of cost-benefit. **Systems thinking** is a way to examine problems by looking at them in the context of the system in which they occur, rather than as isolated issues. Diagrams of systems using systems thinking tend to be circular or iterative, where one part of the system influences or is influenced by another part of the system. For example, a systems diagram of pouring your morning cup of coffee may look like the diagram in Figure 9.6. The desired amount of coffee in your cup influences the angle at which you hold the coffee carafe, which affects the rate at which your cup fills with coffee, which in turn influences the coffee level in your cup. This process continues until the cup is filled to the desired level. Such a feedback loop shows all the participating structures in the system, and leads to a deep understanding of the roles of each of the structures in the system. Using systems thinking, behaviour is influenced by organizational structures such as the norms, the management practices, and the human capital and social capital within the firm.[59] Viewing organizations from a systems thinking perspective leads away from viewing actions or behaviours as the sources of problems, and looks to the role of structures in influencing problems. Systems thinking provides a method to understand the forces that must be influenced in order for change to take place.

Senge suggests that the five disciplines are interdependent, that each requires the other in order for a learning organization to be realized.[60] For example, vision in the absence of systems thinking cannot lead to a rich understanding of how the vision can be implemented successfully. Without vision, personal mastery is not possible, since individuals cannot achieve the necessary creative tension without understanding where one needs to be (i.e., vision) in relation to where one currently stands.

FIGURE 9.6

SYSTEMS THINKING MODEL OF POURING COFFEE INTO A CUP

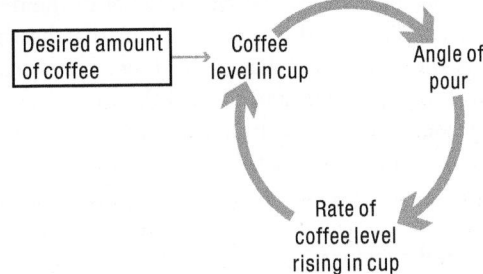

Overall, the five disciplines of a learning organization are vitally important to enabling emergent change. One principle of emergent change is that the order that governs chaos arrives through simple rules that are widely understood. In the context of a learning organization, these simple rules can be represented by the organization's shared vision. Shared mental models and a shared vision ensure that the organizational structures and processes that emerge through chaordic change are in line with organizational needs and environmental constraints or opportunities. Learning organizations permit change as a bottom-up process as well as a top-down process by essentially putting everyone "on the same page" and then allowing them to fill in the lines together. As line-level employees learn new methods to improve products or new ways to satisfy customers, learning organizations build the structures to permit that learning to move up through the organization, where those new methods become incorporated into the organization's practices and get implemented back down throughout the firm. Using organizational learning, firms remain in a constant state of change, or adaptation, by taking in new learning, wherever it is experienced within the firm, and diffusing through the entire organization. In this way, emergent change occurs spontaneously and as needed, rather than as a planned reaction to an event.

// BRINGING IT ALL TOGETHER

After reading this chapter, you are probably aware that change is a dynamic and unpredictable process. Any process that can be described in this way must be approachable from multiple perspectives, with multiple methods. A change process that makes use of the materials from this chapter would include the following features:

IDENTIFY THE PROBLEM

Starting with the firm's strategy and the activities that implement the strategy, identify the problem. Double-loop learning and the principles of a learning organization will facilitate the identification of the primary issues. Once the problem has been identified and clearly expressed, the need for change must be spread throughout the organization.

UNFREEZING

There must be widespread understanding of the need for change, and an associated path that moves toward a solution. This stage of the change process is difficult because of the many challenges in bringing about a mutually held belief in the need for and direction of change. A force-field analysis based on the problem that has been identified is an excellent tool to identify the factors that may be leading to resistance to change and the factors that can help to leverage movement toward the intended change. At this point in the process, change leaders must use their political and persuasive skills to ensure that as many stakeholders as possible agree that the status quo is no longer acceptable, and to develop a shared vision of the firm's future. HR practices must be monitored for the extent to which they align with the change, and adjusted to move the culture away from the status quo and toward the change.

MOVING

The principles of emergent change and a learning organization are apparent in the moving stage. Moving toward the new direction is fraught with uncertainty and the high risk of unanticipated consequences. Changes to policies, work activities, and organization structures should be associated with short-term goals, so that stakeholders can understand when change is moving in the intended direction, and to celebrate these small victories. An organization that empowers its employees to act autonomously, that can effectively communicate its strategic intentions around change, and that can challenge its existing mental models will be more likely to demonstrate emergence in this stage of change. This means that employees will be able to adapt spontaneously to the requirements to implement effective change based on their understanding of what needs to be done.

REFREEZING

After change has been implemented, the new state must be reinforced, or the organization is likely to revert to its pre-change state. To balance the driving and stabilizing forces around the new status quo, HR practices, employee tasks, organizational structure, or other organizational policies must be put into place and monitored for success. For example, an organization that has moved from a focus on production efficiency to more of a customer-focused perspective could measure the extent to which a customer service climate is developing among employees, and the extent to which customer satisfaction is changing, while at the same time monitoring production efficiency.

// SUMMARY

Organizations are complex, open systems that both influence and are influenced by their environment. The interconnected nature of organizational structures, processes, practices, members, and the changing environment renders the prediction of change outcomes a practical impossibility: the chances of unforeseen events or interactions and of unintended consequences are simply too high. At their root, both the planned and emergent approaches to change share an emphasis on the importance of learning, of having a shared sense of purpose, and of being able to adapt the change implementation as it progresses. As organizations move toward flatter structures, more fluid job roles, and greater employee autonomy, they will likely turn increasingly toward efforts to institutionalize a culture of change, and incorporate elements of both planned and emergent change into change efforts. Both the planned and emergent approaches to change can influence how organizations move toward that path.

KEY TERMS

action research p. 233
chaos theory p. 239
double-loop learning p. 223
force-field analysis p. 230

WEB LINKS

Some very good overviews of action research:
http://web.net/robrien/papers/arfinal.html#_edn3
http://www.ascd.org/publications/books/100047/chapters/What-Is-Action-Research¢.aspx

Excellent resources around managing change:
http://hrweb.mit.edu/learning-development/learning-topics/change

A valuable resource around HR planning and change management:
http://www.conferenceboard.ca

DISCUSSION QUESTIONS

1. What are the main reasons that planned approaches to change might fail?

2. Can emergent change be intentional? How can emergent change be used to bring about a specific end result?

3. What are some of the benefits of shared mental models within organizations? Are there any drawbacks to widely shared mental models within firms?

EXERCISES

1. Conduct a force-field analysis of a change from an in-class course delivery format to an online course delivery format for this course. What is your change question? What are the main driving and restraining forces? What actions can you recommend to strengthen the driving forces and reduce the potency of the restraining forces?

2. The opening vignette about Yahoo! discusses some of the steps initiated at Yahoo! to move the firm through an organizational change. Marissa Mayer has been heavily criticized for several of the decisions made during this implementation. What could Mayer have done to reduce the amount of controversy around these policy changes?

3. Think of an organization that you know well or admire. Can you state that organization's purpose? Rather than focusing on organizational goals, try to think of a purpose as something bigger than the organization that is related to society in general.

What might be some of the simple guiding principles that guide emergent change at this organization?

4. A friend of yours has just returned from a vacation and brought you a gift of a very special and valuable kind of tea. Unfortunately, you know nothing about this specific tea. Using action research as a guide, describe how you would learn how to brew the perfect pot of this tea.

CASE STUDY   CHANGE AT TIGER BOOTS

Tiger Brand Boots has been manufacturing high-quality leather boots and shoes primarily for use in the skilled trades and heavy construction work markets since 1935. Tiger Boots are built tough, to withstand potentially dirty and demanding working conditions, and last for years. In addition to being tough, Tiger Boots must be comfortable to wear and work in all day long. Tiger Boots is one of only three boot/shoe companies in the United States that still performs all manufacturing activities in the United States. This adds the distinct benefit of a made-in-America label to a boot that has built a solid reputation as being among the best work boots available. Tiger currently sells its footwear through retailers of work and safety clothing and goods, as well as its own nine factory-owned retail stores and an on-line store within the United States. With 250 factory workers, 50 corporate employees, 30 workers in distribution, and 45 retail employees, Tiger generates roughly $200 million in revenues yearly.

While the cost of American labour is much higher than the labour rates available to the majority of the boot and shoe manufacturers who use overseas manufacturing, the cost disadvantage is partly offset by the fact that Tiger Boots has its own tannery. The animal hides used in the production of leather boots and shoes must be put through a lengthy treatment process before being dyed and then used to make boots or shoes. This ancient art is performed in tanneries, of which there are only a few remaining in North America. With so few tanneries in the world and the importance of high-quality leathers in the production of boots and shoes, tanneries can have a strong influence on the price and quality of leathers available to manufacturers. Thus, Tiger Boots' tannery is an important resource to the firm. Tiger Boots are priced at the top end of the market for work boots and shoes. The average price for a pair of Tiger Boots is around $300, with a range from $250 to roughly $450 for the company's products, whereas many of their competitors in the boot/shoe industry price their products at $100 or less. However, Tiger Boots claims that many of their boots that were purchased five years ago or more are still being worn today, and that with proper care and maintenance, a Tiger boot has an indefinite lifespan. To support this claim, Tiger's website shows many of the aspects of the company's production methods, which involve a high degree of highly skilled hand-crafted work and include a recrafting service. Once the sole wears out of the boots or shoes, owners of Tiger Brand Boots can return their footwear to the company where the boot will be completely stripped down and rebuilt with a new sole and refinishing the leather on the equipment used to originally produce the boot, all for a modest fee (around $125).

The market for work boots has been steady over the past 25 years, and production can be forecast relatively easily using economic indicators of growth in the construction and skilled trades industries. Tiger Brand Boots has a very strong brand name in these markets and its market share has remained steady at around 10 percent. However, while 80 percent of its production is purchased in the construction and skilled trades market, the other 20 percent of production goes to the casual menswear fashion market, and this trend is increasing. It seems that young men are increasingly wearing high-quality leather boots and shoes as part of current fashion trends, and Tiger Brand's cachet in the construction and skilled trades market gives it added value as a choice of menswear. Tiger does not have the manufacturing capacity or organizational capabilities to adequately serve the growing casual menswear market without making changes, and management is at a crossroads. Dave Davenport, the CEO, believes that this represents a tremendous opportunity for Tiger Brand Boots to create a new market and become a bigger company. Preet Gupta, the head of operations is not so convinced; she points out that in order to develop this market, Tiger will need to adopt an entirely new marketing strategy, deepen relationships with popular retailers like Aldo and The Gap, to say nothing about the differences in boot and shoe design between the construction market and the casual menswear market. Do buyers in the casual market really want a steel-toed dress shoe? New designers will need to be hired, and the manufacturing needs of the as-yet-unknown boot and shoe designs will need to be assessed. On top of all this, the cost of leather is increasing due to the increased global demand for leather goods. Tiger's boots are currently double the cost of the average buyer's boot/shoe. As the cost of production continues to increase, will Tiger have to price itself out of the market altogether, or cut its quality to better compete with the lower end of the market? Finally, expanding into this market would require hiring and training another shift of workers. Given that Tiger uses skilled workers, training will take more than a month to bring a new employee to the point of being self-sufficient on the production line.

Dave has countered that this expansion would take advantage of Tiger's tannery, which would protect Tiger from many of the effects of the increase in the price of leather. Dave also believes that these other required capabilities can be developed quickly, or that Tiger could consider producing a new "economy" line of boots and shoes for the casual menswear market that uses the same leathers as the premium footwear, but is glued together rather than hand-stitched, and so cannot be recrafted. This line of footwear would not require the level of skilled production of the premium line, but would retain much of the Tiger look and feel that customers have come to appreciate. Cecily Wan, head of marketing, bristles every time she hears this suggestion, and warns that such a line of economy boots would threaten Tiger Boot's value proposition and threaten Tiger's strong brand value. However, she is excited by the possibility of expanding into a new market, and the enormous opportunity that an expansion could hold for Tiger Brand Boots.

At the most recent corporate meeting, senior management agreed that this expansion is worth the risk. However, they are not certain how to introduce this idea to employees, or how to proceed with the change. Some of the questions and concerns even among senior management are not yet fully answered or addressed, and the line employees are likely to raise many issues as well, especially around the ways in which their jobs may be affected as a result of the proposed changes. Although they are not unionized, the employees are highly skilled and Tiger Boots holds their long-standing employees in very high regard.

QUESTION

1. Would you recommend that Tiger Boots take a planned approach, emergent approach, or blended approach to this change effort? If you think they should take a blended approach, what portions of the change should be planned and what should be emergent? Explain your choice of approach with a draft of your change plan.

// REFERENCES

1. Source: Based on interview with Jason Flick, President and CEO, You.i, and Deborah Naczynski, Head of Education and Outreach, You.i.

2. Senge, P.M., A. Kleiner, C. Roberts, R.B. Ross, and B.J. Smith. 1994. *The Fifth Discipline Fieldbook.* New York: Doubleday

3. Crossan, M J., M.J. Rouse, J.N. Fry, and P.J. Killing. 2008. *Strategic Analysis and Action* (7th ed.). Toronto: Pearson Prentice Hall.

4. Beer, M., and N. Nohria. 2000. *Breaking the Code of Change.* Boston: Harvard Business School Press.

5. French, W.L., and C.H. Bell. 1999. *Organizational Development: Behavioral Science and Interventions for Organizational Improvement* (6th ed.). Upper Saddle River: Prentice-Hall.

6. Burnes, B. 1992. *Managing Change: A Strategic Approach to Organizational Development and Renewal.* London: Pitman Publishing.

7. Ibid.

8. Argyris, C. 1991. "Teaching Smart People How to Learn." *Harvard Business Review, 3*: 99–109.

9. Ibid.

10. CDC. 2010. *Multistate Outbreak of Salmonella Typhimurium Infections Linked to Peanut Butter, 2008–2009 (Final Update).* http://www.cdc.gov/salmonella/typhimurium/update.html. Retrieved March 11, 2015; CNN. 2014. "Unprecedented Verdict: Peanut Executive Guilty in Deadly Salmonella Outbreak." http://www.cnn.com/2014/09/19/us/peanut-butter-salmonella-trial. Retrieved March 11, 2015; . CTV News. 2009. "Georgia Peanut Plant Owner, 2 Others Found Guilty in Salmonella-poisoning Trial." http://www.ctvnews.ca/health/georgia-peanut-plant-owner-2-others-found-guilty-in-salmonella-poisoning-trial-1.2015335. Retrieved March 11, 2015.

11. Hayes, J. 2010. *The Theory and Practice of Change Management.* (3rd ed.). New York: Palgrave MacMillan.

12. Beer, M., and N. Nohria. 2000. *Breaking the Code of Change.* Boston: Harvard Business School Press.

13. Kotter, J.P. 1990. "What Leaders Really Do." *Harvard Business Review, 68,* 112–117.

14. Tetenbaum, T.J. 1998. "Shifting Paradigms: From Newton to Chaos." *Organizational Dynamics, 26,* 21–32.

15. Krackhardt, D., and J.R. Hanson, J.R. 1993. "Informal Networks: The Company Behind the Chart." *Harvard Business Review, 71*, 104–111; Ferris, G.R., D.C. Treadway, P.L. Perrewe, R.L. Brouer, C. Douglas, and S. Lux. 2007. "Political Skills in Organizations." *Journal of Management, 33*, 290–320.

16. Ibid.

17. Appelbaum. S.H., J. Roberts, and B.T. Shapiro. 2009. "Cultural Strategies in M&As: Investigating ten case studies." *Journal of Executive Education, 8*: 33–58.

18. Burnes, B. 2004. "Kurt Lewin and the Planned Approach to Change: A re-appraisal." *Journal of Management Studies, 41*, 977–1002.

19. Surowiecki, J. 2004. *The Wisdom of Crowds.* New York: Random House.

20. Dickens, L., and K. Watkins. 1999. "Action Research: Rethinking Lewin." *Management Learning, 30*(2): 127–140.

21. Clausen, K.W. 2014. "Action Research: Not Just for the Classroom." *Canadian Journal of Action Research, 15*: 1–2.

22. Beaulieu, R.J. 2013. "Action research: Trends and variations." *Canadian Journal of Action Research, 14*: 29–39.

23. Burnes, 2004.

24. Flood, R.L., and E.R. Carson. 1993. *Dealing with Complexity: An Introduction to the Theory and Application of Systems Science.* New York: Plenum Press.

25. Hultman, K.E. 1995. "Scaling the Wall of Resistance." *Training and Development, 49:* 15–28.

26. Schein, E.H. 1999). *The Corporate Culture Survival Guide.* San Francisco, CA: Jossey-Bass.

27. Argyris, C. 1991. "Teaching Smart People How to Learn." *Harvard Business Review, 3*: 99–109.

28. Kotter, J.P. 2007. "Leading Change: Why Transformation Efforts Fail." *Harvard Business Review, 85*: 96–103.

29. Ibid.

30. Tetenbaum, 1998.

31. Senge, P.M. 2000. "The Puzzles and Paradoxes of How Living Companies Create Wealth: Why Single-Valued Objective Functions Are Not Quite Enough." In M. Beer and N. Nohria, eds., *Breaking the Code of Change,* pp. 59–82. Boston: Harvard Business School Press.

32. Tetenbaum, 1998.

33. Ibid.

34. Levy, D. 1994. "Chaos Theory and Strategy: Theory, Application, and Managerial Implications. *Strategic Management Journal, 15*: 167–178.

35. Ibid.

36. Hock, D. 2000. "Birth of Chaordic Change." *Executive Excellence, 17*: 6–8.

37. Tetenbaum, 1998.

38. Ibid.

39. Reynolds Engineering & Design. (n.d.). *Boids.* http://www.red3d.com/cwr/boids.

40. Tetenbaum, 1998.

41. Senge, P.M. 1990. *The Fifth Discipline: The Art and Practice of the Learning Organization*. New York: Doubleday.

42. Senge, 2000.

43. Ibid.

44. Senge, 1990.

45. Ibid.

46. Ibid.

47. Mathieu, J.E., G.F. Goodwin, T.S. Heffner, E. Salas, and J.A. Cannon-Bowers. 2000. "The Influence of Shared Mental Models on Team Process and Performance. *Journal of Applied Psychology, 85*: 273–283.

48. Gauffroy, C., and P. Barrouillet. 2009. "Heuristic and Analytic Processes in Mental Models for Conditionals: An Integrative Developmental Theory." *Developmental Review, 29*: 249–282.

49. Smith-Jentsch, K.A., J.E. Mathieu, and K. Kraiger. 2005. "Investigating Linear and interactive effects of shared mental models on safety and efficiency in a field setting." *Journal of Applied Psychology, 90*: 523–535; Burtscher, M.J., M. Kolbe, J. Wacker, and T. Manser. 2011. "Interactions of Team Mental Models and Monitoring Behaviors Predict Team Performance in Simulated Anesthesia Inductions." *Journal of Experimental Psychology, 17*: 257–269.

50. Argyris, C. 1991. "Teaching Smart People How to Learn." *Harvard Business Review, 3*, 99–109.

51. Chermack, T.J., and R.A. Swanson. 2008. "Scenario Planning: Human Resource Development's Strategic Learning Tool." *Advances in Developing Human Resources, 10*: 129–146.

52. Senge, 1990.

53. Ashforth, B.E., S.H. Harrison, and K.G. Corley. 2008. "Identification in Organizations: An Examination of Four Fundamental Questions." *Journal of Management, 34*, 325–374; Fujita, K., Trope, Y., Liberman, N., and M. Levin-Sagi. 2006. Construal levels and self-control. *Journal of Personality and Social Psychology, 90*(3), 351–67.

54. Conger, J.A. (1991). Inspiring others: The language of leadership. *Academy of Management Executive, 5*, 31-45.

55. Wikipedia. (n.d.). NeXT. Retrieved from http://en.wikipedia.org/wiki/NeXT

56. Conger, J.A. (1991). Inspiring others: The language of leadership. *Academy of Management Executive, 5*, 31-45.p.45.

57. Senge, 1990.

58. Ibid.

59. Ibid.

60. Ibid.

CHAPTER

HR ASSESSMENT AND ANALYTICS

CHAPTER LEARNING OUTCOMES

AFTER READING THIS CHAPTER, YOU SHOULD BE ABLE TO:

- Understand the importance of measuring the effectiveness of HRM activities through workforce analytics.

- Outline five aspects of HRM that can be evaluated using the 5C model for measuring effectiveness: compliance with laws and regulations, client satisfaction, culture management to influence employee attitudes, cost control of the labour component of the budget, and the contribution of HR programs.

- Discuss methods of assessment, such as cost–benefit analysis, utility analysis, and auditing techniques.

- Identify the challenges in measuring HR activities and determine the metrics that are important to the stakeholders in organizations.

Jane Haberbusch, vice-president of HR for Enbridge Gas Distribution, is a keen supporter of the HR scorecard, which she discusses below.

The scorecard works like this: Motivated employees provide great customer service, which results in overall customer satisfaction, which is then correlated with reduced operating costs and increased net profit margins.

Our customer satisfaction ratings are the highest in our sector. We know that motivated and engaged employees provide the best levels of customer service. If you had a workforce that was highly motivated and actively engaged, what types of evidence would you see?

- *Low levels of employee turnover, especially of the "critical keepers"*
- *High levels of employee engagement and employee satisfaction (usually measured through employee feedback instruments)*
- *Low levels of absenteeism and "presenteeism" (showing up for work but not necessarily being productive)*
- *High levels of alignment to company goals and objectives*
- *Effective development of succession candidates to ensure leadership continuity*
- *Enhanced levels of innovation and creativity in response to business challenges*

Using these types of outcomes as measures and assigning stretch targets ensures focus and alignment of all HR-related initiatives. So, for example, before we introduce an HR practice such as a mentoring program for high potentials, we need to establish the connection or the "line of sight" to the company's overall goals.[1]

Source: Courtesy of Jane Haberbusch.

Aligning HRM programs and policies with organizational goals is the beginning of the strategic HR planning process. Assessing whether these policies and practices were effective is the end of one cycle in the planning process, because HR professionals need to know how their programs and policies are performing.

// WORKFORCE ANALYTICS

Corporate scorekeeping allows organizations to make the adjustments necessary to reach their goals. The scorecard, with its measures of key indicators, focuses managers' and employees' attention on what is important to the organization. Focusing on desired results increases the ability to attain the results. Measures allow us to make judgments about the relative effectiveness of various policies and practices, just as baseball scores and statistics allow fans to track the success of baseball teams. In business, the motivation to measure is driven by the need to improve results. A recent study by Deloitte showed that the use of workforce metrics (or analytics) resulted in improved financial, leadership and recruiting performance. However, only about 14 percent of companies in the study used workforce analytics to plan future workforce initiatives.[2]

The use of workforce analytics (first introduced in Chapter 8) has a variety of meanings. In its simplest form, it is about how HR metrics, such as turnover and employee engagement, are used to describe the workforce. For others, the comparison of these metrics (called benchmarking and discussed later in this chapter) elevates the value of workforce analytics. For many, the value lies in being able to use the metrics to predict outcomes (for example, high turnover in a store will predict lower customer satisfaction

and lower sales). This definition captures all of the above: **HR analytics** is an evidence-based approach for making better decisions about employees and HR policies, using a variety of tools to report HR metrics and to predict outcomes of HR programs.[3]

The model of strategic HRM planning outlined in Chapter 1 called for the measurement of the success of the plan. The tracking of customer satisfaction or absenteeism rates not only measures progress but also pinpoints weaknesses and identifies gaps. Just as organizations keep scorecards on their financial effectiveness, so too must the HR department track the effectiveness of its programs.

<aside>
HR analytics
HR analytics is an evidence-based approach for making better decisions about employees and HR policies, using a variety of tools to report HR metrics and to predict outcomes of HR programs.
</aside>

// THE IMPORTANCE OF EVALUATING HRM

Over the past ten years, there has been a noticeable demand from executives for HR to take on the role of strategic partner, and demonstrate its value in measurable terms.[4] This is an evolution from the service and administrative roles of the HR function previously. For example, an article in *Fortune* magazine called for the abolition of the HR function, arguing that HR managers are unable to describe their contribution to value except in trendy, unquantifiable, and "wannabe" terms.[5] The author also proposed that efficiencies could be increased by outsourcing legislated activities (such as payroll and equity) and returning "people" responsibilities to line managers. His exact words were "Blow up the HR department." Senior executives who read *Fortune* asked themselves, "Does HR make a difference? Does it add value?" Nearly a decade later, another journalist wrote an article called "Why We Hate HR," and said that HR practitioners did not have a seat at the table; they didn't even have a key to the boardroom.[6] Clearly, until HR managers can talk about the contribution and value of HR activities in the numbers language of business, the HR department and the HR profession will be vulnerable to destructive proposals such as those listed above. What is the numbers language of business? It means developing a case for any HR program by positing that "if we implement this safety program, we will reduce lost-time injuries and accidents by 50 percent, saving $500 000 annually."

Increasingly, the HR department is being treated like other operational units—that is, it is subject to questions about its contribution to organizational performance. In the simplest terms, HRM must make a difference; if it doesn't, it will be abolished. Decision makers within organizations view HR activities, such as training courses, as expenses. They view results as value. The deliverables, not the doables such as training, are what make a difference to the organization. Measurement of the HR function is critical for improving both the credibility and the effectiveness of HR. If you cannot measure contribution, you cannot manage it or improve it. What gets measured gets managed and improved.

Business is a numbers game. Some surveys have shown that HR practitioners, while familiar with some numbers (such as the number of people employed in the organization), can't always recite other key numbers (such as the sales volumes, market share, profit levels, and rates of return for their organization). When asked to assess their contribution, most HR professionals describe it in terms such as "number of training courses" or "new hires." They do not provide numbers for outcomes. They say things such as, "One hundred twenty people attended the training course," and rarely state, "The training courses resulted in a 15 percent improvement in customer satisfaction."

RESISTANCE

Some HR managers resist measuring their work. Indeed, according to the 2008 IBM Global Human Capital Study, only 6 percent of those HR managers interviewed felt that they were very effective at using data to make decisions about the workforce. Years later, only half of the companies surveyed use data to make decisions. One reason for this low level is the lack of integration of human resources information systems (HRIS) with each other and with operational systems (finance, sales, and so on).[7] Another reason is that HR professionals have limited knowledge of measurement models and limited skills in measurement design. There is an acute shortage of HR professionals with skills in spreadsheets, HRIS and statistics. Even if consultants can be hired to do the measurement work,[8] HR professionals need to know how to understand, interpret, and explain the measures.

HR managers also argue that HR activities cannot be measured, because outcomes such as employee attitudes or managerial productivity are impossible to calibrate meaningfully or precisely. They assert that they cannot control the labour market. But the finance department cannot control the inflation rate, and the marketing department has little control over product quality, and yet each of these departments measures its activities and is accountable for results.

Measuring is expensive, but not as expensive as continuing an ineffective program. The main reason HR is not measured is that there is no standard way of measuring. Think of finance and accounting with their widely accepted principles of measurement.[9]

As the field of HR evolves, the analytic and data-based decision-making capability will develop.[10] There may evolve two types of HR, with one branch similar to sales and accounting transactions, and the other more like the marketing and finance strategic decision making.[11] For example, the necessary transactional work (similar to accounting) might be handled by a personnel department and the strategic work by the HR department. The HR function needs to develop a set of analytic measures that can be used to describe, predict, and evaluate the quality and impact of HR practices.[12] The challenge is to not only develop measures, but also choose the measures that are important to the organization, not just the HR function. Boudreau describes business problems as often a case of "too much information and too few frameworks to interpret the information.[13]

Very few organizations measure the impact of HRM; about two-thirds of HR professionals in Fortune 500 companies measure HR productivity.[14] However, those that do measure are more likely to be treated as strategic partners.[15] Interest in measuring HR is growing slowly, fuelled by:

- Business improvement efforts across organizations
- Attempts to position HR as a strategic partner
- The need for objective indicators of success to accompany the analysis of HR activities

There are other pressures that make measurement a hot topic in HR. For example, *Sarbanes-Oxley* (American legislation that affects Canadian companies operating in the U.S.) requirements force HR to provide information about executive compensation, pension plans, and whistle-blower protection. More HR professionals are now trained in the field of measurement and capable of developing HR scorecards and measuring human capital. There is an increased awareness among leaders that investments in HR can impact customers and then the bottom line.[16]

RATIONALE

There are nine compelling reasons for measuring HRM effectiveness:

1. Labour costs are most often a firm's largest controllable cost.

2. Managers recognize that employees make the difference between the success and failure of projects and organizations. Good performance can be rewarded objectively.

3. Organizations have legal responsibilities to ensure that they are in compliance with laws governing the employer–employee relationship.

4. Evaluations are needed to determine which HR practices are effective, because at this point managers and HR professionals cannot distinguish between a fad and a valid change program.[17] HR is often criticized for communicating with executives with PowerPoint (rhetoric), not Excel (results).[18] Professor Terry Wagar of St. Mary's University in Halifax has studied fads and determined that many of the practices are not integrated with other HR systems, and that they are fragile and do not survive.[19] HR professionals should be skeptical of potential fads, as research has shown that 90 percent of them lose their popularity within a decade rather than become accepted practice.[20] The characteristics of fads are outlined in HR Planning Notebook 14.1.

5. Measuring and benchmarking HR activities will result in continuous improvements. Performance gaps can be identified and eliminated.

6. Audits will bring HR closer to the line functions of the organization. The practices must demonstrate that they enhance competitive advantage, not just that they are efficient or "best-in-class."[21]

7. Data will be available to support resource allocations.[22]

8. Investors want this information. Why? The market-to-book ratio suggests that for every $6 of market value, only $1 appears on the balance sheet. This money would represent tangible assets such as buildings and equipment, and financial assets such as cash and marketable securities. The remaining $5 represents intangible assets. For example, the market capitalization of Microsoft (i.e., the price per share times the number of shares outstanding) is $300 billion, while the total value of its tangible assets is only $20 billion. The $280 billion difference lies in its intangible assets such as brand equity and employee commitment. Likewise, Google has a market cap that was 2500 percent greater than the company's equipment, property, and plant.[23] So when a metric such as employee commitment rises, investors can use this number to predict increases in customer satisfaction, retention, and sales.[24]

9. HR managers are more likely to be welcome at the boardroom table, and to influence strategy, if they use measures to demonstrate the contribution of their function.[25]

The next section describes the areas in which HRM departments can be evaluated.

WHAT IS A FAD?

Over 100 magazines are devoted to business issues, 30 000 business books are in print, and 3500 new ones are published every year. These books often contain contradictory advice: "the first-mover advantage" or "the second mouse gets the cheese." Fads, such as "emotional intelligence," become popular very quickly, and then undergo a steep decline.

A fad has a typical life cycle:

Stage 1: Ascendency:

- Language such as "Something new and revolutionary is here" and "Out with the old, in with the new"
- Descriptions and how-tos
- Great praise and high promise

Stage 2: Maturity:

- Exhortations to jump on the bandwagon
- Initial questions asking whether the technique is a fad
- Suggestions and pleas to look beyond the superficial

Stage 3: Decline:

- Problems, pitfalls, and failures
- Questions asking if there is anything worth saving

A fad can also be defined by these characteristics:

1. It is simple and claims to solve complex problems.

2. It claims to apply to and help anyone.

3. It is not anchored or related to any known and generally accepted theory.

4. Proponents hesitate to present it in academic settings or write about it in referred journals.

5. Proponents cannot tell you exactly how it works.

6. It is a "track" topic at 75 percent of the conferences that you have attended.

7. Its proponents claim that it has changed their lives and that it can change yours too.

8. Its greatest proponents are those with the least experience in the field.

9. It is just too good to be true.

Organizations often adopt a practice simply because others are doing it. This will occur if a large number of organizations are doing it (frequency-based mimicry), if large visible firms are doing it (trait-based mimicry), or if other firms seem to be successful by adopting it (outcome-based mimicry).

The solution for HR professionals when confronted with a consultant proposing "another fine idea"? Ask for evidence that it works. If you are tempted, implement the concept in one small unit, and measure the outcomes. For example, one might ask: What is the evidence that this concept will work in our organization, and what is the risk of implementing this practice?

Sources: A. Garman, "Shooting for the Moon: How Academicians Could Make Management Research Even Less Relevant," *Journal of Business and Psychology*, Vol. 26, No. 2 (2011): 129–133; B.S. Klass, "Outsourcing and the HR Function: An Examination of Trends and Developments Within North American Firms," *The International Journal of Human Resource Management*, Vol. 19, No. 8 (August 2008): 1500–1514; J. Pfeffer and R.I. Sutton, "Evidence-Based Management," *Harvard Business Review*, January 2006: 63–74; D. Miller, J. Hartwick, and I. le BretonMiller, "How to Detect a Management Fad and Distinguish It from a Classic," *Business Horizons*, Vol. 47 (July/August 2004): 7–16; D. Ulrich, *Human Resource Champions* (Boston, MA: Harvard Business School Press, 1997), p. 63.

// THE 5C MODEL OF HRM IMPACT

Executives, investors, customers, and HR professionals themselves make judgments in many ways about the effectiveness of the HR function. The numerous areas that are

judged can be grouped into five clusters—the "5 C's" of evaluating HRM: compliance, client satisfaction, culture management, cost control, and contribution.[26]

COMPLIANCE

Senior management depends on HR expertise to ensure that organizational practices comply with the law, and many HR departments were started because of the need to record compliance with employment standards, such as hours worked and overtime payments. Legislation dealing with the employer–employee relationship is increasing, and the areas of safety, health, employment equity, and industrial relations are all highly regulated. Indeed, some people estimate that 20 to 30 percent of the increase in the salaries of HR professionals is due to the need to trust someone with the responsibility for compliance.

Highly publicized cases of safety violations in which board members of industrial organizations have been fined hundreds of thousands of dollars or threatened with jail time serve as another wakeup call. Other public cases that have cost organizations not only the expense of fines but also loss in business have occurred because managers have been held responsible for the sexual harassment of their subordinates. HR can make a difference by ensuring that managers and employees comply with the law, thus saving the company legal costs, fines, and damaging publicity.

Currently, HR is being asked to ensure not only that the organization complies with laws but also that it is ethical. This means the development of a code of conduct, protection for whistleblowers, and the redesign of orientation and training programs to include curriculum on ethics.

CLIENT SATISFACTION

Across Canada, many organizations are tracking their success by measuring customer satisfaction or soliciting input on client complaints and attitudes. These measures have been found to predict financial performance, on a lagged basis. This means that if employee morale drops, management can expect to see customer satisfaction levels drop in about six months.

Stakeholders, who include external and internal clients, are those people who can influence or must interact with the HR department. External clients of HR comprise candidates for positions, suppliers of HR services such as technology, and government regulators. Internal clients include employees grouped by occupation, union leaders, and managers. These stakeholder groups were discussed in Chapter 3.

Managers are turning to client or stakeholder perceptions of the HR department for input about the effectiveness of HR performance. This approach stems from earlier efforts in total quality management and tries to reconcile the gaps between client expectations and levels of satisfaction. The bigger the gap, the less effective the HR department. This qualitative approach surveys stakeholders about their perceptions of the effectiveness of the HR function. However, recent surveys have indicated that only one-half of managers and employees rate HR's overall performance as good.[27] "Keeping the clients happy" has important political repercussions for the HRM department, as "clients" such as the CEO control the purse strings and have the authority to approve HR policies and programs.

HR professionals need to survey managers about their satisfaction levels.

ADVANTAGES OF MEASURING CLIENT SATISFACTION

The advantages of measuring client satisfaction with the HR department include the following:[28]

- Measuring client satisfaction reminds the HR department that it is indeed a "service" that must deal with the expectations of its clients. The clients, in turn, use assessment criteria that are important to them, such as response time and assistance required to meet their goals.
- Surveying clients about their unmet needs increases the credibility of the HR function.
- Initiating and managing change by surveying stakeholders before, during, and after a change program increases the possibility that the HR department will understand the clients' perceptions; identify resistance to change and overcome such resistance; and prove that the change program meets its goals.

METHODS OF MEASURING CLIENT SATISFACTION

Information can be gathered from clients in several ways.

INFORMAL FEEDBACK Stakeholder perceptions can be obtained informally, as part of the feedback process, whenever the HR professional is undertaking an assignment or completing a routine task such as filling a position. People can simply be asked if they are satisfied with the service.

Informal feedback is of limited use, however, for several reasons. Line managers might be reluctant to give honest feedback face to face; an individual HR officer might not be able to see patterns in the feedback because there is no method for measuring the frequency of problems; and HR professionals have little incentive to report negative feedback to superiors in the organizational hierarchy. For these reasons, a more systematic method must be developed to identify gaps in the performance of the HR department.

SURVEYS Surveys can be used to solicit feedback confidentially, anonymously, and from a larger number of stakeholders. One approach is to list the HR activities, such as selection, and ask specific questions about them, such as questions about satisfaction with the time it takes to fill a vacant position and the satisfaction with a new employee's performance. Some questions that might be included in such a survey are:

- To what degree do you find the HR department cooperative?
- How would you rate the quality of service given?
- To what degree are HR employees available to deal with problems?
- Do you have confidence in HR advice?
- How would you rate the effectiveness of HR solutions?
- What is your opinion on processing time?
- To what extent does HR understand the needs of your department?
- Overall, how satisfied are you with the HR department?

HR PLANNING NOTEBOOK 14.2

HR ROLE ASSESSMENT SURVEY

The following is a sample of the type of survey clients can expect:

Please rate your satisfaction with the HR department on the following items* (1 = low; = 5 high):

HR helps the organization accomplish business goals.

HR participates in the process of defining business strategies.

HR makes sure that HR strategies are aligned with business strategies.

HR is effective because it can measure how it helps make strategy happen.

HR is a business partner.

*The selected items measure the strategic role of HR.

Another survey, developed by Ulrich, asks managers to rate the quality of the various roles that HR plays in strategy formulation.[29] HR Planning Notebook 14.2 contains a sample of the questions used in this survey.

Managers might be asked to list the chief strengths and principal weaknesses of the HR department. Line managers might be asked questions about what the HR department has been doing particularly well or particularly poorly, what it should not be doing, how it might contribute more effectively, and so on.[30]

CRITICAL INCIDENT METHOD In the critical incident method, clients are asked to describe a situation in which the HR department provided assistance that was particularly useful, the consequences of this help, and why it was seen as helpful. Similarly, they are asked to describe a situation in which the assistance was not at all useful, and why. Clients' responses help the HR department identify issues and services that affect unit effectiveness.

PROBLEMS WITH MEASURING CLIENT SATISFACTION

Measuring client satisfaction is not without its weaknesses.

HIGH EXPECTATIONS OF CLIENTS The goal of surveying clients is to identify gaps between their expectations and their satisfaction. If the clients in one business unit have extremely high expectations, their dissatisfaction scores will also be high, even though the level of HR service is constant across units. The temptation on the part of the HR department might be to promise or commit to less with regard to programs so as to appear to have performed better.

CONFLICTING EXPECTATIONS Another problem occurs when different stakeholders have competing or conflicting expectations. The employee group might desire extensive counselling (a nurturing role) from the HR department, while senior managers might be concerned about maximizing productivity per employee (an efficiency goal). One group will be dissatisfied because it is difficult for the HR department to be both nurturing and efficient.

PROFESSIONAL AFFILIATIONS Furthermore, gaps between expectations and performance might occur because HR professionals are more closely tied to the norms and values of their profession than to the norms of managers or line operators.[31] For example, line managers might value how fast a job is filled, while the HR professional might value the creation of a valid selection test. In other words, the HR professional might be trying to do what is right in the profession ("validate the selection test"), rather than what managers consider important ("just hire someone quickly").

Whatever the problems with the client satisfaction approach, the important message is that the viability of the HR function depends to a large extent on stakeholder perceptions of value and effectiveness. These must be measured and managed.

CULTURE MANAGEMENT

Highly effective organizations seek to influence employee attitudes through the development of an appropriate culture that will support optimum performance. (Remember that culture can be defined as the set of important beliefs that members of a community share—"the way we do things around here.") Executives carefully monitor cultural programs (such as that of empowerment) through attitude surveys of employees. The results of these surveys can then be linked to the objective results of the department.

The assumption underlying the culture management model is that HR practices can have a positive influence on employee attitudes, which in turn influence employee performance.

Attitudes, in an organizational context, can be defined as perceptions or opinions about organizational characteristics. Some examples include the attitudes expressed in these statements: "I think that management expects too much for the resources it gives me" or "I feel that I can talk to management about any problems I am experiencing."

The most frequently measured attitudes in the organization are job satisfaction and commitment. Surveys of satisfaction and commitment measure attitudes toward supervisors, colleagues, pay, promotions, and the work itself. The research supports the proposition that attitudes affects behaviours. Highly committed employees will make personal sacrifices for the job, perform beyond normal expectations, work selflessly, endure difficult times, and will not leave the organization for personal gain.[32] A Towers Perrin study of 40 global companies over three years showed that companies with employees with high engagement scores had more than 3 percent in net profit margin over those with low scores.[33] The study also showed that in Canada only about one-quarter of employees report high engagement, about the same as in the United States. A landmark study of 800 Sears stores demonstrated that for every 5 percent improvement in employee attitudes, customer satisfaction increased by 1.3 percent and corporate revenue rose by 0.5 percent.[34] Employees with the highest levels of commitment perform 20 percent better and are 87 percent less likely to leave the organization. Employees at Molson Coors, the beverage company, who reported high levels of engagement, were five times less likely to have a safety incident and seven times less likely to have a lost-time safety incident.[35] Canadian organizations are realizing the benefits of high employee engagement: Telus receives about 75 percent fewer complaints than its competitors and attributes this to its world-leading employee engagement scores. WestJet has one of the most admired corporate cultures (with high employee engagement) and is one of the most profitable airlines in North America.[36]

HR Planning Notebook 14.3 examines the different terms that organizations may use when measuring employee attitudes.

Attitudes
Perceptions or opinions about organizational characteristics

HR PLANNING NOTEBOOK 14.3

MEASURING EMPLOYEE ATTITUDES

Organizations use different terms in measuring employee attitudes:

- *Satisfaction:* This is a passive measure of employee contentment with little relationship to performance.

- *Motivation:* This measure probes whether employees feel stimulated in their role and are driven to meet work and organizational goals. Motivation is strongly related to productivity measures.

- *Commitment:* A measure of the alignment between the strategy, objectives, and values of the organization, commitment is strongly linked to employee loyalty and customer service excellence.

- *Advocacy:* This is a measure of whether employees will speak highly of the organization as an employer, and as an organization with products and service. Advocacy is strongly linked to sales growth and employee attraction.

- *Engagement:* If an employee scores highly on motivation, commitment, and advocacy, then she would be classified as engaged. Engaged employees are more productive, deliver higher customer satisfaction levels, deliver the brand promise more effectively, create stronger growth, and generate higher profits.

Organizations should pay attention to employee attitudes and should attempt to manage the culture to improve individual and organizational performance. HR managers might want to ask the managers in their organizations about the effectiveness of the engagement surveys being used by asking questions such as:

1. Does the survey prompt discussions with your direct reports?
2. Does the survey help you identify actions that can be taken to improve the engagement scores?[37]

COST CONTROL

Traditional organizations continue to see personnel as an expense. The labour component of the production process in service organizations, such as universities and government departments, is an organization's single largest expense. This cost represents up to 85 percent of the expenses in white-collar organizations. The cost of employees consists of pay and benefits, the cost of absenteeism, and the cost of turnover. HR practices can reduce labour costs by reducing the workforce while attempting to get the same volume of work done with fewer employees. There are three ways to reduce labour expenses by reducing the size of the labour force:

- *Technology:* One of the most frequently used ways to cut labour costs is to increase the use of technology. Technology to process benefits claims and pursue e-learning has replaced HR staff, resulting in cost savings of about 30 percent.[38]

- *Outsourcing:* Firms are also outsourcing major activities in order to manage the costs of labour. However, there are detrimental effects of cutting costs in this way. Core talent may be lost and the capacity for innovation diminished.[39] See Chapter 13 for a more detailed discussion of outsourcing.

- *Downsizing:* Chapter 10 provides an analysis of the processes for restructuring.

Often, companies try to reduce the headcount in the HR department as part of a strategy to save costs. But the savings can be deceptive. For example, a financial services company cut its HR headcount by 30 percent (around 300 people). But then the line managers hired their own staff to handle the HR issues, and the shadow organization of HR specialists now numbers 150.[40]

HR departments can reduce expenses associated with employees in at least two other ways. The first is to increase the efficiencies of those working (i.e., achieve the same results at lower costs or faster speeds), and the second is to reduce the costs associated with behaviours such as absences or turnover that are, to some extent, under the control of the employee.

INCREASING EFFICIENCY

Efficiency is expressed in terms of the results achieved (outputs) in comparison to the resource inputs. Measures of efficiency include the following:

- Time (e.g., average time to fill an opening, process a benefits claim)
- Volume (e.g., number of people interviewed to fill a job, number of requests processed per employee)
- Cost (e.g., cost per training hour or per test).

HR managers should measure these resource inputs and then attempt to improve the measurements over time or across units. The use of benchmarks is critical in comparing one organization's efficiency ratios against the best in the field. Data revealing a cost per hire of $500 or turnover rates of 15 percent are meaningless without relevant comparison points. For example, a turnover rate of 15 percent among senior executives indicates a problem; a turnover rate of 15 percent in a fast-food restaurant is very low.

The ratios generated must be interpreted and analyzed by comparisons made over time, across departments, and against the benchmarks of best practices. These benchmarks allow the HR manager to make the following kinds of statements: "The cost per hire is $500, which is $50 less than last year and $60 less than another company. That shows we are doing a better job than we did last year and than other HR departments." HR Planning Notebook 14.4 provides examples of these measures.

These efficiency measures must be managed with effectiveness in mind. Conceptually, it is possible to reduce training costs to zero, but the performance of employees would suffer in the long run. Therefore, most companies add a qualifier to the ratio when judging efficiency. For example, lowering the cost per trainee would be acceptable only if job performance remained the same or improved.

COST OF EMPLOYEE BEHAVIOUR

The costs of absenteeism, turnover, and occupational injuries and illnesses can all be measured, benchmarked, and managed. Any introductory textbook in HRM will describe how to measure these factors and will provide prescriptions for reducing the costs related to them. To control the expenses associated with employees, organizations should carefully track and compare the rates of absenteeism, turnover, and occupational injuries and illnesses. Here are some figures to think about: On average, each full-time employee missed 6.9 days over the year (with health and government sectors reporting higher rates at 10.9 and 8.9 respectively).[41] Across all sectors, average turnover is about 15 percent annually, and highest in services, retail and health care (around 22 percent to 27 percent).[42]

The costs of turnover, which include termination, replacement, loss of revenue when the position is vacant, and the learning time for new employees to become productive, are estimated at between 6 and 18 months of the employee's annual compensation. At Taco Bell, the stores with the lowest turnover yielded double the sales and 55 percent higher profits than stores with the highest turnover rates.[43]

In keeping with the trend to view employees as investments, and not just as expenses, the next section examines how organizations measure the return on this investment.

> **Efficiency**
> Results achieved compared to resource inputs

CONTRIBUTION

Unless HR can demonstrate its impact on the bottom line, it will continue to be seen as "overhead," as a department that grabs resources while contributing nothing. Many executives feel that it is time for the HR department to identify and evaluate its contribution, as other departments are expected to do.

The thesis underlying the contribution model is that HRM practices shape the behaviour of employees within an organization, and thus help the organization achieve its goals. In other words, the effective management of people makes a difference in how well an organization functions. Research has shown that HR practices can affect organizational performance in measurable ways. Studies have established that sophisticated and integrated HRM practices have a positive effect on employee performance: They increase knowledge, skills, and abilities; improve motivation; reduce shirking; and increase retention of competent employees. These best practices have a direct and economically significant effect on a firm's financial performance.

// HOW HR CONTRIBUTES TO ORGANIZATIONAL PERFORMANCE

The majority of published studies find an association between HR practices and firm performance.[44] HR matters. The basic causal model shows that HR practices impact collective commitment, operational performance, expenses, and profits.[45]

We will look now at two ways of measuring contribution: financial measures and measures of managerial perceptions of effectiveness.

FINANCIAL MEASURES

SURVIVAL

Private or for-profit organizations can measure a dramatic indicator of success: survival. This can be considered a zero-sum index. If the company survives—that is, does not go bankrupt or cease business—the organization is a success. Survival is the first measure of effectiveness, and the contributions of HRM practices should be judged against this life-or-death index.

When researchers tracked the survival rates over five years of new organizations listed on the stock exchange, they found that HR practices were associated with this ultimate measure of a firm's performance.[46]

This crude measure is not satisfying for most businesspeople, however, because it doesn't give relative measures of success. (Teachers who give a pass or fail, rather than an A, B, C, D, or F grade, leave the same sense of dissatisfaction among students.) Most employees desire a relative measure, and will even ask "How am I doing compared to the others?" at performance evaluation interviews. The most common measures of business success provide these points of comparison, which allow judgments to be made across divisions, companies, and even sectors. They are the bottom-line measures such as profits.

PROFITS OR RETURN ON INVESTMENTS

All businesses track sales, or revenues, return on investment (**ROI**), return on equity (**ROE**), expenses relative to sales, and other financial ratios. These indices measure the relative success of an organization in meeting its goals. Any HRM practice that contributes to these measurements likely would be endorsed by senior management. Measuring the impact of HRM investments in training or performance appraisal allows HR professionals to use the same language (e.g., basic costs, ROI) as other corporate units and provides a rational way of making decisions. HR Planning Today 14.1 illustrates how this might work.

> **ROI**
> Return on investment
> **ROE**
> Return on equity

There are some limitations to financial analyses, however; they capture certain immediate aspects of performance, but they do not capture managerial perceptions of effectiveness.

MEASURES OF MANAGERIAL PERCEPTIONS OF EFFECTIVENESS

Sometimes financial measures are not available to researchers who are studying privately owned organizations, and sometimes financial measures are not appropriate for public-sector organizations. It is meaningless to talk about government departments in relation to profits, for example. Therefore, other measures have been sought. One method is to ask managers to assess their organization's performance relative to the performance of sector competitors.[47] Despite the biases that might be introduced into such a measure, these perceptions have been found to correlate positively with objective measures of a firm's performance.[48] The principal advantage of using a perceptual measure such as this one is the ability to compare profit-seeking firms with public organizations.

RIGHTS NOT AVAILABLE

Templer and Cattaneo argue that organizational effectiveness is not easily defined.[49] Measures beyond survival and those discussed above might include the achievement of one group's political objectives at the expense of a competing interest group and the adaptation of an organization to its environment (which obviously contains an element of the survival measure).

The measure that supersedes all these might be one of goal optimization. Templer and Cattaneo combined these various perspectives to conclude that "an effective organization is one in which the behaviour of employees contributes towards the attainment of organizational goals and enables the long-term adaptation of the organization to its environment"—that is, survival and effectiveness.[50]

Which is the best measure of HRM performance? Managers will choose whichever of the 5C measures meets their needs for information. Some will require measurement of all the five C's; others will focus on one important indicator, such as cost control. Some companies are moving toward a balanced approach.

We have examined five areas in which HR practices and policies should be tracked. Now we turn to an examination of the various approaches to measuring the effectiveness of HR policies, practices, and programs.

// APPROACHES TO MEASURING HRM PRACTICES

This section outlines a number of quantitative and qualitative approaches to measuring the impact of HRM policies and practices. Typical ways of measuring HR activities are:

- *Activity-based measures:* The number of employees completing training; the number of employees hired
- *Costing measures:* The cost of the training program, the cost per hire
- *Client satisfaction:* The manager has a problem solved; the HR department changed an employee's benefits information quickly

Most of these methods use numbers, which can measure the impact of HRM in the language of business: costs, days lost, complaints, and so on. But the question has to be asked: Where is the added value? See HR Planning Notebook 14.5 for a description of added value.

The next three approaches—cost–benefit analysis, utility analysis, and benchmarking—attempt to prove value.

COST–BENEFIT ANALYSIS

HRM activities, such as the process of selecting employees, cost money. Most organizations absorb the costs of these activities without conducting analyses to determine benefits. **Cost–benefit analysis** examines the relationship between the costs of a program and its benefits.

> **Cost–benefit analysis**
> The relationship between the costs of a program and its benefits

Costs included in these calculations are classified in several ways. **Direct costs** are those that are used to implement the program, such as the cost of selection tests or training materials. **Indirect costs** are those that an organization absorbs, such as the trainee's time away from work. Indirect costs often go unrecognized, and sometimes are not included in cost–benefit analyses. HR Planning Notebook 14.6 presents an example of a cost–benefit analysis.

Most programs can be subjected to a cost–benefit analysis if hard data are available, or the value of a program can be estimated from soft measures such as supervisors' estimates of productivity.

HR should always measure the direct and indirect costs of training.

HR PLANNING NOTEBOOK 14.6

MEASURING THE CONTRIBUTION OF HRM PRACTICES

A wholesale produce company hired, and then fired, seven ineffective sales representatives over a two-year period. The company calculated the costs of these actions.

Costs

Training	$493 738
Recruiting	$30 100
Management time to train and terminate	$25 830
Lower profits and higher waste due to poor performance	$1 612 000
Total costs	$2 161 668

The HR department interviewed line managers to develop a profile of the ideal sales representative and identified 12 critical success factors. Then the company's HR department developed a solution involving three types of training:

- Behaviour-based interview training for managers

- A training program for newly hired sales representatives to accelerate performance readiness or weed out those who didn't meet the standards

- Performance counselling training for managers so that they could learn to discuss performance problems and ensure that trainees accepted responsibility for their own learning and performance.

The cost to implement these three programs was $15 400 (development and attendance costs).

The savings that resulted from this solution were then calculated.

Savings

Cost of the problem	$2 161 668
Cost of the solution	– $15 400
Total savings	$2 146 268

The cost–benefit ratio is as follows:

$$\$2\,146\,268 \div \$15\,400 = 139{:}1$$

Source: Adapted from material originally published as "Increase HR's Contributions to Profits," by D.M. Burrows, *HR Magazine*, September 1996, pp. 103–110. © 1996, Society for Human Resource Management, Alexandria, VA. Used with permission. All rights reserved.

UTILITY ANALYSIS

Senior managers are often faced with decisions about the most effective programs. For example, to motivate employees, should HR managers implement a leadership training program or a pay-for-performance program for new supervisors? To hire the best candidate, should HR managers use peer interviews or the new selection test? HR managers would have much to gain if they were able to estimate if program A provided a greater return than program B. The training director, for example, might argue that grouping 100 managers in a classroom for training is more expensive and less effective than e-learning.

A tool that calculates, in dollar terms, the costs and probable outcomes of decisions would assist HR managers in making choices among programs. **Utility analysis** is such a tool. It is a method of determining the gain or loss to the organization that results from different courses of action. Faced with a decision, managers use utility analysis to help them choose the strategy that produces the outcomes the organization is seeking.[51] This method measures the utilities (gains and losses) by using human resources accounting. Human resources accounting uses standard accounting practices to calculate and report an organization's human assets (or employees) in economic terms. The costs of recruiting, selecting, training, and retaining employees are calculated, and then these costs are amortized over the employees' working lives. It seeks to quantify, in dollars, the value of improvements in HR activities, particularly selection. In utility analysis, which is an extension of cost–benefit analysis, the costs and benefits of alternative solutions to a problem are calculated and compared. The decision maker then can use the quantitative data that result from utility analysis to choose the alternative with the highest net value. HR Planning Notebook 14.7 provides an example of how utility analysis can be used to reach a decision.

> **Utility analysis**
> A method of determining the gain or loss that results from different approaches

---

HR PLANNING NOTEBOOK 14.7

AN EXAMPLE OF UTILITY ANALYSIS

Utility analysis is statistically complex, but it can be illustrated by the following simple example.

An organization has a choice between two types of selection procedures (or can use neither). The utility of a selection procedure is the degree to which it results in a better quality of candidate than would have been selected if the selection procedure had not been implemented. Quality can be measured by tenure (Did the employee selected using the selection procedure remain with the organization at least one year?) or performance (Did the new employee rate above average in performance after one year?) or other objective outcomes (Did the employee sell more accounts or process more files?). The costs of using procedure one (an ability test), procedure two (peer interviews), or the usual selection method (or base rate) of managerial interviews are calculated. Then the benefits of the candidates chosen under each of the three methods are determined. If tests resulted in higher-performing candidates but cost more than the performance increase is worth, the tests have little utility. If peer reviews result in greater performance at no greater cost, peer reviews have great utility.

Source: M.L. Blum and J.C. Naylor, *Industrial Psychology: Its Theoretical and Social Foundations*, rev. ed., New York: Harper-Row, 1968.

Utility analyses have been used in various studies. However, the computations involved are beyond the competencies of most managers.[52]

BENCHMARKING

A plan needs an audit. An **audit** measures progress against goals. If the goal of the HR function is to train 100 managers, at some point data need to be gathered to determine if that goal was achieved. Audits keep the HR department on track and are the primary tool to assess current performance to develop action plans and future goals.[53] Audits can be done annually or quarterly, but a consistent checking against the plan ensures no year-end surprises and allows managers to take corrective action. For example, if the goal is to achieve 4 out of 5 on an employee satisfaction scale, and an audit shows pockets of low satisfaction, the HR department can target those areas for remedial action before year-end. Nevertheless, the audit is not the last step in the cycle of plan, execute, and measure.

Benchmarking is concerned with enhancing organizational performance by establishing standards against which processes, products, and performance can be compared and subsequently improved.[54] It is searching for the industry's best practices and then trying to achieve improved performance by adopting superior practices.[55] Benchmarking can be used to accomplish the following:

- Stimulate an objective review of processes, practices, and systems
- Motivate employees to perform to a higher standard by providing a common target for improvement
- Provide objective comparative data with best-in-class organizations
- Raise questions and stimulate discussions about better ways of operating[56]

The process starts by targeting an area for improvement, such as university recruitment in the staffing function. Key measures are identified for comparison. In recruitment these might be cost per hire, quality of hire, processing times, and percentage of acceptances from first-choice candidates. The next step is to identify the best-practice organizations through publications, associations, experts, and awards ceremonies. There are four sources of benchmarking partners:

- Internal (e.g., compare university recruitment with high-tech recruitment, or compare previous year recruitment with this year's recruitment).
- Competitive (compare exact functions of a competitor).
- Sector (some conditions may differ for your organization)—some sector associations establish HR benchmarking subcommittees, which share information. There is a Human Resources Benchworking Network, which gathers data for health care, municipal governments, and not-for-profits. The BC HR association has a benchmarking service.
- Best-in-breed organizations (whose products, culture, and so on may not be comparable)—many of these organizations are willing to share this information if there is an incentive for them, such as a copy of the report, access to your metrics, and so on. Disney World and South West Airlines are examples of best-in-breed organizations whose HR practices are often analyzed and benchmarked.

Benchmarking can be done by either internal or external consultants. Internal consultants have the advantage of knowing more about the organization and being trusted by the staff supplying the information. However, external consultants might be more objective, have greater numbers of outside references or benchmarks, and be more likely to convey bad news to management. Sometimes an independent body, such as the Conference Board of Canada, will act as the project manager for the benchmarking study so that confidentiality is not an issue in data collection. This third-party intervention helps with the obvious question: Why would competitors want to reveal their best practices? And if they do so, is it because they have developed even more powerful processes that they do not share?[57] Obviously, the results obtained from audits can be compared with benchmarks obtained from previous years, with other organizational units, or with other companies.

After the data have been collected and compared, the differences will be obvious. The best organization might have metrics such as a 6-week processing time, while your organization might process applicants in 12 weeks. Interviews during or after the data collection might reveal the reasons for the speed—perhaps the entire processing is done on the Internet. The goal then becomes to match the best target for each of the indices.

For instance, the training function can be examined as a percentage of payroll spent on training, training dollars spent per employee, profits per employee, training costs per hour, and so on. The results of these examinations can be compared to comparable figures for other organizations. As an example, in Canada, organizations spend about $705 per employee on training.[58] These benchmark statistics can be used as guidelines. If statistics are available on the best-performing companies, organizations can attempt to match those figures.

Benchmarking is popular because the measures are easy to collect and the numbers have a superficial credibility, but there is no published research that supports a relationship between HR benchmarks and ultimate firm performance.[59] We all like to know benchmarks such as the facts that Apple has the highest profit per employee at half a million dollars and LinkedIn at $55 000 per employee.[60] But these numbers are relatively meaningless. For example, an organization can have one HR professional per 1000 employees because it has outsourced most of the HR work. Knowing that your organization's cost per employee is higher than the sector benchmark does not provide you with anything of value, anything that would lead you to a cause and a solution. Finally, you cannot build competitive advantage by copying it, because the best capabilities (like the culture at Southwest Airlines) are complex and difficult to imitate. An organization has to create its own capabilities.[61]

THE HR SCORECARD

Although the most popular way of measuring HR is benchmarking, the HR balanced scorecard is gaining momentum, with about two-thirds of Canadian companies using this method.[62] The **balanced scorecard** rests on the assumption that any successful business satisfies the requirements of investors (financial performance measures), customers (market share, customer commitment, and retention), and employees (employee satisfaction and organization commitment).[63]

The idea of a balanced scorecard arose from the idea that financial measures alone do not capture the true performance of an organization, and that these measures tend to reflect past performance and are not necessarily predictive. Other measures deemed of

> **Balanced scorecard**
> A balanced set of measures to show contribution to organizational performance

value to the analysis of a company included not only financial performance but also customer satisfaction and employee engagement. The balanced scorecard provides answers to these four basic questions:

1. How do customers see us? (The customer perspective)
2. What must we excel at? (The internal business perspective)
3. Can we continue to improve and create value? (Innovation and learning perspective)
4. How do we look to shareholders? (The financial perspective).[64]

The process starts with the organization's strategy and then HR looks for ways that the HR processes and practices can support that strategy. What can HR do to support the organization's goals, and how can this be measured? For example, the goal at a pipeline company was to increase revenues; one way to accomplish this was to reduce downtime for repairs. The HR goal in this case was to increase the amount of time devoted to preventive maintenance, by increasing employee skills sets in repairs, and to change the compensation system to include incentives to perform preventive maintenance.[65] This set of linkages is more fully described in Figure 14.1.

MEASURING THE WORTH OF EMPLOYEES

Many company presidents say, "Employees are our greatest assets," or, as the president of Dofasco said, "Our product is steel; our strength is people." What do they mean?

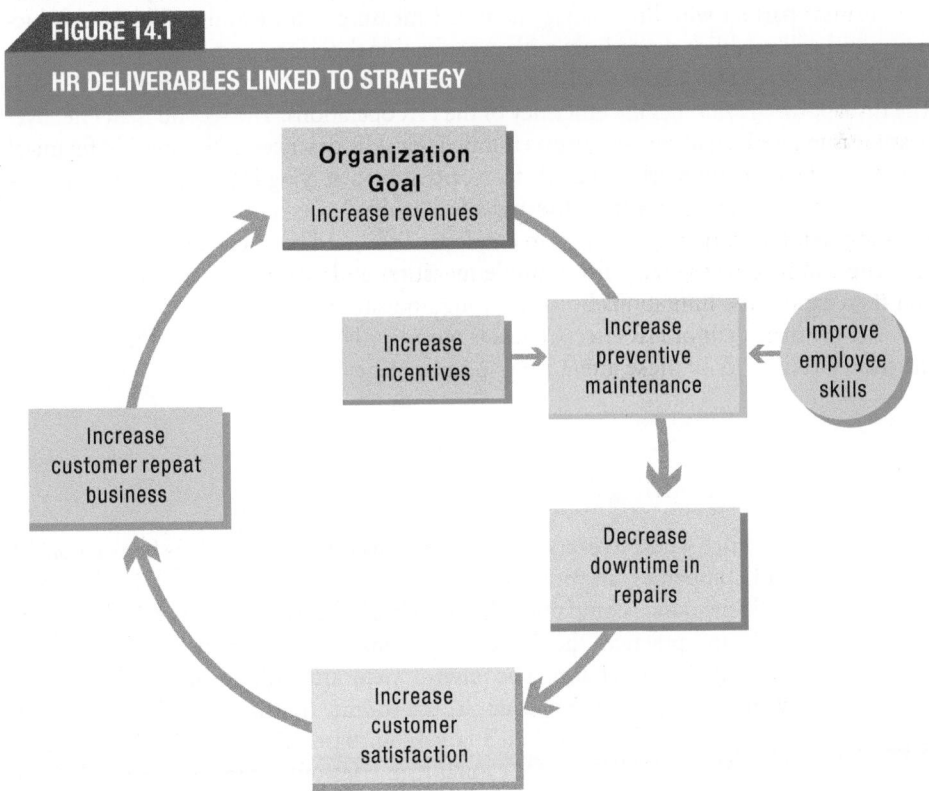

FIGURE 14.1

HR DELIVERABLES LINKED TO STRATEGY

Analysts posit that human capital and financial capital drive business results. Human capital can refer to factors such as the employees' knowledge, skills, capabilities, and attitudes that impact performance.[66] Remember that it is not just the sum total of employee competencies, but also the application of these competencies in a way that has value to the organization, that provides the true measure of human capital.[67]

The productivity of most organizations entering the 21st century is highly dependent on the intellectual capabilities of their employees. The balance sheet cannot capture the value of this human capital. As indicated earlier, this human capital represents a significant asset, representing up to 85 percent of a corporation's value.[68]

There have been attempts to measure the worth of employees by counting them, and then attempting to put a number value on their knowledge. Those who measure the worth of employees want to bring attention to the fact that human resources are of strategic and competitive importance. Another reason is that the value of these resources must be expressed in financial terms to bring credibility to the HR department.[69]

Assessing the worth of intellectual capital or human capital in an organization is incredibly complex and still in the developing stages to produce meaningful measures and none are universally accepted. Our focus here is not on measuring the worth of employees, but on measuring the effect of HR practices and policies.

Readers interested in a fuller description of measuring HR effectiveness should consult *Research, Measurement and Evaluation of Human Resources*.[70] The choice of measurement tool depends to a large extent on the organization's strategy and the stage of sophistication of its HR department. For example, an HR department that continues to focus on administration in a support role to employees and managers will measure efficiencies. Reports from HR will include statements such as "Processed 1250 benefits questions; trained 10 percent more employees than last year." An HR department that is a business partner with line management will measure culture and employee productivity, and will establish direct links with organizational performance.

The measurement options available to HR professionals are summarized in Table 14.1. The first approach examines the efficiency of the HR operations. The second is an effectiveness measure, looking at the link between individual HR practices and a specific financial outcome. The third approach is the HR scorecard approach tying HR activities to business activities. The last approach is the cause-and-effect analysis, which focuses on measuring the links between HR programs, the links to employee links, and business outcomes.

The columns in the table list example measures and advantages of each approach, and then expose the limitations by asking tough questions.

The measurement of HR effectiveness is not easy. The next section outlines some of the difficulties faced by those attempting to track HR effectiveness.

UNIVERSALITY OF BEST PRACTICES

No single best practice works in every situation. Some companies, such as banks, consist of many different companies, all with unique characteristics; in the case of banks, these companies include insurance companies, discount brokerages, and venture capital firms. The HRM policies and practices that benefit performance in the bank may hinder performance in the venture capital arm. The environment and culture of the parts of the larger company are very different. For example, the routine transaction work of the bank lends itself to compensation systems based largely on base salaries, while the entrepreneurial, risk-taking nature of the venture capital firm cries out for incentive-based pay.

TABLE 14.1

SUMMARY OF HR MEASUREMENT ALTERNATIVES

MEASUREMENT APPROACH	EXAMPLE MEASURES	PRIMARY APPEAL	TOUGH QUESTIONS
Efficiency of HRM operations	Cost-per-hire, time-to-fill, training costs, ratio of HR staff to total employees	Explicit currency-value calculations. Logic of cost savings is easy to relate to accounting. Standardization makes benchmarking comparisons easier.	"Wouldn't outsourcing cut costs even more?" "Do these cost savings come at the price of workforce value?" "Why should our costs be the same as the industry's?"
HR activity, "best practice" indices	Human capital benchmarks, human capital index	HR practices are associated with familiar financial outcomes. Data from many organizations lends credibility. Suggests there might be practices or combinations that generally raise profits or sales, and so on.	"What is the logic connecting these activities with such huge financial effects?" "Will the practices that worked in other organizations necessarily work in ours?" "Does having these practices mean they are implemented well?"
HR scorecard	How the organization or HR function meets goals of "customers, financial markets, operational excellence, and learning"	Vast array of HR measures can be categorized. "Balanced scorecard" concept is known to business leaders. Software allows users to customize analysis.	"Can this scorecard prove a connection between people and strategic outcomes?" "Which numbers and drilldowns are most critical to our success?"
Causal chain	Models linking employee attitudes to service behaviour to customer responses to profit	Useful logic linking employee variables to financial outcomes. Valuable for organizing and analyzing diverse data elements.	"Is this the best path from talent to profits?" "How do our HR practices work together?" "What logic can we use to find more connections like this?"

Source: From M. Effron, R. Gandossy, and M. Goldsmith, *HR Measurement Alternatives* (New York: John Wiley, 2003), p. 85. Reprinted with permission.

Furthermore, organizations and businesses may have different strategic goals. The goal of the financial sector is to maximize ROE, while the goal of Citizenship and Immigration Canada might be to implement the government's immigration policy, which might include increasing the number of immigrants with certain skills. Within a single organization, the goals of one business unit might be to maximize market share (at the expense of profit), while another unit might be attempting to maximize profit. These differences lead to the conclusion that the impact of HRM must be measured against unit goals, not against some generality such as growth or profits. Moreover, some experts suggest that organizations not adopt best practices, but focus on fit. They argue that aligning HR practices with an organization's strategy (influenced by its environment) will result in greater performance than the method of copying other HR strategies (best practices and benchmarking).[71] This is described in Figure 14.2.

SEPARATION OF CAUSE AND EFFECT

The perennial problem in measuring the impact of HRM practices is separating cause and effect. For example, if a profitable company shares its profits with employees through bonuses, does the possibility of earning such a bonus make employees more productive and their companies more profitable? Research suggests that businesses

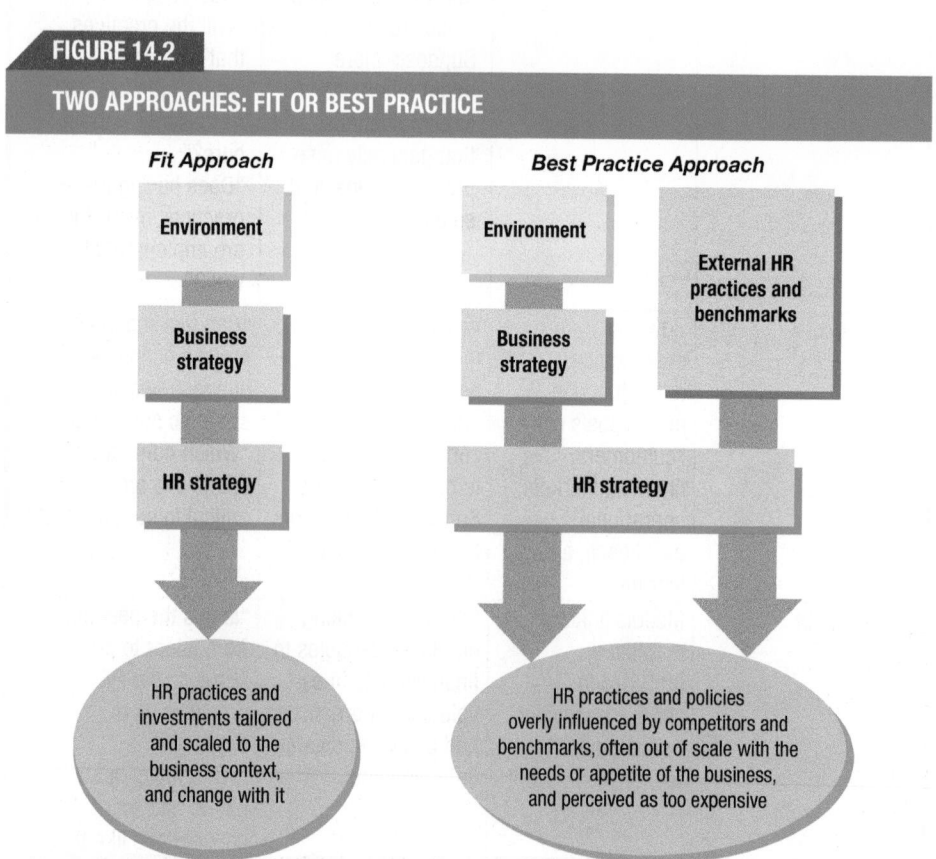

FIGURE 14.2

TWO APPROACHES: FIT OR BEST PRACTICE

that are profitable invest in HR practices and that this investment pays off in improved financial performance.[72] However, once a new HR practice is implemented, it may take years before its effects are observed. Experts have suggested that it takes two years to design and deliver an HR program and another two years before an organizational outcome can be measured.[73] Obviously, a leading indicator is more valuable for predicting future performance than a lagging indicator, as discussed in HR Planning Notebook 14.8.

HR PLANNING NOTEBOOK 14.8

LEADING AND LAGGING INDICATORS

HR professionals need to be able to understand the link between HR activities and results. For example, is turnover a leading or a lagging indicator? A leading indicator anticipates, predicts, or affects the future. Higher employee turnover can precede outcomes such as lower customer satisfaction, which in turn can predict lower customer retention and sales. A lagging indicator represents information that results from an event or a change. The lagging indicators in the above example are the lower customer satisfaction, retention, and sales.

Associated with the lack of confidence in the explanation of causal links between specific HRM practices and organizational performance is the observation that the culture of an organization may explain more than a specific HRM practice. The day-to-day norms of an organization may influence employee behaviour more than any specific practice. For example, if an organization is deeply committed to valuing employees, the day-to-day actions of all managers have more powerful effects than a standalone program such as 360° feedback. Other challenges are outlined in HR Planning Notebook 14.9.

HR PLANNING NOTEBOOK 14.9

CHALLENGES OF EVALUATING HRM

- The work of assessing HR practices is costly; it can add 5 percent to the HR budget.
- HR professionals may not have the time or skills to evaluate.
- HR is not solely responsible for the behaviour of employees. A weak manager may influence productivity more than any HR practice.

- The numbers game—do the numbers reflect reality? Customers have been asked by service providers to give them a good rating when the evaluation agency phones, as their bonus depends on receiving a 10 out of 10.
- What if the result shows no impact of HR practices? How will this information be used? What is the risk to the HR professional's career?

SUCCESSFUL MEASUREMENT

As you have just read, there are many ways to measure the contributions of the HR function. Organizations seem to focus on background, functional, and efficiency measure. According to a study of Canadian leaders, the most frequent measures are headcount and hires and terminations.[74] Other popular operational measures can be found in HR Planning Today 14.2.

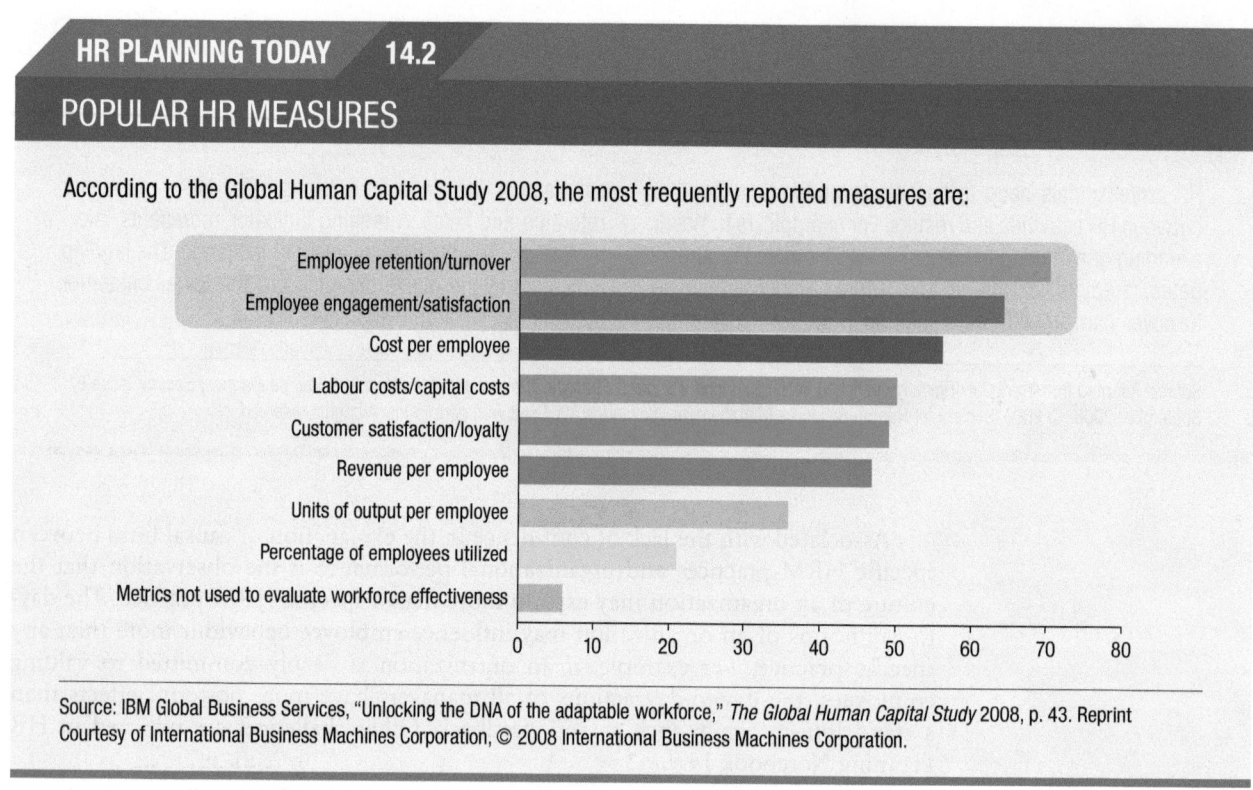

HR PLANNING TODAY 14.2

POPULAR HR MEASURES

According to the Global Human Capital Study 2008, the most frequently reported measures are:

Measure	Value
Employee retention/turnover	~71
Employee engagement/satisfaction	~65
Cost per employee	~57
Labour costs/capital costs	~50
Customer satisfaction/loyalty	~49
Revenue per employee	~47
Units of output per employee	~36
Percentage of employees utilized	~21
Metrics not used to evaluate workforce effectiveness	~6

Source: IBM Global Business Services, "Unlocking the DNA of the adaptable workforce," *The Global Human Capital Study* 2008, p. 43. Reprint Courtesy of International Business Machines Corporation, © 2008 International Business Machines Corporation.

Unlike the accounting profession, which has a set of accounting principles used and understood universally, the HR profession has yet to create a set of generic measures. A recent study identified three hurdles to the development of these HR metrics:

1. Identifying measures that are grounded in research and theory and are practical
2. Gaining acceptance of these measures by the stakeholders
3. Applying these measures consistently and over time[75]

However, the Society for Human Resources Management, (with 250 000 members) is preparing guidelines for standardized measures of HR metrics in an attempt to codify metrics already used by HR professionals and enable increase benchmarking.[76]

There has been a tendency for HR practitioners to report isolated or averaged numbers, which are meaningless to managers. A meaningful measure is one that allows the managers to identify and solve the problems and report the results.[77]

Whatever measure you decide to use should have the following characteristics:

- *Alignment:* The measure and the potential results must offer some value to the strategy or goals of the organization. Measuring the ratio of HR professionals to the number of employees does not. Measuring the impact of the performance management system on customer satisfaction does. If your organization does not have clear goals, then choose metrics that are meaningful. Why measure cost per hire if you don't know if this number should be increased or decreased? Decreasing it might result in less qualified candidates who are easier to find, but ultimately result in poor quality work or increased turnover, thus increasing costs. In other words, the full cost of reducing or increasing these measures must be calculated.

- *Actionable:* As Albert Einstein said, "Not everything that can be counted counts, and not everything that counts can be counted." Choose only those measures that you can control. Why choose to measure work–life balance issues if your organization is not prepared to make substantial investments in changing working hours or options? Obtain metrics on things like employee commitment or turnover, items for which you can develop action plans.

- *Trackability:* A good metric must be trackable over time so that improvements, as a result of the introduction of solutions, can be assessed. Some measures, such as time to hire, should be tracked weekly for all positions; others, like employee engagement, may be tracked semiannually with a stratified sample.[78]

- *Comparability:* Try to choose measures that can be compared across units and even with best-in-world organizations. To obtain an employee engagement number of 4.5 is not helpful, unless you know that this is lower than in other departments, and much lower than, for example, that of the best employers.

- *Drill deep*: An average turnover figure of 10 percent is meaningless. You need to know that the turnover rate for new hires is 50 percent (a serious problem) while the turnover rate for key executives is 5 percent (not a problem). Employee engagement scores of 90 percent for the company may hide the fact that the operation in Jasper, Alberta, is at only 15 percent.

- *Report and communicate a limited number of measures:* The availability of databases allows us to accumulate mountains of data, but very little meaningful information. Information overload is a more serious problem than not measuring at all. Decide on five to ten key measures, and report on these in the same way over time. This should be both historical (lag) and predictive (lead) measures. These key metrics almost always include indices of employee engagement, retention rates by occupational group and unit, absenteeism by occupational group and unit, productivity measures, and cost–benefit analyses for the introduction of any new program.

Another approach might be to listen to the questions being asked by line managers, such as "How can I improve the quality of our service?" and provide programs and then measure these programs to prove the increase in quality service.

All these measures can be arranged in a hierarchy:

Level 1: Basic data–headcounts, number of positions, etc.
Level 2: Operational data–training days, number of grievances, etc.
Level 3: Employee data–levels of engagement, absenteeism, turnover, etc.
Level 4: Organizational data–the correlations between turnover and sales; between engagement and unit performance,[79] etc.

Each of these levels is of interest to different levels in the organization, and would be provided to those managers. The reporting of measures may differ not only by level but by strategy. One study found that companies with a differentiation strategy preferred to receive measures of employee innovative capacities, while those with a cost leader strategy wanted measures of their employees' abilities to manage costs.[80] The lesson here is that the metrics provided have to be of value to the recipients.

The HR department can increase its credibility and power to help managers, and change the perception of the function from a cost centre to one that contributes to profits. HR professionals should continually identify instances of contribution such as "That executive search would have cost the organization $50 000, and we did it for $10 000"; "We have worked with the union and reduced grievances by 20 percent, saving 1500 hours of managerial time"; and "We changed our benefits provider and saved the company 10 percent."[81]

At this time, metrics seem to inform strategy rather than drive it. Measurement is the key to the management of human capital, and the art of managing people is turning into the science of HRM. This trend will continue as more HR practitioners will be well educated in their discipline, certified and regulated, and adept at validating their profession through the measurement of its activities.

REPORTING TO BOARDS OF DIRECTORS AND SHAREHOLDERS

Increasingly, external stakeholders want to know the human capital numbers, because they know that these are often linked to the future performance of the organization. For example, Aviva, the world's fifth-largest insurance group, provides the following information:

- Percentage of employees who consider that management supports diversity in the workplace
- Percentage of staff who feel that employees in the business are treated with respect
- Percentage of employees who participated in the Global Employee Climate Survey and rated us favourably on leadership index and engagement index[82]

We started this chapter with a description of some of the metrics used by Enbridge Gas Distribution. Enbridge reports on four "people" metrics under the heading "Develop a Healthy and Productive Workforce"—employee engagement, critical retention, attraction/recruitment effectiveness, and career learning opportunities. Executives and shareholders are now very interested in these measures, and HR professionals are increasingly able to supply them.

Stakeholders are interested in data to establish the worth of HR programs.

// SUMMARY

This chapter attempts to close the loop in the strategic HR planning process by examining assessment; when managers implement a plan, they need to know whether the plan was successful. In addition, it is important to measure the impact of HRM so as to prove the value of HR and to improve its performance. The 5C model for measuring HR effectiveness has five areas: compliance with laws and regulations, client satisfaction, culture management, cost control, and contribution. Methods to measure the impact of HRM include cost–benefit analysis, utility analysis, and audits. Benchmarking is a valuable tool that provides comparative data on key ideas and stimulates discussion about better ways to operate. However, there are challenges in measuring HR effectiveness: Overall organization goals might not be applicable to all branches or subsidiary companies; it is difficult to relate cause and effect; and some HR professionals do not see the benefit in such measuring. The chapter concludes with a discussion of ensuring that the metrics chosen have value to stakeholders in the organization.

KEY TERMS

attitudes p. 375
audit p. 384
balanced scorecard p. 385
benchmarking p. 384
cost–benefit analysis p. 381
direct costs p. 382
efficiency p. 377
indirect costs p. 382
ROE p. 379
ROI p. 379
utility analysis p. 383
workforce analytics p. 367

WEB LINKS

A detailed list of HR metrics can be found at HR Metrics Service:
**http://www.hrmetricsservice.org/wp-content/uploads/2013/07/
HR-Metrics-Standards-and-Glossary-v7.3.pdf**

John Sullivan, a noted expert on HR, also publishes a list of the best metrics for a large organization at:
**http://www.ere.net/2004/07/26/what-are-the-best-hr-metrics-for-a-large-
organization /**

DISCUSSION QUESTIONS

1. Your HR director has asked you to determine whether your organization (a group of about 50 non-unionized, full-time managers and professionals working in scientific

services in Alberta) has an absenteeism problem. You go to the Statistics Canada website and search for absenteeism data from the Labour Force Survey, where you are happy to discover that the average absenteeism rate in Canada (in 2011) is 9.3 days, and the employees in your organizations take an average of 9 days per year. Therefore, you do not have an absenteeism problem. Your manager tells you to "drill down." In other words, she wants data on the absenteeism rates by sector, by occupation, and so on. Does your organization have an absenteeism problem?

2. A company wishes to increase the sales performance of its staff. It has been determined that for each $15 product sold, the company makes $5 in profit. Currently, employees who are paid $20 an hour sell an average of four products an hour. A consultant is persuading the company to purchase a four-hour training course. The consultant guarantees that sales capacity will increase by 25 percent and that the effect will last one year (50 weeks of selling time, assuming an eight-hour day). The cost of the course is $400 per employee. Should the company buy the training course for its ten sales representatives? Conduct a cost–benefit analysis to determine the answer.

3. The Canada HR Centre provides a turnover calculator for estimating the costs of an employee quitting. In groups, choose a real job (for which you have compensation information) and calculate the cost of turnover for this position.

EXERCISE

1. You are the HR manager of a retail organization with 10 000 employees across Canada. The executive team and the board of directors want you to prepare an annual HR report. Choose ten measures that you want to include in the report. Explain why you chose these, how you will measure them, and why this information will be useful for the executives and directors to know. (The web links suggested above may be helpful.)

CASE STUDY 1	TALENT MANAGEMENT AND WORKFORCE ANALYTICS AT FRITO-LAY

Frito-Lay, a manufacturer of well-known brands such as Ruffles and Doritos, is a division of PepsiCo, which employs about 10 000 people across Canada. An employee group, called the Route Sales Representatives, was considered a key talent group. A Route Sales Representative (RSR) performed three key tasks:

1. Driving and delivery–taking the products from distribution centres to stores
2. Merchandising–managing in-store inventory and product placement
3. Sales–taking orders and negotiating for additional shelf space in order to increase sales

However, Frito-Lay was experiencing low productivity and high turnover among this group. Frito-Lay decided to use workforce analytics to identify the source of the problems. The company surveyed both the RSRs and their supervisors, and analyzed recruitment sources and successes, and the characteristics of successful RSRs.

Using advanced statistical techniques, the work uncovered several causes. Their traditional labour pool of high school graduates was shrinking, at the same time as the complexity of the job was increasing. The company began increasing the compensation rate to reflect the new job demands. It also found that on larger routes, the RSR was unable to find the time to merchandise, so a dedicated merchandiser was hired for these large routes. Analyzing the profiles of successful candidates resulted in a change to the hiring profile to include prior sales experience.

This process of analysis required a great deal of managerial and employee commitment, and a time frame of about six months.

Source: Based on Levenson, A."Using Targeted Analytics to Improve Talent Decisions," *People and Strategy*, 34, 2, June 2011, p. 34. http://pepsico.ca/en/brands/frito-lay-canada.html.

QUESTIONS

1. What methods were used in this case to identify the causes of high turnover and low productivity? What other methods could have been used to obtain better data?

2. Though their efforts resulted in improved retention and productivity, what is missing from this case?

CASE STUDY 2 — MEASURING CULTURE TO SUPPORT GROWTH AT CMA

Certified Management Accountants of Ontario (CMAO) provides the CMA designation to certify professional accountants and resources to optimize enterprise performance. CMA of Ontario has approximately 25 000 members. CMA Ontario has 83 employees and has doubled in size from five years ago. Its annual revenue has also doubled from five years ago when a new strategic vision was adapted and propelled the not-for-profit organization to perform like a Fortune 500 company. Development at CMA has been fuelled by the need to offer members and prospects more value with an aggressive growth target of 5 percent annually.

"If we are going to compete in today's marketplace, it's not enough to be a sleepy not-for-profit. We must operate similarly to our membership, many of whom are running successful Canadian businesses," says Christine Thrussell, Manager of Human Resources for CMA Ontario, who recalls the push for change when she first started with the organization. Thrussell made it her objective to be a designation of choice for employees in the not-for-profit sector. "To be competitive, we have to ensure we have the resources employees are looking for."

As part of having the necessary resources, CMA Ontario knew the importance of having a culture to support new work designs. As a result, it was important to the leadership to tap into how their employees valued their workplace. In combination with its balanced scorecard system, CMA Ontario implemented a culture audit assessing employee satisfaction with technology, training, benefits, etc.

At the beginning of Thrussell's career at CMA Ontario, the employee climate survey indicated the organization was in the bottom 10 percent of companies of similar size and revenue base. After four years of improvement and changes under the current leadership, CMAO reached the top 10 percent of the survey. For example, four years ago, 52 percent of employees believed they had the technology needed to support the business. Today, 88 percent indicate they have appropriate technology to do their work.

CMA Ontario reports back to employees on these improvements at quarterly town halls and senior leadership and management team meetings. "Employees are able to see the benefits. They've been able to draw a line of sight from what they *had* to what they have today," says Thrussell. "We have a different mindset now, where the focus is on a world-class customer service experience. It's all about implementing the strategy and doing it with discipline."

Source: Correspondence with Christine Thrussell, Human Resources Manager, CMA, June 2011.

QUESTIONS

1. If you were the manager of HR, how would you rationalize to your members investing in a culture audit?
2. What additional measures would you use to show the value of investing?

// REFERENCES

1. Courtesy of Jane Haberbusch.
2. Bersin by Deloitte "Organizations with High Impact Talent Analytics realize major financial , leadership and recruitment gains." www.bersin.com/News/Content.aspz/id=1692. Retrieved November 6, 2014
3. Adapted the definition by Bassi, L "Raging debates in HR analytics." *People and Strategy* 34, 2, June 2011: 14.
4. Lawler, E. and J. Boudreau. 2009. "What Makes HR a Strategic Partner?" *People and Strategy*, Vol. 32, No. 1: 14–22.
5. Stewart, J. 1996. "Blow Up the HR Department." *Fortune*, January 15.
6. Hammonds, K.H. 2005. "Why We Hate HR." *Fast Company*, 97 (August): 41–47.
7. IBM Global Services. "Unlocking the DNA of the Adaptable Workforce." *The Global Human Capital Study 2008*. Somers, NY: IBM Global Business Services. P. 42. https://hbr.org/2013/12/change-your-company-with-better-hr-analytics/ Retrieved November 11, 2014.
8. Tootell, B., M. Blackler, P. Toulson, and P. Dewe. 2009. "Metrics: HRM's Holy Grail? A New Zealand Case Study." *Human Resource Management Journal*, Vol. 19, No. 4: 375–392.
9. Toulson, P.K., and P. Dewe. 2004. "HR Accounting as a Measurement Tool." *Human Resource Management Journal*, Vol. 14, No. 2: 75–91.
10. Lawler, E.E., A.R. Levenson, and J.W. Boudreau. 2004. "HR Metrics and Analytics: Use and Impact." *Human Resource Planning*, Vol. 27, No. 4: 27–36.

11. Boudreau, J.W., and P.M. Ramstad. 2005. "Talentship and the New Paradigm for Human Resource Management: From Professional Practices to Strategic Talent Decision Science." *Human Resource Planning*, Vol. 28, No. 2: 17–27.

12. *The 2007–2008 Workplace Trends Report.* 2008. Washington, DC: Society for Human Resources Management.

13. Boudreau, J. W. 2010. *Retooling HR.* Boston: Harvard Business School Publishing. P. 127.

14. Corporate Leadership Council. 2001. *The Evolution of HR Metrics.* May, Cat. No. CLC13LNPC.

15. Lawler, Levenson, and Boudreau, 2004.

16. Anonymous. 2005. "Getting Real and Specific–With Measurements." *HR Focus*, Vol. 82, No. 1: 11–12.

17. Dolan, S.L., and A. Belout. 1997. "Assessing Human Resource Effectiveness: The Emergence of the Stakeholder Approach." *HRM Research Quarterly*, Vol. 1, No. 1 (Spring).

18. Hesketh, A. 2008 "Should It Stay or Should It Go?" *Strategic Outsourcing: An International Journal*, Vol. 1, No. 2 (2008): 154–172.

19. Wagar, T. 2002. "Seemed Like a Good Idea, but . . . The Survival (and Death) of High Involvement Work Practices." *HRM Research Quarterly*, Vol. 6, No. 1 (Spring).

20. Schumpeter, G. "The holes in holacracy." *The Economist* July 5yh, 2014.

21. Huselid, M.A. 1994. "Documenting HR's Effect on Company Performance." *HR Magazine*, Vol. 39, No. 1: 79–85; Boudreau, J.W., and P.M. Ramstad. 2003. "Strategic HRM Measurement in the 21st Century: From Justifying HR to Strategic Talent Leadership." In Goldsmith, M., R.P. Gandossy, and M.S. Effron, eds., *HRM in the 21st Century.* New York: John Wiley, 2003. Pp. 79–90.

22. Fitz-enz, J. 2000. *The ROI of Human Capital.* New York: AMACOM.

23. Schiemann, W. 2007. "Measuring and Managing the ROI of Human Capital." *Cost Management*, Vol. 21, No. 4: 5–15.

24. Cascio, W. F. 2011. "Becoming the Evidence Based Manager: Making the Science of Management Work for You." *Personnel Psychology*, Vol. 64, No. 1: 266–269.

25. Lawler, Levenson, and Boudreau, 2004.

26. Belcourt, M. 2001. "Measuring and Managing the HR Function: A Guide for Boards." *Ivey Business Journal*, January/February 2001: 35–39.

27. Pfau, B.N. "The State of HR." Presentation at Human Resources Planning Society Conference, April 27, 2004.

28. Tsui, A.S. 1987. "Defining the Activities and Effectiveness of the Human Resource Department: A Multiple Constituent Approach." *Human Resource Management*, Spring: 35–70; Dolan and Belout, 1997.

29. Ulrich, D. 1996. *Human Resource Champions.* Boston: Harvard Business School Press.

30. Rothwell, W.J., and H.C. Kazanas. 1988. *Strategic Human Resources Planning and Management.* Englewood Cliffs, NJ: Prentice Hall.

31. King, A.S., and T.R. Bishop. 1991. "Functional Requisites of Human Resources: Personnel Professionals' and Line Managers' Criteria for Effectiveness." *Public Personnel Management*, Vol. 20, No. 3 (Fall): 285–298.

32. Meyer, J.P., N.J. Allen, and C.A. Smith. 1993. "Commitment to Organizations and Occupations: Extent and Test of a Three Component Conceptualization." *Journal of Applied Psychology*, Vol. 78: 538–551.

33. TowersPerrin. 2008. *2007–2008 Global Workforce Study*, www.towersperrin.co, retrieved on June 15, 2010.

34. Kiger, P.J. 2002. "Why Customer Satisfaction Starts with HR." *Workforce*, Vol. 81, No. 5: 26–32.

35. Lockwood, N. 2007. "Leveraging Employee Engagement for Competitive Advantage: HR's Strategic Role." *HR Magazine*, Vol. 52, No. 3: S1.

36. Colgate,M. "Cracking the customer service code" *The Globe and Mail*, October 3, 2014. B12.

37. Gable, S.Y. S. Chyung, A. Marker, and D. Winiecki. 2010. "How Should Organizational Leaders Use Employee Engagement Surveys? *Performance Improvement*, Vol. 49, No. 4: 17–25.

38. Caudron, S. 2001. "How HR Drives Profits." *Workforce*, Vol. 80, No. 12: 26–31.

39. Wright, P.M., and S.A. Snell. 2005. "Partner or Guardian? HR Challenges in Balancing Value and Values." *Human Resource Management*, Vol. 44, No. 2: 177–182.

40. Rison, R.P., and J. Tower. 2005. "How to Reduce the Cost of HR and Continue to Provide Value." *Human Resource Planning*, Vol. 28, No. 1: 14–18.

41. http://www.conferenceboard.ca/topics/humanresource/questions.aspx. Retrieved November 11, 2014

42. Krell, E. 2011 "5 ways to manage turnover." *HR Magazine*, 57, 4, p.63-65.

43. Fitz-ens, 2000.

44. Guest, D., J. Michie, M. Sheenan, and N. Conway. 2003. "A UK Study of the Relationship Between Human Resources Management and Corporate Performance." *British Journal of Industrial Relations*, Vol. 41: 291–314.

45. Wright, P.M., T.M. Gardner, L.M. Moynihan, and M.R. Allen. 2005. "The Relationship Between HR Practices and Firm Performance: Examining Causal Order." *Personnel Psychology*, Vol. 58, No. 2: 409–447.

46. Welbourne and Andrews, 1996.

47. Delaney, J.T., and M.A. Huselid. 1996. "The Impact of Human Resource Management Practices on the Perceptions of Organizational Performance." *Academy of Management Journal*, Vol. 39, No. 4: 949–969.

48. Powell, T.C. 1992. "Organizational Alignment as Competitive Advantage." *Strategic Management Journal*, Vol. 13: 119–134.

49. Templer, A., and R.J. Cattaneo. 1995. "A Model of Human Resource Management Effectiveness." *Canadian Journal of Administrative Studies*, Vol. 12, No. 1: 77–88.

50. Templer and Cattaneo, 1995: 79.

51. Brealey, R., and S. Meyers. 1991. *Principles of Corporate Finance*, 3rd ed. New York: McGraw-Hill.

52. See A. Saks, *Research, Measurement and Evaluation of Human Resources* (Toronto: Thomson Nelson, 2000) for a detailed treatment of decision making using utility analysis.

53. Tyler, K. 2001. "Evaluate Your Next Move." *HR Magazine*, Vol. 46, No. 11: 66–71.

54. Pemberton, J.D., G.H. Stonehous, and D.J. Yarrow. 2001. "Benchmarking and the Role of Organizational Learning in Developing Competitive Advantage." *Knowledge and Process Management*, Vol. 8, No. 2: 123–135.

55. Moffett, S., K. Anderson-Gillespie, and R. McAdam. 2008. "Benchmarking and Performance Measurement: A Statistical Analysis." *Benchmarking: An International Journal*, Vol. 15, No. 4 (2008): 368–381.

56. Fitz-enz, 2000.

57. Maire, J.L., V. Bronet, and M. Pillet. 2005. "A Typology of Best Practices for a Benchmarking Process." *Benchmarking: An International Journal*, Vol. 12, No. 1: 45–60.

58. Thomlinson, A. Learning and Development Outlook 2014: Strong Learning Organizations, Strong Leadership, *The Conference Board of Canada*, February 18, 2014.

59. Becker, B., and M. Huselid. 2003. "Measuring HR?" *HR Magazine*, Vol. 48, No. 12: 56–66.

60. http://nypost.com/2014/02/28/apple-has-biggest-slice-of-profits-per-employee/ Retrieved November 12, 2014

61. Woodcock C.P., and P.W. Beamish. 2003. *Concepts in Strategic Management*, 6th ed. Toronto: McGraw-Hill Ryerson.

62. http://www.business.mcmaster.ca/mktg/nbontis/ic/publications/MetricsScotia.pdf. Retrieved November 12, 2014

63. Ulrich, D. 1997. "Measuring Human Resources: An Overview of Practice and a Prescription for Results." *Human Resource Management*, Vol. 36, No. 3 (Fall): 303–320.

64. Kaplan, R.S., and Norton, D.R. 2005. "The Balanced Scorecard: Measures That Drive Performance." Reprinted in *Harvard Business Review*, Vol. 83, No. 7: 1–10.

65. Becker, B., M.A. Huselid, and D. Ulrich. 2001. *The HR Scorecard: Linking People, Strategy and Performance*. Boston: Harvard Business School Press.

66. Chen, J., Z. Zhu, and H.Y. Xie. 2004. "Measuring Intellectual Capital: A New Model and Empirical Study." *Journal of Intellectual Capital*, Vol. 5, No. 1: 195–212.

67. Elias, J. 2004. "Evaluating Human Capital: An Exploratory Study of Management Practice." *Human Resource Management Journal*, Vol. 14, No. 4: 21–40.

68. DiBernardino, F. "The missing link: Measuring and managing financial performance of the human capital investment" *People and Strategy*, 34, 2, June 2011, p. 44.

NEL

225

69. Bullen, M., and K.A. Eyler, 2010. "Human Resource Accounting and international Development." *Journal of International Business and Cultural Studies*, Vol. 22, No. 1: 1–16.

70. Saks, A.M. 2000. *Research, Measurement and Evaluation of Human Resources*. Toronto: ITP Nelson.

71. Samnanai, A.K., and Singh, P. 2011 "Stop Chasing Best Practices: Focus on Fit for Your HR Function." *People and Strategy*, Vol. 34, No. 1.

72. Wright et al., 2005.

73. Van de Voorde, K., J. Paauwe, and M. Van Veldhoven. 2009. "Predicting Business Unit Performance Using Employee Surveys: Monitoring HRM Related Changes." *Human Resource Management Journal*, Vol. 20, No. 1: 44–63.

74. Uyen, V. 2003. "Finding the Right Numbers to Measure HR." *Canadian HR Reporter*, Vol. 16, No. 15: 1.

75. Tootell, B., M. Blackkler, P. Toulson, and P. Dewe. 2009. "Metrics: HR's Holy Grail?: A New Zealand Case Study." *Human Resource Management Journal*, Vol. 19, No. 4: 375–392.

76. www.businessweek.com/articles/2012-07-09 hr-group-creates-workforce-metrics. Retrieved July 29, 2014.

77. Cook, I. 2011. "How Can HR Metrics Help Companies Grow?" *Canadian HR Reporter*, Vol. 24, No. 9 (May 26). ABI/INFORM Global, retrieved on June 20, 2011.

78. Anonymous. 2005. *Strategic HR Review*.

79. Robinson, D. 2009. "Human Capital Measurement: An Approach That Works." *Strategic HR Review* (Chicago), Vol. 8, No. 6: 5–13.

80. Gates, S., and P. Langevin. 2010. "Human Capital Measures, Strategy and Performance: HR Managers' Perceptions." *Accounting, Auditing, and Accountability Journal*, Vol. 23, No. 1: 111–132.

81. Cascio, W.F. 2000. *Costing Human Resources*. 4th ed. Cincinnati: South-Western College Printing.

82. *Aviva plc Corporate Social Responsibility Report 2008*, www.aviva.com/reports/csr08. Retrieved March 31, 2012.

Index